"Meticulously researched, Margery Metzger's Hidden Demons, uncovers the harrowing atrocities committed by serial killer, Lewis Lent Jr, and the traumas he inflicted on a small, bucolic town in the Berkshire mountains of Massachusetts. The time consuming and exhaustive investigations into Lent's crimes, conducted by a task force of multiple law enforcement agencies, ushered in new protocols for investigating serial killings that continue to be utilized by the FBI's Behavioral Analysis Unit today. For fans of true crime, Hidden Demons is essential reading."
—Kathy Stearman, author of memoir IT'S NOT ABOUT THE GUN: Lessons from My Global Career as a Female FBI Agent

***

"EVERYTHING about this ripped-from-the-headlines book is compelling: the graphic writing, the people whom Metzger brings to life and the haunting and true tale of a murderer and his madness."
—Roselle Kline Chartock, author, THE JEWISH WORLD OF ELVIS PRESLEY

***

"An inside and compelling look at perhaps the most notorious child abuse / murder case in the history of western Massachusetts. The book reads like a novel, but its historical accuracy reveals stomach turning details which to date have not been part of the public consciousness. It is a must read for anyone who appreciates true crime stories."
—Daniel A Ford, Retired Superior Court Judge

***

"A harrowing true tale of an elusive serial killer run amok in the pristine Berkshires of Massachusetts, Margery Metzger's HIDDEN DEMONS is a tour-de-force of cold case investigative reporting."
—Christian Barth, author of THE GARDEN STATE PARKWAY MURDERS: A Cold Case Mystery

HIDDEN DEMONS

EVIL VISITS A SMALL NEW ENGLAND TOWN

MARGERY B. METZGER

WILDBLUE
PRESS

WildBluePress.com

HIDDEN DEMONS published by:
WILDBLUE PRESS
P.O. Box 102440
Denver, Colorado 80250

WILDBLUE PRESS is registered at the U.S. Patent and Trademark Offices.

ISBN 978-1-957288-87-1 Hardcover
ISBN 978-1-957288-88-8 Trade Paperback
ISBN978-1-957288-86-4 eBook

Cover design © 2023 WildBlue Press. All rights reserved.
Interior Formatting by Elijah Toten
www.elijahtoten.com

Book Cover Design by Tatiana Vila
www.viladesign.net

HIDDEN
DEMONS

Dedicated to:
Harriette Boyington
beloved mother, grandmother, and friend

Seymour Bernstein
As a child when I asked you a lot of questions
you would reply, "Are you writing a book?"
"Yes Dad, I am writing a book."

CONTENTS

PREFACE

Some changes happen gradually, almost imperceptibly. As waves lap against the shoreline, sands shift, shells and creatures from the sea wash ashore, then vanish as the waves recede. Swimmers jump the waves, surfers and boogie boarders catch the perfect ride into shore. The rhythmic ebb and flow mesmerize, inducing tranquility and harmony.

Yet some changes occur beneath the surface without our even noticing. A hidden riptide tugs at revelers frolicking in the ocean, suddenly and violently sweeping them off course or pulling them under.

Profound changes crept into the Berkshires. Some changes were transitory, making only minimal impact. On the other hand, some changes have remained indelibly etched into the fabric of our ways of life. Some scars were overtly presented, while others festered inside. The physical landscape of beautiful Western Massachusetts prevailed, yet the soul of Berkshire County hardened.

In January 1994, events involving a father and daughter changed the bucolic Berkshires forever. Memories of events run together, becoming fuzzy. Some folks are no longer alive to share their memories. Some do not feel at liberty to discuss these events. Some folks find the memories too painful to rehash. Some remember the impact more clearly than the facts. And for some folks, the memories are crystal clear. I have tried to piece together the most truthful understanding of the events.

What other changes happen without our awareness?

What other changes in our lives are hidden in plain sight?

PROLOGUE

I sit behind bars an innocent man. I sit behind bars condemned by public opinion. I sit behind bars condemned of murder of innocent children. I sit behind bars condemned by a psychologist who has never met me, of being an "unfeeling animal!" I sit behind bars listening to all they say about me on the outside and ask my Lord "why"!

CHAPTER 1

THE BERKSHIRES

At the westernmost end of Massachusetts lies Berkshire County, 900 square miles, population somewhere between 150,000 and 155,000 (varying over the years), thirty towns, and two cities. The Berkshires, glorious in nature's beauty, have a rich history of industrial innovation, of the settlement of one of the longest lasting religious utopian sects, and as a magnet for the ultrawealthy.

In the early 1900s, the county's natural resources and rail access from New York and Boston made it ideal for burgeoning industries such as paper, iron, textiles, and spinning and weaving. The Housatonic River provided the power needed for the rapidly growing number of paper mills, an industry that survived in the Berkshires for two hundred years.

The Shakers, originally from England, migrated to the Albany, New York area in the late 1770s. The Shakers, short for Shaking Quakers because of their charismatic worshipping style, believed in pacifism and egalitarianism of the sexes. A celibate society, their numbers increased strictly through recruiting new followers, proselytizing members who wanted to live with this egalitarian, communal, religious utopian sect. In the 1780s, a member of the sect donated farmland in Hancock, Massachusetts, thus establishing an ideal environment for the third of what would become nineteen Shaker communities in the United States.

The Shakers maintained a self-sufficient community that was exemplary in its governance and its contributions to 19th-century society. They made significant contributions in the areas of architecture, education, agriculture, science, medicine, and craftsmanship. Their influence in architecture and furniture style remains popular to this day.

Post-Civil War American industrialists accumulated great wealth. These *nouveau riche* magnates, many from New York and Boston, discovered the beauty of the Berkshire Hills, choosing to build seasonal retreats in this picturesque corner of Massachusetts. The upper crust crowd moved within their social circle, with various homes built in the most favorable locations to enjoy the changing seasons, each competing for the most scenic views.

The estates and mansions built by the likes of Vanderbilt, J.P. Morgan, Stokes, Choates, author Edith Wharton, and sculptor Daniel Chester French were designed in the fashion of European grandeur—an Italian villa, a French palace, or an English estate. Hundreds of craftsmen, artisans, and horticulturists were commissioned to work their magic, creating exquisite structures with magnificent grounds. Laborers by the hundreds, many of them immigrants, provided the workforce and household staffing. With the influx of these estates came the great economic class divide between the very wealthy and their servants, laborers, factory workers, and farmers.

The Berkshires abounded with pride as the birthplace and home of great thinkers and social activists: jurist and legal scholar Oliver Wendell Holmes, advocate for women's rights Susan B. Anthony, and historian and civil rights activist W.E.B. Dubois. These environs nurtured the creative muse of great American writers Nathaniel Hawthorne, Edith Wharton, and Herman Melville. As Melville gazed out the window of his home, Arrowhead, at the distant Mount Greylock, the contours of the landscape reminded him of a humped back of a sperm whale, thus inspiring the novel *Moby Dick.* Nathanial Hawthorne wrote *The House of Seven Gables* and his series of children's stories *Tanglewood Tales* in his little red cottage in Stockbridge.

The arts flourished with world renowned cultural venues such as Tanglewood (summer home of the Boston Symphony Orchestra), Jacob's Pillow Dance Festival, Williamstown Theater Festival, the Sterling and Francine Clark Art Institute, Shakespeare and Company, the Berkshire Theater Festival, the Norman Rockwell Museum, Chesterwood (home and studio of sculptor Daniel Chester French), the Berkshire Museum, and Hancock Shaker Village, along with the restoration of some of the great estates of the 1800s.

Nestled in the scenic and tranquil Berkshire Hills lies the larger of the two cities—Pittsfield. Forty-three square miles with a population of between 50,000 and 35,000 (varying over the years), Pittsfield boasted of being a wonderful place to raise a family with the local Bousquet ski mountain, beautiful Onota and Pontoosuc Lakes, parks, hiking trails, and Wahconah Park baseball stadium, one of the oldest stadiums dating back to 1919. Built with home plate facing west into the blinding, setting sun, action at this vintage wooden baseball stadium routinely pauses for sun delays, adding to the stadium's quirky charm.

Despite the beauty and charm of this New England city, changes were happening. In1982, Massachusetts passed Proposition 2 ½, an initiative spearheaded by Citizens for Limited Taxation. This law limited municipal governments from increasing assessed property taxes to no more that 2.5% each year. Although a triumph for anti-tax advocates, local government coffers felt the pinch.[1]

---

1. **Proposition 2 ½** (*Wikipedia—https//en.wikipedia.org/wiki/Proposition 2 1/2).*

The '80s also brought the disastrous shutdown of General Electric's transformer division. GE's arrival in Pittsfield in 1907 revived the old mill town economy of the 19th century. In a city of 50,000 at its height in the 1940s, GE employed 13,000. Pittsfield gave itself over to its one mega-industry. The GE workers were paid well, received generous benefits, living and working as a close-knit community. The company's benevolence and community involvement were legendary. After eighty years GE swept out of town, leaving PCB contamination in its wake. Pyranol, a coolant used in the manufacturing of small transformers, was later discovered to be a dangerous carcinogen.[2] It is estimated that one and a half million pounds of PCBs were leaked or dumped into the Housatonic River. PCB laden soil was even donated to Berkshire County cities and towns as clean landfill.[3]

The trickle down effected the entire local economy. Pittsfielders, who had once flocked to North Street aka "upstreet" to shop, found their favorite stores closing or moving away. Hoping to revitalize the downtown's main drag with a shopping mall just did not cut it with the locals and the plan never happened.

Yes, things were changing. Pittsfield was a shrinking city, struggling to redefine itself. As this quiet city came to life in the early morning hours of a typical, snowy Berkshires winter day, January 7, 1994, Pittsfield was about to put itself back on the map.

2. **GE Left Behind a Complex Legacy in Pittsfield, How PCBs Came to be Used and Leaked** (http://www.wbur.org/radioboston/2016/06/29/ge-andpittsfield).

3. www.thebeatnews.org/BeatTeam/pcbs-dumped/).

CHAPTER 2

THE HUNT

The headaches gnawed at his temples. The sunglasses filtered the harsh light that pierced his eyeballs. Some days, he holed up in his bedroom riding out these waves of pain. At night he worked at his job in the dimly lit theater, still wearing sunglasses. He was warned that his work was getting sloppy. More pressing thoughts niggled in his mind. Although he showed up for work, the quality of his job performance finally got him fired.

Somewhat peeved, yet somewhat relieved, he had more time to pursue his passion. He was free to travel around. He was free to start a construction project he dreamed of building in his apartment. He was free to pursue his "master plan."

Friday Morning, January 7, 1994

Holiday season over, the tedium of long, cold, gray, snowy months lay ahead. The plows and sanders were out early to stay ahead of the snow not enough to shut down schools, just enough to cast a foreboding dullness.

Usually groggy after filling in for a colleague on the midnight to seven shift at the hospital, nursing assistant

Russell Davis's adrenaline was pumping. Called upon to administer CPR to a patient in cardiac arrest just prior to the end of his shift, he left Berkshire Medical Center as the darkness lifted. Forgetting to remove his glasses, which he usually wore just for night driving and work, he stepped out into the frigid blast of a New England January morning and headed home to see his young sons off to school.

At 6:55 AM, while dropping off his son at Reid Middle School located on North St. (aka Rte. 7) just north of downtown, William Mullett noticed a dark pickup truck with a white cab parked on the north side of the building. At this early hour, it was unusual to see people around the school. According to the direction the pickup truck faced, it appeared as though the truck had circled around the back of the building parking facing upper North St. As Mr. Mullett pulled farther into the driveway, the driver started up his truck, driving past the Mulletts. According to Mr. Mullett, as he passed by in his car the truck driver looked away "as if he didn't want us to see who he was." In just the short time he saw the driver, William Mullett noticed that the man was scruffy looking, with facial hair slightly graying, was of medium build, and was wearing wire-framed glasses. Mullett asked his son if he had ever seen this truck before, to which the son said no. The pickup truck abruptly exited the driveway, heading south toward the center of Pittsfield.

Kenneth Card arrived at work just before 7:00 AM. That morning he dropped his wife Lois off at work, not wanting her to drive in the early morning snow. Ken, who worked for Scarafoni Property Management, immediately started snow blowing the sidewalk in front of the Fleet Bank at the corner of West and North Streets. He then worked his way down West Street to the KB Toys headquarters, wanting to have the walks cleared when the bank and the KB employees arrived for work.

The Berkshire Hilton stood on the corner of West and South Streets, across the street from the KB Toys headquarters. At 7:00 AM, groundskeeper Guy Harris was out shoveling snow from the sidewalk in front of the hotel when something caught his eye. A black pickup truck with a white cab made its way, unusually slowly, up the West Street hill. Reaching the intersection with South Street, the driver turned right.

A few minutes later, the same truck again ascended the hill very slowly, although the weather conditions did not seem to warrant such caution. As the truck stopped at the traffic light, out of curiosity, Mr. Harris noted the GM logo on the back of the truck and that there was just one person in the vehicle.

In 1989, Janie Ray was taking care of a young girl while on the job working for the Berkshire County ARC, an organization that provided a wide range of services for persons with disabilities. At that time, she met the cabulance driver who picked the child up each day. After the girl died that year, Janie no longer saw the driver until three years later, when she started dating her boyfriend, Phil Shallies.

Staying at Phil's house, Janie woke up at 7:15 to get ready to go to work. Besides her job with BARC, she was a well-known videographer who worked with several Berkshire nonprofits and organizations. That morning, she had an 8:00 appointment to film animals for adoption at the Humane Society. While waiting for her curling iron to heat up, she asked Phil to press the button on the answering machine for the time, which was 7:30. She hurried outside to start up her car and to grab the newspaper. While outside, she saw Phil's friend, the former cabulance driver, returning Phil's pickup truck that he had borrowed the previous day. She waved to him as he got out of the truck that was backed into the lower driveway on the Shallieses' property. She invited him in, but he wanted to shovel the upper driveway where his inoperable van and Janie's car were parked. Waiting for him to finish shoveling made her slightly late for work.

Phil Shallies lived in Lanesboro, Massachusetts with his mother, Sarah "Sally," Phil's Aunt Eleanor Turner, and Eleanor's boyfriend and tenant, Chester "Chet" Forfa. Phil often loaned his truck to his friend, whose decrepit van sat in Phil's upper driveway broken down, waiting for Phil to patch it together, administering frequent repairs.

This fellow ingratiated his way into a friendship with the Shallies family. Starting out slowly, upon referral, this new customer took his van to Phil Shallies, who worked as an auto mechanic from his home garage. Phil, who was blind, had an exceptional talent for fixing cars. Despite his lack of vision, he used his other senses to diagnose and repair cars. Phil could feel his way around a vehicle and listen to the subtle sounds of the engine to determine the problem.

The well-worn, often broken-down van frequently sat in the Shallieses' driveway waiting for Phil to patch it together. In exchange for the auto maintenance, the customer worked side by side with Phil doing household repairs and transporting Phil and the elderly ladies to appointments, using Phil's pickup truck or Chester Forfa's sedan. Like

Phil, his mother was blind and most appreciative of the help this man offered. He was a godsend.

The Time Was Right

At 7:00, Rebecca "Becky" Savarese, a twelve-year-old seventh grader at Notre Dame Middle School, headed out the door of her apartment in a mixed income apartment complex where she lived with her single mom, Christine Paoli. Each morning, Rebecca made the one-mile trek to Notre Dame Middle School through well trafficked, downtown Pittsfield.

Bundled up in her ski jacket, carrying her purple LL Bean backpack, earplugged into her Walkman, this slender, fair complexioned preteen with curly brown hair, braces on her teeth, and wire-rimmed glasses made her daily walk to school, totally absorbed in the music of the Smashing Pumpkins. Rebecca turned right from the driveway of Riverview West Apartments onto West Street, passing Berkshire Gas Company, then crossing the street in front of the Salvation Army, past the Big Y supermarket, up the hill approaching the corner of West and North Streets, the exact center of town where North, South, East, and West Streets converged at the city's central rotary.

Notre Dame, a small Catholic school, was located just off North Street, the main thoroughfare and shopping district in the heart of the city. On the corner of North and Melville Streets stood the Pittsfield YMCA. Around the corner on Melville Street buzzed the hub of youth activity at the Notre Dame Middle School, St. Joseph's High School, the Boys' Club, and the CYC (Catholic Youth Center), all on one short block.

While at Big Y supermarket, he spotted Rebecca Savarese walking east toward the center of Pittsfield on her way to school. He felt he had a relationship with the preteen. He had often seen her and her friends' comings and goings from school and about town. He followed the young people, cataloguing their whereabouts and their patterns of movement. Rebecca was alone, seemingly distracted, and the first youngster he had seen that morning. He was more than ready to make his move. Getting in his truck, he drove in the opposite direction from where he had been seen earlier. Circling around, he parked in front of the bank on North Street near the intersection with West Street.

Walking up West Street, as Rebecca approached North Street, a scruffy-looking man with a mustache walked past her, then suddenly appeared alongside of her. He warned her, "Do you see the gun I have?"

"At first, I thought he was just joking," Becky told authorities. "He seemed like a nerd to me."

He approached her, a yellow shirt draped over his arm, and came even closer to her. Coaxing her up to North Street with a gun pointing at her ribs, he commanded, "Do everything I say, and everything will be all right. See that black pickup? I want you to get into it."

As the kidnapper led her up the street to his truck, Becky remembered the words her mother repeated to her daily: *"Becky, you stay on the main road and walk where it's well traveled. If anyone is behind you, duck into a business—*

kick, bite, scream, punch, spit—anything to get attention."[4]
Fearing for her life, Becky later said, "I was afraid if I got into the truck, I would never see my mom again. I would be lying in some ditch dead."

Within feet of the truck, Rebecca suddenly pretended to hyperventilate, faking an asthma attack. Breathlessly, she asked her attacker, "Can I sit down for a minute?" This stellar performance from a child who never had asthma was enough to catch the kidnapper off guard. As she began to sit down, the kidnapper felt a jerk on his hand as she wiggled loose from the backpack. The split second it took her to slip her arms out of her backpack, she took off running down West Street, leaving him holding the backpack. She flagged down Kenneth Card as he cleared the sidewalks. He took the agitated girl into his office and immediately called the police.

Stopped at the traffic light on North Street, Russell Davis observed something unsettling happening on the sidewalk next to his car. At first, he thought a father and daughter were having a heated argument, although with his car windows up he could not hear what they were saying. However, when this slight young girl freed herself from the man's grasp and took off running, his curiosity turned to suspicion. Ironically, Russ had just had the discussion with his sons about "stranger danger." Russ looked directly at the man, who now appeared to realize he was being watched.

As the man calmly walked back to his truck, Russ observed the partial license plate number on the front of the vehicle through his rearview mirror. Fortunately, because

4. Caldwell, Jean. (January 12, 1994). **Drug abuse Resistance Education.** *The Boston Globe.*

Russ had forgotten to take off his glasses, the man's face and the license plate numbers that he noted were in clear focus. While trying to process what was happening, Russ's attention was diverted as the truck pulled away, passing him on the right and running two red lights. Convinced that he had witnessed an attempted crime in progress, Russ tried to follow the truck down South Street, losing the suspect as the truck turned left a block away onto East Housatonic Street just as the light turned red. Not being able to follow the truck anymore, Russ looked for a place to stop to call the incident into the police. He did not have to go far before he spotted a police car at the corner Mobile station/Lipton Mart.

Just as Kenneth Card was placing a call to the Pittsfield Police Department, Russell Davis approached Officer Delmont Keyes at the Lipton Mart on South Street. Davis explained that he had just witnessed what he thought was an attempted abduction at the corner of North Street. Within minutes, the Pittsfield Police Department received both calls. The police knew they had a major incident on their hands, but little did they suspect the extent of the event.

The Man

He was up at 5:30 AM, making himself a pancake breakfast. Leaving the apartment at 5:45, the ride should have taken thirty-five minutes from North Adams south on Rte. 7 to downtown Pittsfield. Being early gave him time to stop off at Reid Middle School before the buses arrived, then proceed to the Pittsfield Big Y supermarket on West Street not long before 7:00. He later claimed that he cashed in $.60 worth of soda cans, although the computer on the recycling machine registered its first deposit of the day at 8:00.

It was not unusual for him to borrow his friend Phil's truck or Phil's tenant Chet's car to run errands, to transport the older folks, or to use as a loaner while his van was being repaired. Although the man's appearance could often be unkempt and his van a mess, he occasionally would return Phil's truck or Chet's car in pristine condition, detailing the insides of the loaned vehicles.

What struck Janie and Phil as unusual on this day was how early their friend arrived at their house. He usually rolled in at around 10:00 AM. Occasionally, he would even sleep in his van, which he would park in Phil's lower driveway, still not waking up and coming into the house until later. Arriving early that snowy morning, he parked Phil's truck in the lower driveway, threw some snow on the truck, then walked to the upper driveway where he unloaded something from the borrowed truck into his disabled van. He then began to shovel the driveway.

When his friend finished shoveling the driveways, Phil invited him in for breakfast. Phil planned to work on his friend's van that day, which he did in exchange for the work the customer provided for the Shallies family. The two worked on the van from 10:00 AM to 1:00 PM. The men then borrowed Chester Forfa's car to head down to Pittsfield to Smith's Auto Electric to have the coil from the van tested, then to Reddington Auto Parts on Wahconah Street for some wiper blades for Chet's car, which they installed right there. They returned to Phil's and worked on the van briefly until lunchtime at about 1:45 in the afternoon.

What a Story!

Patrolman Patrick Barry, the first officer on the scene, escorted Rebecca to the police station.

Shortly after sending her daughter off to school, Chris Paoli received the call from the police that her daughter was safely at the station following an attempted abduction. With their adrenalin pumping, Rebecca's mother and maternal grandparents, who were an integral part in the upbringing of their granddaughter, rushed right over. The family's shock was palpable. Due to the surreal circumstances surrounding the incident with her granddaughter, and out of her own fear and wishful disbelief that this incident happened to Becky, Grandma Paoli immediately responded with, "Are you sure she's not lying?" The family quickly realized the incident was shockingly true.

Detective Joe Collias had recently been transferred to the detective bureau from the juvenile bureau, where he investigated child physical and sexual assaults. He understood the nuances of interviewing children. He recalled that morning. "In the early morning, she came to the police station with her mother. Her mother sat back and let her daughter talk. The girl sat at my desk with me, and she was just this happy kid. And I asked her what happened."

Without giving much detail, she simply said, "I was just walking up West Street. This guy walked along side me, grabbed me and was trying to force me into a van."

Collias replied, "Oh, really."

Rebecca said, "And I got away from him. I ran away from him. Then he got in his van and drove away."

Collias stated, "I got up from my chair, took a break, and walked around a bit. I was talking to one of my colleagues. 'Man, that's a screwy story. She's telling me this story as if it's no big deal.' Then I got a call at my desk from the dispatcher. A man just reported that he was on his way home from work this morning when he saw something on the corner of North and West Streets. A guy was trying to force a young girl into a van, and she got away."

"My jaw dropped to my chest. Are you kidding me? She wasn't scared or crying. Probably most of it was nervousness because she was smiling. So, I went back and started from the beginning to take a typewritten detailed statement. "

"So, Becky, can you describe the man to me?" Collias probed.

This time, Becky filled in details of her ordeal for Detective Collias. "At first, I thought he was just another weirdo walking downtown. He looked like a nerd who was sloppy. The man was white, maybe in his forties or older. He was a little taller than me, maybe about five-foot-six, and thin. He needed a shave and looked like he had wrinkles on his face. He had glasses with silver frames, a mustache, dark brown hair, and, I think, brown eyes. He was dirty looking with dirty, ratty-looking jeans and clothes. He had on a dark-blue knit cap pulled over his ears, and a dark-blue or green jacket. He had a yellow cloth or shirt over his arm that hid the gun he had poking in my side."

"Becky, how did you get away?"

"I pretended to have an asthma attack. I asked him if I could sit down for a minute. As he was pulling on me, I sort of slumped down, pretending I couldn't catch my breath. As he pulled, I slipped out of my backpack and ran as fast as I could to the first adult that I saw. The man was plowing snow off the sidewalk. He took me right into his office and called the police."

"What can you tell me about his vehicle?"

"It was a black pickup truck with a white top over the back end of the truck."

"Did you ever see that truck before?"

"Yeah. I've seen that truck a few times before as I was walking home from school with my friends, and I think at the cinema center."

"Do you remember ever seeing the man before?"

"No."

"Becky, we're going to need you to work with another officer to put together a picture of the man."

Patricia "Patti" Driscoll was one of the few female Massachusetts State Police in the 1990s who had worked her way up to detective. Assigned to the Massachusetts State Police Crime Prevention and Control Unit housed in the Berkshire County District Attorney's office, she headed over to the police station with a Smith and Wesson Identikit, referred to by the police as "Mr. Potato Head," to work with Rebecca to construct a composite sketch of the suspect. Patti guided Rebecca in the task by asking specific questions regarding the perpetrator's appearance.

The composite was not intended to be an exact picture of the person; rather, as close of a likeness as possible. The questioning usually began with the hair, working the way to the eyes, nose, lips, etc. The features would overlap, refining the overall picture until the likeness was as accurate as possible. Again, Becky performed this challenging task remarkably well. The police wasted no time circulating the composite to all the local law enforcement agencies.

Russell Davis returned to the station after he got his sons off to school to give his account of the incident he had witnessed to the detectives. He had not been sure of what was happening with the young girl and the man until she took off running. He still had his doubts until the truck pulled out into the main intersection in the center of town and recklessly ran two red lights.

Davis caught sight of part of the license plate numbers in his rearview mirror before the truck driver took off. Because he had a mirror image of the license plate, he was unsure if the numbers he saw were the first three or the last three of the license plate. He confirmed Rebecca's description of the pickup truck as black or dark blue with a white cab.

District Attorney Gerard Downing

Detective Patti Driscoll knocked on Gerard Downing's office door. Berkshire County District Attorney Gerard Downing and First Assistant DA David Capeless had just returned to the office. Driscoll entered and announced, "We were advised by the Pittsfield Police Department that there was an attempted kidnapping early this morning."

"Oh, really? Where?" replied DA Downing.

Patti walked over to the window and pointed to the street below. "She's a seventh grader at Notre Dame."

Downing asked, "What's her name and how late was she for school?"

"Her name is Rebecca Savarese and there was an eyewitness."

"Holy crap. That's one of my son Ben's classmates."

The shocking audacity of this crime gave pause to the DA as well as to Rebecca's family.

Timing is everything. Downing and Capeless were just beginning their biggest murder case since taking office three years earlier. Less than two years after becoming DA, Downing and Capeless faced one of the most sensational and highly publicized cases in the history of Berkshire County—the Wayne Lo Case.

Wayne Lo immigrated to the United States from Taiwan at age seven. The Lo family moved back and forth from Taiwan twice before finally settling in Billings, Montana when Wayne was in seventh grade. A brilliant student and accomplished violinist, Wayne received the W.E.B. Dubois Minority Scholarship to Simon's Rock College of Bard in Great Barrington, Massachusetts.

Simons Rock, an adjunct of Bard College, provided a unique niche educational experience for extremely bright, creative teens who were not best served educationally in a traditional high school. Skipping their junior or senior years in high school, the average age of the students was sixteen. Highly selective students came from all over the country to this nurturing rural campus that offered a liberal learning style with small classes where students and faculty operated on a first name basis.

On Monday, December 14, 1992, eighteen-year-old college student Wayne Lo traveled by taxi, a forty-five minute ride from his Great Barrington campus to Dave's Sporting Goods store in Pittsfield, where he easily purchased, on the spot, an SKS semiautomatic assault rifle with no questions asked. He only needed an ID proving he was of legal age. Just days before, he had readily purchased armor-piercing ammunition by mail order using his mother's credit card. The package marked "ammunition," delivered to the school, sat in the mail room. Again, no questions were asked.

Returning to school from Dave's, Lo loaded the rifle with the armor-piercing ammunition, going on a shooting rampage. Perhaps it was the naiveté of the times, but Wayne Lo's privacy had priority over the red flags hidden in plain sight. Two days prior to the incident, an unopened package of ammunition from the North Carolina company, Classic Arms, had been delivered to the mail room and brought to the attention of school officials. When questioned, Lo responded that the ammunition was a Christmas gift for his father. Lo's room was searched, but nothing was found. Bullets were hidden in the weight room of Lo's dorm. A caller warned the school that Lo had a gun just prior to the shooting.[5] Yet all these warning signs remained unheeded. First Assistant District Attorney David Capeless later pointed out, "The Simon's Rock shooting was one of the first in the modern wave of school shootings."

The biggest case of District Attorney Gerard Downing's and Assistant DA David Capeless's careers was now in its second day. The Wayne Lo case received such a

---

5. Bellow, Heather. (December 17, 2017). Shooting at Bard College at Simon's Rock/25 Year Later. *The Berkshire Eagle*.

preponderance of pretrial publicity that all parties agreed the defendant could not get a fair trial in Berkshire County. The trial, which had been moved fifty-five miles east to Springfield, MA, presented all sorts of logistical issues. Witnesses included a myriad of former Simon's Rock students—many of whom were no longer living in Massachusetts—college faculty, Great Barrington Police, local emergency personnel, the gun shop owner, and more. Although jurors were selected from Springfield, everyone else involved with the trial had to be transported back and forth daily.

Jury selection began on Thursday, January 6, 1994. Anticipating the process of seating a jury amenable to both the prosecution and the defense would take at least two days, the district attorneys marveled that this task was accomplished in just one day. Well organized plans for the next day were implemented and carried out without a hitch. Jurors were escorted by van to Simons Rock College in Great Barrington to the scene of the crime for a "view."

On Friday morning the jury, along with the defense and prosecuting attorneys, the judge, and the court reporter retraced the steps taken by Lo on that horrifying day when he went on his shooting rampage. Starting at the security guard gate at the college entrance, Wayne Lo shot guard Teresa Beavers twice in the abdomen at point blank range with an incredibly powerful rifle. Remarkably, she survived. As professor Nacunan Saez drove through the gate, he was shot and killed. As Galen Gibson came out to help, he, too, was shot dead.

Lo then moved into the library, where he shot through the card catalogue with the bullet penetrating and embedding into the thigh of Thomas McElderry, who was sitting in the library. Moving on to the dorm, Lo shot and wounded Matthew David and Joshua Faber, who were standing inside a glass enclosed stairwell. Lo then fired at and missed another student. His rampage came to a halt as his gun jammed upon entering the student union. He grabbed a student and ordered him to call the police, and the cops soon arrived. By 11:00 in the morning, Lo had surrendered to the Great Barrington Police without a struggle.

By noon, the jurors—cold, overwhelmed, and emotionally spent from their outing to Simon's Rock—were treated to lunch at the Red Lion Inn on Main Street in Stockbridge. This historic inn, featured in Norman Rockwell's famous painting *Main Street at Christmas,* gave the jurors the needed respite from their morning ordeal in this tranquil, picture perfect New England setting.

The snow, which had begun early in the morning, was becoming a full-blown blizzard. Rather than taking time out for lunch, District Attorney Downing and Assistant DA Capeless returned to their office in Pittsfield to prepare for the opening day of the Lo trial on the following Monday. They were just beginning to work on the evidence portion of the trial when Detective Driscoll broke the news of the kidnapping to the DAs.

Gerard Downing anxiously waited until his son Ben got home from school. Ben remembers his father calling him and saying he needed to talk about something serious. "You may have heard about something with a classmate and we're trying to check into it. Just tell me something about her."

Of course, the students in Rebecca's class had heard the news. For this tight knit seventh grade class, a combination of shock, terror, and disbelief permeated the classroom. Ben and Becky had grown up together. Their families both belonged to St. Theresa's Parish. They had started together at Sacred Heart Elementary School and then gone on to Notre Dame Middle School. Becky was friendly and well-liked by everyone. There was a genuine, no nonsense, no excuses quality about this girl that her classmates instinctively appreciated.

"As I walked to school and basketball practice," Ben reflected, "I never heard my father say anything, but I can imagine his thinking that could easily have been Ben or my sister, Maggie, who is a couple of years younger." This was hitting too close to home for the district attorney.

CHAPTER 3

THE SEARCH

At 11:15 AM, Detective Owen Boyington, as well as all the other detectives, received a call from Pittsfield Police Department's Lieutenant David Boyer to come in to work as soon as possible in response to a man with a gun who tried to physically force a twelve-year-old girl into his pickup truck. By noon, the detectives had assembled and were assigned to search various quadrants of the city to look for a '70s model GMC black pickup with a white cab over the bed of the truck and having a partial Massachusetts license plate number 878. This information submitted to the DMV for a statewide search turned up a few possible matches. One match occurred in the neighboring town of Lanesboro.

Detective Boyington canvassed the northwest quadrant of the city, checking parking lots of businesses, barrooms, restaurants, public housing, etc. Finding nothing in his section of Pittsfield, he requested permission to search the nearby towns of Hancock and Lanesboro. As he drove over the Pontoosuc Lake causeway, approaching Lanesboro, blizzard-like snow squalls caused near whiteout conditions. Turning left past the lake, he headed north on Rte. 7 (main thoroughfare running the length of Berkshire County) to the Lanesboro Police Department to inform them that he was in their jurisdiction and to drop off a composite photo of the kidnapping suspect. As Boyington drove past steeply inclined Summer Street, he thought, *In this treacherous weather someone coming down that hill might not be able to stop and would slide right into traffic on busy Rte. 7.*

Arriving at the Lanesboro PD, located up a steep driveway about 100 yards past Summer Street, Boyington checked in with Officer Timothy Sorrell. Sorrell, having received the Be on the Lookout (BOLO) from Pittsfield PD, had already canvassed local motels and made a few rounds of the parking lot of the nearby Berkshire Mall. Deciding that there was no point continuing farther into Lanesboro, Boyington left the station to head back to Pittsfield when, by chance, he looked to his left, across the lane of traffic, up Summer Street, and noticed a dark blue pickup with a white cab backed into the driveway of the second house on the north side of the road.

Boyington felt it was divine intervention that he had just happened to look up the road at that moment, especially because he was traveling in the opposite lane. His daughter Amy insisted that, rather than divine intervention, her father looked up that street because he was very ordered and not easily distracted from a task. The vigilance he had acquired as a Marine in Vietnam honed his ability to focus.

Driving a short distance, Boyington swung around in the parking lot of Bob's Country Kitchen, backtracked to Summer Street, flooring his Queen Victoria rear wheel drive patrol car, fishtailing up the road's steep grade to get a better look. He saw that the front plate of this dark blue truck was Mass Reg 878-735. He returned immediately to the Lanesboro PD, informing Officer Sorrell of the truck, then he called Pittsfield PD. Detective Danford ran the plate and found that the truck was registered to Phillip Shallies of Summer Street, Lanesboro. Boyington and Sorrell took off to check things out.

Owen Boyington

Owen Boyington, as well as his parents, Owen Sr. and Harriette (nee Dallmeyer), were born and raised in the Berkshires. Owen Sr. grew up in a good natured, rowdy clan of fifteen children. Owen described his mother Harriette Dallmeyer's family of fourteen children as old, staunch Baptists. Both Owen Sr., "Ozzie," and Harriette had worked hard their entire lives. Ozzie had to quit school after the seventh grade to help support the family. He spent his life working as a laborer, often taking on several jobs.

During World War II, Boyington Sr. joined the navy, seeing action at Iwo-Jima, Okinawa, and the Philippines. As with many men, the war had a profound effect on their lives, which they bore silently. Returning home, Sr. settled into family life. The couple purchased the house on Essex Street, where Harriet was born and raised. Along with the house came his mother-in-law, who was not particularly fond of her daughter's husband.

The family house remained the hub of the Dallmeyer family, never quite feeling like it was the Boyington domain. Now with three children—Roger, Owen, and Helen—life at home was uncomfortable for Ozzie. He worked a few jobs and began drinking heavily. Much of the responsibility fell on Harriette. She raised her two sons and her daughter with an iron fist. Tall, stern, and sturdy, Harriette was known for radiating kindness and for having a wicked sense of humor. An optimistic realist, she provided structure for the family. Although she was a no frills kind of gal, Harriette possessed a natural, rugged beauty.

Depending on whether Ozzie had a job, Harriette intermittently provided the sole support for her family, working as the chief cook at Berkshire Nursing Home. She possessed the natural ability to turn a house into a home on a shoestring. She could sew as well as any seamstress and cook as well as any chef. Hard working, thrifty—perhaps better described as frugal—she expected the same from her children. Harriette did her best to rein in her two rambunctious boys. Although she was a church-going woman, the boys just did not feel the spirit.

At age seventeen, the oldest son, Roger, quit school. He joined the navy, doing two tours of duty in Vietnam, flying aircraft, bombing North Vietnam. Although never estranged from his family, once Roger finished his tours of duty, he never returned to live in Pittsfield.

On the other hand, Owen Boyington met Judy in high school, where they became inseparable. Both middle children had an alcoholic parent and were tasked with financial and emotional responsibilities beyond their years. Their support for each other evolved into a deep love.

After high school, Owen worked in an auto body shop until he enlisted in the Marines at a time of great upheaval in our country. As much as one could, Boyington was a man who lived on his own terms. He wanted to be a Marine, yet he knew two years of active duty was plenty for him. With family responsibilities and his sweetheart Judy waiting for him at home, he expected to enlist for a two-year stint and no more. However, the Marine Corps now required either three or four years' service. Owen would have none of this. As he was about to walk, the recruiter realized that he did not want to lose this man to the army and agreed to Owen's terms—two years with induction after Christmas and New Year's so he could spend the holidays with Judy and his family.

Serving in Vietnam from July 1968 until August 1969, the height of the war following the Tet Offensive in January 1968, US military strategy changed from search and destroy to winning the hearts and minds of the South Vietnamese. Combined action groups of twelve to fifteen US Marines embedded themselves in small Vietnamese villages. As a heavy equipment motor vehicle operator moving supplies to these villages within the third combined action perimeters, Owen dodged sniper fire, landmines, and miserable jungle diseases such as "the fevers" or "jungle rot."

Although US troops served as military advisors for ten years, the first Marine combat ground troops arrived in Vietnam in 1965. The Vietnam draft finally ended in 1973 but still, boys were being swallowed up by the military to do their patriotic duty and proudly serve their country. A dense fog of anticipation and despair descended on our country, which was deeply divided. Draft age males, their spouses, girlfriends, parents, and extended families lived in fear. For most, the Vietnam "conflict" was a leap into the unknown somewhere in Southeast Asia. Many Americans had never heard of Vietnam. Never before had our young men been summoned to put their lives on the line for a cause they did not understand. The draft swept up those who honestly believed that if Uncle Sam beckoned, they must defend our nation no matter what—no questions asked—as well as those who opposed the war or just did not know what was happening to them.

Draft-aged boys not willing to voluntarily go to war had several options. They could continue their education at college to bide time; or they could enlist, be drafted, escape to Canada or Mexico (being declared traitors who would be arrested when they tried to return to the US), maim themselves, have a doctor declare them unfit for service or 4F, or become conscientious objectors. They could make their families and country proud or be perceived as weak, unpatriotic embarrassments. Except for those young men who could afford to stay in school, the choices were bleak. As so vividly described by Hamilton Gregory in his book *McNamara's Folly: The Use of Low IQ Troops in the Vietnam War,* desperate for bodies to fight this divisive conflict, Secretary of Defense Robert McNamara maintained his military census by enlisting thousands of our nation's poorest, least educated, minority, powerless young men by making deceptive promises and waiving medical, educational, and psychological deferments. The toll on these poor souls proved enormous.

On the home front, the hippie movement of "love children" with their mind-blowing psychedelics, "mellow yellow," "love, peace, and rock & roll," helped to blur the harsh realities of the racial and political strife happening in the real world. The non-violent struggle for racial equality and civil rights led to sit-ins and strikes culminating on August 28, 1963, with over 200,000 people participating in the March on Washington, where Dr. Martin Luther King delivered his "I Had a Dream" speech. These acts of civil disobedience finally led the government to take notice, passing the Civil Rights Act in 1964, the Voting Rights Act in 1965, and the Fair Housing Act in 1968.

But cities throughout the country were seething with discontent. Ella Baker, feeling Martin Luther King was out of touch with the younger Blacks, began the Student Nonviolent Coordinating Committee (SNCC). Malcolm X captured people's attention with his Nation of Islam philosophy of Black Power, nationalism, and the right for self-defense. Bobby Seale, Huey Newton, Eldridge Cleaver, and the Black Panther Party encouraged Blacks to fight for their rights. Ten years of demonstrations and race riots including Watts, Detroit, and as many as 100 other cities throughout the country wracked the nation.[6]

Acting as a voice of conscience for the US in his famous "Beyond Vietnam" speech delivered at the Riverside Church in Manhattan on April 4, 1967, the Reverend Dr. Martin Luther King Jr. decried the Vietnam War, speaking for himself and for clergy of all faiths. As the winner of the Nobel Peace Prize in 1964, he could not, in good conscience, remain silent about the inhumanity of this war and America's twisted ideals of democracy. He spoke out about how the

---

6. Civil Rights Movements. *Wikipedia.*

war was sucking up the enormous manpower, skill building, and money needed by our most poor and vulnerable. King railed against the disproportionate number of African American men relegated to attend inferior, segregated schools, to drink out of segregated water fountains, to eat in segregated restaurants, and forced to withstand a multitude of other indignities. Yet these were the young men being forced into military service and dying for our country. King questioned America's cherished values of family when we were destroying both families and villages in Vietnam.[7]

The United States reeled from the assassinations of Medgar Evers, Dr. Martin Luther King Jr., President John F. Kennedy, and later, Robert Kennedy and Malcom X. The public's rapidly increasing disapproval of the war led to numerous anti-war demonstrations. As the war escalated, the largest and probably the most famous protest took place in October 1967, when over 100,000 people demonstrated in Washington, DC, congregating at the Lincoln Memorial. In 1969, with the advent of the draft lottery, college campus anti-war demonstrations escalated. In 1970, with the US military moving into Cambodia, a new wave of protests broke out, resulting in the National Guard opening fire on student demonstrators at Kent State University, killing four students.[8]

No soldier returns from war unscathed. The adjustment to civilian life affects each person differently. The United States, however, did not welcome these returning warriors as heroes. Oh yes, many families honored their sons and daughters, but the country did little to pay homage to our returning military. The returning soldiers became pariahs. The wounded received treatment at VA hospitals, but the emotionally scarred and drug addicted were left to fend for

7. *Kingencyclopedia.stanford.edu/encyclopedia/documentarysentry/doc_beyond_ Vietnam.*

8. **Williams, Yohuru. Sound Smart: Vietnam War Protests.** *www.history.com/topics/vietnam-war-protests.*

themselves. Unless blatantly psychotic, PTSD was either untreated or just unidentified.

One of the challenges of returning to civilian life was finding gainful employment. A few extra points for having served in the military were added onto civil service tests, but lack of training and jobs just added to the challenges of the young soldiers as they attempted to transition back into home life.

Upon his discharge from the Marines, Owen Boyington was ready to move on with his life. He and Judy burned all his letters from Vietnam. One month after Owen's return, they were married. The couple understood the chaotic upbringing they had had and were determined not to repeat the mistakes their parents made. Judy, twenty-two, and Owen, twenty-four, began building a family of their own.

Steady, living wage employment was difficult to find. Being independent and perhaps stubborn, Boyington was determined to make it on his own. He finally thought he was set when he landed a job with the New England Telephone Company. However, after a few years working with a steady, living wage, shockingly he was laid off. By then, he and Judy had two children. Attempts to break into the laborers' union was next to impossible. Not knowing where else to turn for living wage employment in the Berkshires, Owen was feeling frustrated and desperate about providing a future for his family.

A Marine buddy living in Oklahoma convinced Owen that he would have no trouble providing for his family out there. With no other apparent options locally, Judy and Owen decided to take a chance. They were packed and ready to go, with their house under contract for sale, when Owen's sister, a young mother with an infant and a newborn, was killed in a tragic car accident.

Owen's mother Harriette was shattered by the agony of her daughter's death and by the tragedy of her daughter's two young children suddenly being left motherless. Piling on the pain of no longer having her two remaining sons, her daughter-in-law, and Owen and Judy's daughters, whom she adored, nearby was an added burden Owen could not inflict upon Harriette.

Deciding to remain in Pittsfield, Owen took a civil service test, willing to accept whatever job presented itself first. That job happened to be with the Pittsfield Police Department.

In many ways, Boyington's tour of duty in the Marines prepared him for his career on the police force. While in the Marines, he lived the microcosm of what was happening on the home front. The racial tensions, the class divides, the educational and social inequities, and the questionable moral compass that fueled the Vietnam "conflict" were all part of his world. Serving in war, soldiers had developed a heightened vigilance, a reliance on instinct, and an understanding of diversity and of actions under stress, all of which became useful in Owen's career in law enforcement.

As a rookie police officer, Boyington worked varied shifts, settling into the midnight to 8:00 AM shift for seven years before switching to the 6:00 PM to 2:00 AM shift. Despite working full time while finishing college and then earning a master's degree in criminal justice, he always made it a point to try to have dinner with his family. Weekend days off were family time. Judy saw her role as wife and mother to support her husband and be there for her children. They were determined to create the family that they both had lacked growing up.

After nine and a half years on the force, Boyington was selected for the newly formed drug unit consisting of just two officers. A year later, by special request, Lieutenant Gerald Lee selected Sgt. Boyington for the detective bureau. Owen Boyington epitomized community policing. He thoroughly knew the community where he had spent most of his life. He was a no- nonsense cop who, at the same time, helped many troubled youths get their lives on track. Gerald Lee described Boyington: "He was a good detective and a good investigator. I liked him, the bad guys didn't. He was like a dog with a bone. He just wouldn't give up. He would get involved with a case and there was no stopping him. He would go until six in the morning—just keep on and on until he resolved the case." Working the 4:00 PM to midnight shift in the detective bureau, Owen recalls the night crew to be the most cohesive, cooperative, and effective group with whom he had ever worked.

The knock on the Door 2:15 PM, Friday, January 7, 1994

Detective Boyington, accompanied by Officer Sorrell, knocked on the kitchen door of the Shallieses' home. Sitting down to lunch were two elderly ladies, Sarah Shallies and Eleanor Turner; an elderly man, Chester Forfa; and two younger men, Phillip Shallies and his friend. Although the residents were somewhat confused when the police showed up on such a nasty day, according to Boyington, "One of the elderly ladies remarked that they knew why we were there and went on to say that they had heard on the radio about the incident with the girl. They all seemed to me very much aware that the GMC pickup in the lower driveway resembled the truck described on the radio. Eleanor Turner stated that Phil had received a phone call from an old friend telling him of the radio broadcast earlier in the day." As the other younger man at the table put down his tuna fish sandwich and turned to face the officers, Detective Boyington noticed an uncanny resemblance to the composite picture circulated by the Pittsfield Police Department.

Detective Boyington asked if anyone had used the truck early that morning. The friend explained that he had borrowed it the night before since his van was broken down.

He came to the house daily to help with chores and, in return, he often used Phil's truck since Phil was blind. The man claimed that he had driven the truck directly from his home in North Adams that morning. The officers asked both men if it would be okay with them if they looked inside their vehicles. Boyington peeked through the car window at the interior of Phil's truck, which was tidy, while Sorrell looked through the window at the interior of the friend's van, which was quite messy. Nothing suspicious was visible by just glancing in the windows of either vehicle.

Detective Boyington and Officer Sorrell asked Phil's friend if he would mind stepping outside so that they could talk. He was agreeable. Everyone in the kitchen was extremely curious about the unfolding events. While Detective Boyington chatted with this man on the covered stoop outside the kitchen, the residents of the house huddled next to the window, trying to listen to the conversation on the porch. Realizing the curiosity of those inside, the conversation moved to a more private location on the lower porch outside the living room.

Detective Boyington asked to see the man's driver's license. He readily produced his license and willingly engaged in conversation with the detective. Boyington and Sorrell were both familiar with many of the locals, but neither of them knew this guy, identified on his license as Lewis Lent.

Boyington probed, "Are you from around here? I haven't seen you before."

Lent responded, "I'm from Upstate New York—Reynoldsville."

Boyington continued, "Where do you work?"

"I'm currently unemployed, but I worked nights as a janitor at the Pittsfield Cinema Center for seven years," replied Lent.

A chill ran down Boyington's spine. Suddenly, he had that stunning "ah ha" moment as a light bulb went on in his mind. Out of nowhere came the moment of crystal clarity. In that instant, Detective Boyington knew he had found the missing link to the Jimmy Bernardo case, a mystery that had baffled the Pittsfield Police for three years. As Sorrell checked out the van, he also felt an unsettling suspicion.

Boyington reasoned with Lent, "We have to get this straightened out. You're a great guy helping blind people. Come on down to the police station and we'll get things sorted out. We'll give you a ride down and back. You give me a statement about why you had Phil's truck. If somebody made a mistake here, I want to straighten it out with you."

Lent agreed to go but asked if Chester Forfa could go with him.

Boyington agreed. He immediately notified Lieutenant Boyer of his suspicions. "Oh man, I'm telling you, I got the guy, not only for the incident this morning, but for Jimmy Bernardo." He requested an officer to come and transport Lewis Lent and Chester Forfa to the station. The department was right on it.

Lieutenant Boyer and Detective Danford arrived quickly to escort Lent and Forfa to the station.

The Pittsfield Police knew the events unfolding could prove the huge break in the Jimmy Bernardo case that they agonized over for three years. They wasted no time setting the wheels in motion. As Lieutenant Boyer and Detective Danford escorted the men to the police station, Detective Boyington and Officer Sorrell returned to the Lanesboro station to pick up a Polaroid camera to take photos of the GMC pickup and the broken-down van.

Jimmy Bernardo

Gerald Lee had joined the Pittsfield Police Department in 1969. Working his way up the ranks, he took over as police chief in November 1992. A seasoned policeman, Chief Lee inherited a heartbreaking and baffling case—the murder of Jimmy Bernardo.

On October 22, 1990, Jimmy Bernardo arrived home from school at approximately 2:45. He dropped off his things, got on his bike, and left home for the Pittsfield Plaza. Routinely, Jimmy would head over to the plaza when he did not have homework to finish first.

Just a half mile from his home, the strip mall was located on heavily trafficked Route 20, which connects the western edge of Massachusetts with New York State. This non-descript, anywhere, USA strip mall hub of activity housed a furniture store, a video rental store, a pool hall, a laundromat, a discount tee and sweatshirt outlet, an appliance store, a karate studio, and a restaurant. The feature attraction of the plaza was the Pittsfield Cinema Center.

The Pittsfield Plaza became the teen gathering place, providing an expansive parking lot for kids to ride bikes, hang out, play video games and pinball machines, shoot pool, and sometimes sneak into the movie theater with the aid of the theater's janitor.

Jimmy, along with a group of friends, frequented the Clean Machine Coin-Op laundromat to enjoy the pinball machine, video games, and pool table provided for the patrons in the rear of the store. He usually hung out with boys a bit older than himself. Jimmy had a reputation for being "mouthy," but the woman working at the establishment never considered him to be a problem.

That afternoon, Jimmy came alone and played the machines from about 3:00 to 3:30. As he was leaving, he told the woman in charge that he was going to the pay phone by the movie theater, although she often let the boys use the laundromat phone. Jimmy returned, asking the woman to exchange his coins for quarters to continue playing the machines.

Jimmy returned home somewhere between 4:20 and 4:30. The family was eating an early dinner that evening to watch a movie on TV that began at 5:00. Jimmy quickly finished an assignment to write a letter to the United State troops in Saudi Arabia and had his parents sign some items for school the next day. After gobbling down dinner, he returned to the Pittsfield Plaza, where he had arranged to meet up with a friend. The friend's family did not finish dinner as early as the Bernardos, so the boys planned to meet at 5:30.

Shortly after 5:00, as the woman working at the laundromat was about to leave work for the day, she spotted Jimmy through the window coming from the direction of the cinema. He sat down on a chair outside the laundromat to sip his A&W root beer purchased in the soda machine in front of the laundromat and wait for his friend. His bicycle was on the sidewalk next to him.

Jimmy's friend left home at 5:30. When he got to the plaza, he rode his bike around for about fifteen minutes looking for Jimmy. At about 6:00, the friend called the Bernardos' house, enquiring about Jimmy. Mrs. Bernardo told him that Jimmy was still outside playing. The friend then rode across the street to the nearby park where Jimmy might have gone. By 6:30, when he still could not find Jimmy, the boy returned home.

The Bernardos could always count on Jimmy being responsible enough to get home before dark. When Jimmy did not return home at his usual curfew, his parents began to worry. Mrs. Bernardo began calling his friends and drove to the Pittsfield Plaza looking for him. Not finding him, Mr. Bernardo went out to the field adjacent to the Pittsfield Plaza parking lot, walking the shortcut that his son often took going to the plaza.

Now Jimmy's parents began to panic and called the Pittsfield Police. The police took down the boy's descriptive information and sent an officer to the Bernardo home for a follow-up interview. The police treated this as a missing person report. They interviewed Jimmy's younger brother Robert, who swore he had no idea where Jimmy could be. All Robert knew was that his brother had said he was going to the Pittsfield Plaza. The Bernardos furnished the detective with a recent school photo of Jimmy, and a missing person bulletin went out from the police department.

At this point, there was no evidence to suggest anything suspicious had occurred. Detective Peter McGuire did some asking around at the Cinema Center. He briefly chatted with the movie theater's janitor, who said he didn't know anybody and hadn't seen anybody around the cinema. His answer seemed plausible, so nothing was noted.

That night, Police Detective Tom Bowler, who lived a block away from the Cinema Center, had a very uneasy feeling about Jimmy. Having received the bulletin, Bowler decided that before returning home after his shift ended at midnight, he would do some searching on his own. He drove around the Cinema Center, where Jimmy had been seen last. He drove around the area surrounding the McDonald's across the street from the plaza. He scouted nearby Gale Avenue and Jason Street and over the railroad tracks. He got out of his car and walked the tracks and then down to a pond at the wildlife preservation where teens partied and often had bonfires.

"I finally returned home. Sitting in my driveway I was thinking, *Something's not right. This is the real deal.* We've had kids who were missing for days. They were staying at a friend's house or out with a girlfriend, but something just didn't set right. I remember calling the detective bureau the next morning and talking to the supervisor and saying, 'Hey, something's up. I checked that whole neighborhood.' I called to find out if he came home," recalled Bowler.

Detective Joseph Collias remembers, "We had no bike, no clothes, nothing. We thought maybe he got rebellious and got mixed up with some people. We just had no idea." Posters with Jimmy's picture circulated throughout Massachusetts as well as throughout the country.

A friend informed police that Jimmy had told him he had wanted to run away. Rumors of sightings of Jimmy swirled, but nothing panned out. Any leads that came in went to the desk and would be checked out. The detective bureau worked the streets while the juvenile bureau followed up with the parents. On November 2, *America's Most Wanted* broadcasted Jimmy's disappearance. New England Missing Person's Bureau helped collect leads. Without any significant evidence, Jimmy remained a missing person until November 18, when two boys discovered his mint-green BMX Mongoose bicycle partially submerged in Silver Lake near the General Electric complex in Pittsfield, across town from the Pittsfield Plaza. This first significant piece of evidence shocked the community. The search for a body began. "Police used helicopters, planes, police dogs, Army and Navy Reserve personnel volunteer searches, kayakers, and scuba."[9]

Just three days later, on November 21, deer hunters found a body approximately 200 feet off a one-lane dirt road in rural Newfield, New York, eight miles south of Ithaca and sixty miles southwest of Syracuse. Sadly, the naked body was at first believed by the hunters to be a young female due to a lack of body hair. The body would soon be identified as that of Jimmy Bernardo. He lay face down at the base of a sapling tree with a ¼-inch clothesline rope tied around his neck in a slip knot, with the other end tied to the tree. The victim's clothes were found approximately 200 feet from the body. The lack of scratches on the boy's legs indicated that he had walked through the bramble underbrush clothed before being stripped at the scene of the murder.

The Onondaga County, New York medical examiner ruled the cause of death as asphyxiation by strangulation.

9. **Lahr, Ellen G. (6/10/96). Jimmy Was Like a Son.** *The Berkshire Eagle.*

With no defensive wounds found on the body, there was no evidence of struggle or beating. The serious bruises on the neck were due to the rope being twisted tightly, closing off the carotid arteries. Although the victim was not found with restraints, lingering residue remained on the victim's feet below the ankles and around the wrists. The tape over the eyes had paper towels wadded up, either for the victim's comfort or to make a better blindfold.

As soon as word came into the police department about the discovery of Jimmy's body some 200 miles away, Pittsfield Police Officers Peter McGuire, Joseph Collias, and senior investigator from the New York State Police Robert Cartwright went together to break the news to Ron and Mary Bernardo, before they found out through the media. McGuire lamented, "It was one of the saddest and hardest things I ever did. The three of us promised we would never give up until we found who had done this to their son. The abduction and murder of a child is something you do not ever forget."[10]

Detective Peter McGuire was assigned to the murder case along with New York State Police Senior Investigator David McElligot. Throughout the ordeal, McGuire kept the Bernardos informed, developing a close relationship with the family. The tragedy hit close to home for McGuire because he also had a twelve-year-old son. He shared the Bernardos' pain and vowed not to let up until justice was served. McGuire marveled, "I cannot say enough about their (Mary and Ron Bernardos') courage and ability to stand up to this ordeal."[11] "Not too many people didn't have a twelve-year old in their life," said Pittsfield Police Chief Lee. "When you see children involved, everyone is affected. When a child is abducted and killed, the police don't forget

10. O'Connor, Gerald. (January 15, 1994) For Bernardos and the Police a Long Road and Sad Conclusion. *The Berkshire Eagle.*

11. Lahr, Ellen G. (June 10, 1996). Jimmy Was Like a Son. *The Berkshire Eagle.*

it."[12] Close family, strong religious faith, and a supportive community embraced the Bernardos, trying in some small way to ease their inescapable anguish and loss.

This tragedy sent shock waves through the community. The once safe city, where people did not feel the need to lock their doors and felt completely comfortable letting their children play outdoors, ride their bikes around town, walk to school alone, or even wait for the school bus without an adult present, took a dramatic turn. Parents felt the need for a new vigilance, watching and protecting their children as never before.

A massive search ensued, including informational roadblocks in the vicinity of the Pittsfield Plaza and in the vicinity of Newfield, where the body had been found. Command centers were set up at the Pittsfield Police Department as well as the Ithaca, New York PD. Reward money started coming in, hoping to generate useful information. There was particular interest in the Pittsfield Cinema Center, since this was where Jimmy had been seen last.

Detectives McGuire and McElligot checked out every lead for over three years. All the businesses in the Pittsfield Plaza were asked to submit employee lists. Richard Baumann, the manager of the Pittsfield Cinema Center where Jimmy had been seen last, handed over his payroll list. It never occurred to him to include all his part-time and contract transitional employees, nor the many delivery people who frequented the facility. He figured that the police already knew of the nighttime janitor who contacted them occasionally when there was a break-in at the theater. Thirty thousand leads, files bulging with information, every name submitted, every known sex offender, every lead followed up, and still there were no clues. There was a vague mention

---

12. Lahr, Ellen G. (June 10, 1996). Jimmy Was Like a Son. *The Berkshire Eagle*.

of the sighting of a light-blue van, but that tip never panned out.

For three years, the Pittsfield Police and the New York State Police followed up on every tip they received. The paperwork on these dead-end leads filled filing cabinets. After three years, the clues led nowhere.

CHAPTER 4

IN CUSTODY

3:30 PM, Friday, January 7, 1994

Arriving at the police station, Lewis Lent had his elimination photo taken. The intent of the photo was to mingle it with those of similar looking males for the victim and other witnesses to identify the perpetrator of the crime. His photo would be inserted among nine other photos. Lent proceeded upstairs to the detective bureau to talk with Detective Boyington.

Shortly after Lent's arrival at the station, Detective McGuire called over to the State Police Troop C in Ithaca, New York to let them know that finally they suspected they had a break in the Jimmy Bernardo case. A background check showed the address on a previous motor vehicle registered to Lent as Burdett, New York, just twelve miles from where Jimmy's body was discovered.

New York State Police Captain Frank Pace, the head of Troop C's Bureau of Criminal Investigation out of Sidney, decided to head over to Pittsfield. He started out but got only as far as the New York Thruway due to blizzard conditions. Troop G, the closest to the Massachusetts border, was notified. Detectives James Ayling from over the New York/ Massachusetts border in East Greenbush and Detective Jack

Murray from Loudonville in the nearby Albany area braved the blinding snow, finally getting through to the Pittsfield Police station. The New York troopers were chomping at the bit for the opportunity to begin to unravel a murder case that had baffled them for three years.

Boyington needed to bide time while the wheels turned to start the investigation and the New York troopers arrived. He began the interrogation with Lent, "There's no big problem here. I just want to talk to you - get to know you."

Lent presented himself as friendly, and he loved to talk. At this point, the suspect had not been read his rights because he was not yet being questioned about the day's incident. Boyington assured Lent that since he was not under arrest, he was not obliged to talk or to stay at the station. Boyington typed away as Lewis Lent talked about what he had done during the day.

In his statement to Detective Boyington, Lent ran through what had transpired when Detective Boyington and Officer Sorrell appeared at the door of the Shallieses' home. He proceeded to explain his whereabouts during the day. In his explanation, he made it clear that he had left his house between 5:45 and 6:00 that morning, driving directly from his apartment in North Adams across to Williamstown and down Rte. 7 directly to Phil Shallieses' home in Lanesboro. Much of the conversation was simply banter about baseball, shoveling snow, and snow blowing. Boyington just wanted to keep Lent talking until the New York authorities arrived. As it was getting late, Boyington sent out to the Highland restaurant for burgers and coffee.

After all this time, Boyington felt as if he was running out of gas. He excused himself and told Lieutenant Boyer, "Look Dave, I have to start throwing some hard balls. I'm done. I have three or four pages of bullshit. I'll just stick with Rebecca Savarese."

Boyer gave him the go ahead. As far as Boyington was concerned, "He ain't leaving, but he doesn't know it. He's under arrest but I haven't told him yet. Lent was not asking to leave. He just kept talking. He was loving being the center of attention."

So now, Boyington read the accused his rights and told Lent he was going to ask him some difficult questions to straighten things out about Phil's truck. Lewis Lent acknowledged that he understood what had just been read to him, and he signed the waiver. Detective Boyington reiterated that Lent was not under arrest. During this time, Lent agreed to whatever was asked of him. He never asked about Chet Forfa, who had accompanied him to the station, nor did he ask to contact an attorney or call anyone.

Up to this point, Lent stuck to the story that he had come to Lanesboro that morning directly from his home in North Adams. He continued talking. Boyington thought things were going well until his supervisor Lieutenant Boyer came in and asked Lent if he had an FID (Firearms Identification card).

Lent replied, "Yes, I do."

Boyer queried, "May I see it?"

Lent handed him the card. He maintained that he did not possess a handgun, nor had he ever shot a handgun. As Boyer walked away holding Lent's FID, he muttered to himself, "You'll never see this again." As reality began to close in on the suspect, Lent just clammed up. It was over. Boyington again read him his rights.

Amy Boyington

At 5:30 Friday afternoon, Amy Boyington called her father, Detective Owen Boyington, at work. Amy found it unusual that all the lines to the Pittsfield Police Department's detective bureau were busy. Trying again later, she finally got through to her father.

"Amy, what's up?" Detective Boyington greeted his daughter.

"Dad, I've got to talk to you."

"Hey, listen. Is everything all right? Got a problem?"

"No."

"Car wreck?"

"No."

"I can't talk to you right now. I'm really, really busy." Boyington needed to get off the phone.

"That's OK, Dad. I'll talk to you tomorrow."

As Owen hung up, he realized, "I never refused a call from my kids before. When the girls called, I always talked to them."

For the past year and a half, Amy Boyington, a senior at Westfield State College, came home on weekends and vacations to work at the Pittsfield Girls' Club. Today, she was still on her Christmas break. A physical education major, she hoped working at this job would lead to full time employment when she graduated in the spring. Although she spent most of her time as a lifeguard and swim instructor, she filled in anywhere she was needed. An ideal find for the club, Amy was an experienced babysitter—hard working, reliable, focused, creative, and athletic. The club had a treasure in her.

This Friday afternoon, due to the bad weather, a usually bustling swim class consisted only of Suzie and Jennifer[13] from the club's after school program. Amy decided to let the girls have the run of the pool with a free swim. After an hour in the water, she rounded up the girls, getting them out of the pool to dress and be ready in case their mothers arrived early to pick them up.

While the girls were still swimming, a nicely dressed man arrived at the Girls' Club's main office, the official check-in area, to pick up his daughter from her swimming lesson.

---

13. Not their real names

He looked respectable, so without further questioning or signing in, he was granted access to the pool area. Even the heartiest of Berkshireites wanted to get home safely during this blizzard and snuggle in for the night.

Suzie and Jennifer made their way up the few steps from the locker area to the changing stalls, giggling and horsing around. As they were changing, Amy's co-worker Lisa, finishing work with the after-school program, came up to the pool to visit. A little before 5:00, Jennifer's mother arrived. After chatting with Amy and Lisa, the mother yelled up to the girls to hurry them along. The girls were in the last two changing stalls at the far end of the hall next to a back room, which was used to store supplies. When the girls came down to the locker room, Jennifer whispered in Amy's ear, "There's a man upstairs in the back room."

Amy and Lisa immediately went upstairs and checked the back room, finding no one. Starting at each end of the long, narrow hallway, they began pulling back the changing stall curtains. When they reached the third stall from the back room, they found the curtain pulled tightly closed, unusual for an empty dressing area. Looking down, they spotted boots under the curtain. Amy waited there while sending Lisa to the pool office to call down to the main office. Unfamiliar with the intercom system, Lisa could not get through to the office. Amy then left the dressing area to help Lisa make the call.

Wanting to keep things quiet until help arrived, Amy, Lisa, and the girls waited in the locker room for backup. Jennifer's mother, however, had a different idea. She stood on the steps leading up to the dressing rooms, calling to the intruder trying to coax him out.

According to Amy, "The man came out of the stall and through the changing area and then down the stairs. The mother, the two girls, Lisa, and I were standing at the bottom of the stairs next to the door that leads to the rest of the building and to an outside exit. I started to question him why he was there. He told me that he did not know, and he started to back out of the door. I told him to wait because I wanted to straighten this out. He continued to back through the door and then ran through an outside exit that led to East Street. He ran eastbound on the sidewalk down East Street."[14]

Growing up with a dad who was both a Marine and a cop, Amy learned by example that, "If you see something, say or do something." Without thinking twice, she took off after the intruder. He was no match for this five-foot-nine, long-legged track team runner. As the suspect reached the parking lot of the Registry of Motor Vehicles down the block, Amy grabbed him by the back of his coat collar. By this time, two male employees for the Girls' Club appeared and the three surrounded the man, gently but firmly leading him back to the club. They escorted the unresisting man through the front door and locked him in the director's office, waiting for the police to arrive.

While the chase was in progress, Lisa had come to the main office to report this incident to the club's assistant director, who called the police. The director of the after school program immediately notified the staff to keep everyone in classrooms. "There has been a situation and the police have been called. I did not want them seeing anything they did not need to see," she stated.

As the suspect was brought back into the building, the after school director thought, *That's Nick Mangiardi. I know him. He doesn't have a daughter. Why would he do such a thing? He looks so normal.*

At 5:09 PM, Officer David Herforth answered the call requesting the police at the Girls' Club on East Street because of a suspicious male in the swimming pool area changing room. Officers Robert Beals and Michael Ortega

---

14. **Boyington, Amy. (January 9, 1994) Pittsfield Police Department, Detective O.W. Boyington Statement.**

were immediately dispatched to the scene. Amy Boyington directed them to the office where the suspect sat.

Now that the police had taken over, Amy immediately called her dad. Unfortunately, she could not get through to the Pittsfield Police Department's detective bureau. She had no idea why all the lines were busy.

After ascertaining the man's identity as Nicholas Francis Mangiardi Jr., the officers inquired what he had been doing in the locker room. Denying anything sexual, he responded, "I arrived early for the 6:00 PM family swim." In truth, the family swim began at 6:30 PM and had been canceled that evening due to the miserable weather. In her later statement to the police, Amy, who worked the family swim every week, said that she had never seen this man before.

When asked the whereabouts of his bathing suit or a gym bag, Mr. Mangiardi told them that he had left his bathing suit upstairs. Officer Beals continued to interview him while Officer Ortega went to search for bathing trunks in the locker room. Upon further questioning, the suspect stated that he "went upstairs, got scared and hid." At this point, Officer Beals advised him of his Miranda rights. When Officer Beals returned to the office with a pair of white shorts, Mangiardi told the officers that he had brought them to the club. However, upon further scrutiny, he admitted that the shorts were not his.

Now Officer Ortega let the suspect know that he was going to interview the two young girls. Nicholas Mangiardi suddenly blurted out, "I was not masturbating. You know how kids exaggerate."

Although quite shaken, Jennifer explained that she and Suzie had been changing in the two back curtained changing stalls. As they finished dressing and were packing their bags, Suzie heard someone in the back room.

"Who is it?" she had asked.

Jennifer went up to the door, opened it just a crack, and asked, "What are you doing back there?"

Looking in, she saw a man crouching, showing some bare skin. She was unsure if it was an arm or a leg. Now both girls looked and saw his bare legs as he sat in the back room. Unnerved, they hurried to the adults in the locker room.

At first denying this account, Nick Mangiardi finally admitted to having his pants down while hiding in the back room. He stated, "I have a younger sister and just like kids. I like to hear them laugh and see them have fun."

The suspect was arrested for lewd and lascivious behavior, transported to the police station, booked, and advised of his rights by Sergeant John O'Neil. Later, the suspect called his mother and said, "Mom, they picked me up tonight, same old thing. I got caught with my pants down."[15]

The Station Buzz

5:30, Friday, January 7, 1994

Just as Detective Boyington took a break from interviewing the kidnapping suspect, Bob Beals, who was working the desk, came up and said, "Did you hear about your daughter and what happened at the Girls' Club?"

"No. She called before, but I couldn't talk to her."

"You won't believe this. There was a guy hiding out in the girls' locker room. He took off, and Amy chased him down the block and caught him at the RMV.

"Damn, the one time I didn't talk to her!"

The police all knew how impetuous, dangerous, and crazy Amy's actions had been, yet, as cops, they all admired her guts and automatic response without thinking

---

15. Beals, Officer Robert J., Ortega Officer Michael. (January 7, 1994) Pittsfield Police Department Robert J. Beals Report to the Chief.

through the potential consequences. As her dad, Owen felt tremendous relief that Amy was not hurt yet felt immensely proud of her courage and quick thinking.

CHAPTER 5

THE ARRESTS

Lent was cooperative, allowing the police to interview him and take his picture. Detective Bowler recounted, "We looked through the mug books to find people with similar characteristics to his. We came up with about nine individuals. We would insert his picture among the nine."

Rebecca Savarese and eyewitness Russell Davis, along with Russell's eight-year- old son, returned to the station in the late afternoon. They were shown the array of photos independently of each other. Usually, witnesses are kept in separate rooms so they cannot influence each other's identification. Due to lack of space in the Pittsfield Police Department, Rebecca and Russell remained in the same room, but at opposite ends. Unlike early in the morning when Lent wore a heavy jacket and a knit cap pulled down covering his hair, police photos of him without the outerwear provided a clearer look at the man. Rebecca and Russell chose the same photo and told Detective Bowler that it looked like the individual they had seen, but not with one hundred percent certainty.

The coincidence of Russell Davis being the witness to the abduction of Rebecca Savarese was prescient. Nancy Davis, Russell's wife, had gone to school and remained friends with Mary Bernardo, Jimmy's mother. The weekend prior to the incident with Rebecca Savarese, Nancy had visited with Mary, at which time she enquired if anything new was happening in the investigation of Jimmy's case. The next weekend, Nancy again stopped over the Bernardos' house and let Mary know that it was her husband who had witnessed the incident with Rebecca and called the police. Little did they know at the time that this incident would be the break in the murder case of the Bernardos' son.

The police escorted Russell Davis and his son to the Shallieses' residence to identify the truck allegedly used in the kidnapping. Davis stood in front of the truck, looking at it through a mirror to see it as it appeared to him that morning through his rearview mirror. Although it looked very much like the same vehicle, he could not identify it with absolute certainty since the vehicle was now covered with snow. Rebecca was also asked to identify the truck. Again, in the dark and with snow on the vehicle, she said that it looked familiar but could not definitively make the connection.

Bowler continued, "So we still did not have a positive identification of our suspect. At some point, the decision was made to try and firm up the identity through the witnesses. There was only one person who could do this and that was Rebecca. We decided among ourselves up at the detective bureau that we would do a physical lineup."

After getting Lent's consent to participate in the lineup, on that cold, blizzardy night, the police visited bars, restaurants, pool halls, and hangouts, rounding up men resembling Lewis Lent. Unlike what one sees on TV, the Pittsfield Police Department was not equipped with a room with a two-way mirror separating the witness from the lineup. Rebecca had to be in the same room with these men. She remained in the records rooms while the lineup was being assembled in a nearby hallway.

Detective Bowler described the process. "We had the seven other guys standing out in the hallway with numbers hanging around their necks. They each held a card, were given a number, and were instructed that when their number was called, they were to say the phrase on the card: 'Do as I say, and I won't shoot you.'

"Rebecca was in the room with me and I instructed her how this was going to take place.

I told her to look at all the men carefully and to take her time. The men would be instructed to turn left and right and to say a phrase. She had a sheet of paper which corresponded with the eight individuals in the lineup. She was to check off the number if there was somebody there that she recognized. And she was to tell us how she recognized that individual."

"She was a little nervous. I'll be honest with you: I was a little nervous because I didn't know how this was going to pan out. I was also somewhat anxious because as an investigator, we are hoping we had our individual and hoping for a positive result here. We were hoping for either of two things—to move forward with this person or to discount him saying he was not involved."

"She fully understood her role and responsibility. When we stepped out into the hallway, she grabbed my arm.

"She said, 'That's him.'

"I said, 'That's who?'

"'That's the man who tried to take me this morning.'

"I said, 'OK, I want you to take your sheet of paper and you mark down the number on the sheet that corresponds with the individual,' which she did. We continued with the process so that everyone in the lineup had a chance to speak and do their part. This was all being video recorded. After we finished, we brought her back in the room. We talked. She was certainly shaken up and nervous."

As a result of the lineup, Lent was also rattled. His defenses started stripping away. He remarked how fearful the little girl looked when she saw him in the lineup. He mentioned that he suffered from blackout spells during which he had no memory of what happened. He explained that when his personality split, his alter ego "Stephen" would appear, and that he had no control over "Stephen's" actions.

Based on Rebecca's ID, Lent was arrested. He was taken downstairs to be processed, and Bowler continued, "But after we arrested him and we went through his wallet in the booking room, we found the receipt from his purchase of a gun from a sporting goods store." Lt. Boyer again questioned Lent about owning a handgun and again Lent denied it. Boyer then showed Lent a receipt from Dave's Sporting Goods Store for a .22 caliber revolver with a six-inch barrel with his signature, dated 2/23/93. Bowler continued, "So now we knew that he was lying to us earlier and things just progressed from there."

It was Desk Sergeant Michael Case's job to supervise the dispatcher and run the station. He was responsible for booking the prisoners. Upstairs in the detective bureau to be sure that all procedures were ironclad and done by the book, Lent was videotaped as he was read his rights. Lieutenant Boyer asked Sergeant Case to stay an extra shift to attend to Lent. He felt that Case would be the one to maintain his cool settling this prisoner in his cell for the night.

Lewis Lent, fearing his first night alone in the basement jail cell, wanted to keep talking. The police befriended him to keep up the momentum. As a delaying tactic, the prisoner complained to Sergeant Case that the cell was crawling with bugs. This, most assuredly, was not the case.

At about 6:30 that evening the New York Police, after braving the elements to make the trip to Pittsfield, arrived at the Pittsfield Police Station. They were chomping at the bit to finally confront the first credible suspect in the murder case of Jimmy Bernardo. Unfortunately for the New York Police, their interaction with the suspect was limited. Pittsfield Police needed to concentrate on the immediate crime—the attempted abduction of Rebecca Savarese. Lent talked and bantered with the Pittsfield Police until 3:00 in the morning. The New York State troopers would have their time with the prisoner over the weekend.

The Pittsfield Police strategized how to proceed with the alleged perpetrator of not only an attempted child abduction, but with a credible suspect in the murder of Jimmy Bernardo. They wanted to make Lent as comfortable as possible for him to let down his guard and begin telling them the truth. They also had to establish ground rules for the roles that the Pittsfield Police and the New York Police would play in questioning the suspect. Lieutenant Boyer wanted New York to stick strictly to the Jimmy Bernardo case while Pittsfield would stick to the Rebecca Savarese case.

District Attorney Gerard Downing and First Assistant District Attorney David Capeless were on hand to confer with the police on how to proceed. There were several things that the police needed to do to establish evidence for future court proceedings. Technicians from Berkshire Medical Center arrived to draw blood for blood type and DNA samples. The DAs also conferred on what forms Lent needed to sign.

Meanwhile, Lewis Lent was contemplating his own strategy. "He was very calm the whole time he was up in our detective bureau. He was trying to cooperate, but at the same time planning what his next step would be," observed Detective Bowler. "He was trying to figure out if his calculations would be correct in the next couple of minutes or the next few hours. How was all this going to pan out? But at the same time, I think he was trying to cooperate to make it look like he wasn't involved in anything. I think it was after the arrest was made that he knew there was no hiding. Things were now going to come out in the open. It was up to him how he was going to play this out."

On the Home Front

As Lent went through his paces at the police station that first night, his friends and neighbors reeled with the turmoil and shock of the events of the day. Downstairs neighbor Linda Domenichini recalled the following in her deposition to the police:

"Phil Shallies called my house and talked to Rick Murdock (Linda's boyfriend). He said Lew was in trouble, and to get rid of the pot plants. We all knew that Lew had some pot plants growing in his apartment. Rick called me on the telephone and told me about the conversation with Phil. I told him to go upstairs and tell Roger Beaudin to get rid of the plants and paraphernalia. Roger broke into Lewie's room (he had done it before so he knew how to get in). Roger brought two plants down to my apartment and put them in my bedroom. Then after I got home, I found the plants in my room and tried to find out what was going on. I watched the six o'clock news and saw the composite of Lew and listened to the description of the vehicle. I knew it was Lew right to the Band-Aid on his nose.

"I called Phil to see if he had heard anything more. Phil had heard nothing at this point that was new, but he filled me in on what he knew to this point. I told Bodie (Roger) to get rid of the paraphernalia or anything concerning pot, because the police would probably be coming. Bodie took the paraphernalia down to the cellar and put it in an old washing machine for the night. About 11:00 Phil called to say there was an arrest. Lewie had been arrested. The police came over about 12 midnight to question Jonathan and Melissa and Roger. The police left and said they would be back in the morning.

CHAPTER 6

THE CRACK IN THE ARMOR

Saturday at the Station, January 8, 1994

Detectives Peter McGuire and Gary Danford reported for work at 8:30 on Saturday morning. Desk Sargent Harold Finn, bringing the detectives up to speed, related that Lent had requested to make a phone call and that Lent mentioned that he remembered some things he could not remember the previous day. McGuire went down to lockup and brought the prisoner upstairs to the detective bureau. Lent was again read his Miranda rights, which he signed before he began sharing his newly found memory.

Lent began, "Last night when I was in the lineup and seeing that little girl, it was like a mirror reflection of seeing her looking scared. It's like I had seen her with the same look on her face somewhere before."

He prefaced his newfound memory by telling the officers that he had difficulty remembering things due to blackout spells. He continued to recall that the previous Thursday, he had borrowed Phil Shallies's truck to help out a friend. Originally, Lent had recounted driving directly from his apartment in North Adams early Friday morning, south on Rte. 7, then turning left onto Summer St, arriving before 8:00 at Phil's house. He now remembered making a right turn onto Summer Street, which meant he must have been heading northbound up Rte. 7 from Pittsfield.

After his denial the previous day about owning or ever handling guns, being presented with contradictory evidence jogged his memory. He remembered that he owned a shotgun, .22 semiautomatic rifle, and a pellet pistol, but denied buying a revolver at Dave's Sporting Goods. The police checked this out at Dave's and a copy of his purchase slip for the revolver was sent to the police. Lent stated for the record, "I do not remember. I do remember going to Dave's Sporting Goods with my woman friend Susan. I remember looking at them."

Confronted with this evidence, McGuire asked Lent if he would give a new statement in writing regarding the purchase of the gun, to which Lent agreed.

Phone Home

Lent then asked to use the phone and have some privacy. McGuire could not allow the prisoner to be left alone in the room. The detective waited by the door at the other end of the room so Lent could be observed without McGuire listening in on the phone conversation.[16]

Lent called his friend and downstairs neighbor Linda Domenichini, asking to speak with his nephew Jon, who happened to be at the neighbors' apartment. Lewis started by saying that Jon probably knew where he was and what happened. Lewis told him he could not remember the kidnapping incident. He asked Jon to feed his cats until he returned home. Lewis also asked him to go upstairs and look behind the refrigerator for a jar and to throw it away before the contents would start to smell and stink up the apartment.

---

16. **Detective Gary Danford (January 18, 1994) Pittsfield Police Department Detective Gary W. Danford Investigation Report.**

Jon and Linda's boyfriend Rick looked behind the refrigerators in the kitchen and in Lewis's bedroom, not finding a jar. The two guys searched the whole apartment but still could not locate the jar. Entering Lewis's bedroom, Jon saw the wall that divided the room in half, which he believed his uncle wanted to use for storage although he had no idea what he had wanted to store. He discovered a plastic shopping bag containing what appeared to be a little girl's sweater. He had no idea why this was in Uncle Lew's room.[17]

New York Investigators Step In

The New York Police moved into action on the home front. They wanted to speak with Lewis Lent's parents. Interviewing them had to be handled very sensitively. While waiting to speak with the suspect in Pittsfield, Detective Ayling assigned Officers Conroy and Stark, from their command post in New York, to engage Lent's mother and stepfather, Lois and Alfred Wood, in an interview about their son. The police hoped to gain a greater insight into Lent's background and his whereabouts.

Mark Wood, Lewis's stepbrother, accompanied his parents in the room during the police questioning. Lewis's arrest hit his family with shock and disbelief. In light of the charges against their son, Mrs. Wood cried, "He wouldn't do that. He is a Christian. He is a preacher!" Mr. and Mrs. Wood knew of the Bernardo case but felt Lewis could not have harmed a child.

The questioning began with their son's visits home. Lewis had visited them several times since his move to the Berkshires. On many of his visits, Lewis brought along his friend Sue, whom his parents believed to be his girlfriend.

17. Witness Statement Sheet, 1/9/94 – Investigator Frank J. Jerome.

Lewis brought a twelve-year-old named Stevie a few times and once a blind friend, Phil. On most of his trips home, Lewis drove Sue's car, first her blue Ford Escort station wagon, then later her newer car, a maroon Ford Escort wagon. The police wondered if he ever came home in his van. They were particularly curious whether he had returned to them in the van between August and November of 1990. He did come home for Thanksgiving 1990, but they could not recall his driving a blue and white van at that time. The interviewers then honed in on Lent's whereabouts during August 1993. Lent mentioned that he had gone to the state fair to watch the demolition derby. His parents knew that Sue had worked at the state fair that summer, but they could not pin down the exact date when he had come by the house.

A lavender button from a man's dress shirt was found at the crime scene near Jimmy Bernardo's body, perhaps torn from the killer's shirt during a struggle. As yet the shirt had not been found. The police inquired if Lewis ever left any of his clothes at the parents' house. The answer was no.

The police mentioned that Lewis had a gun permit and a pistol. Had his parents ever seen him with a gun? During a conversation, Lewis had told his mother that he had a gun and a permit to use it, but not to worry. The police showed them rope and tape and asked if they had seen these before. Again, the answer was no.

Next, they began to ask questions about Lewis's background. Mrs. Wood was unaware of any childhood problems, recent problems, or anything unusual of a sexual nature. Mrs. Wood related that she and Lewis Lent Sr. had separated when her son was one year old. Her ex-husband had remained in the Burdett, New York area for ten years before moving to Florida.

When Lewis moved to Florida, he lived in the same town as his father. That is when she believed that Jr. found out about his father's past. Knowing this scandalous information, she thought her son would have had nothing to do with his father.

The police gleaned little information or insight from Lent's parents. Lois Wood described Lewis as independent and very private, which meant that she could not offer reliable information to the police about her son's behavior and habits.[18]

New York troopers then interviewed Lewis Lent's friend Sue. She explained that she had met Lewis in 1985 when he attended Northeast Bible School of Biblical Studies. She stated, "Lewis is a Christian, and he did some preaching while attending Bible school in Rome, NY and maybe in Utica. Lewis does carpentry work, masonry work, and also does moving jobs for his friends... Lewis and I have been seeing each other and we have been very close friends since 1985. Our relationship has always been strictly platonic due to our religious beliefs."

Sue remembered details about all of Lewis's temporary jobs, about all the cars he had owned or borrowed, about where they went together, about the selling of his first van, about his background and his family, and about going gun shopping with him. She remembered that he had clothesline rope, which she believed he used to tie boxes, and duct tape, which she believed he used to patch up hoses in his van. She believed that the rope the detectives showed her did not match up with what she had seen in his possession.[19]

The officers asked Sue if Lewis had ever talked to her about the Jimmy Bernardo case. Her response was that she and Lewis often watched the local news together. Other than talking about the Bernardo case in passing, he mentioned that everyone at the movie theater had spoken to the police. He never mentioned anyone else. There was no record of a

---

18. **Command Post interview by Troopers Conry/Stark, January 8, 1994.**

19. **Police interview, State of New York, People of the State of New York vs. Lewis Lent.**

police interview with Lent.[20] With his family, as with friends and acquaintances, Lent morphed into whatever he thought someone wanted him to be.

Pittsfield Police Station

Finally, at about 10:00 AM, New York State Police Detectives Murray and Ayling had their chance to speak with Lewis Lent. They wanted to talk to him about a different matter— Jimmy Bernardo—but Lent, in turn, insisted that he wanted to talk with them about the incident from the previous day. Lent expressed to them his concern about the fear he had put the little girl through and wanted to make it up to her. The detectives suggested that he write a letter of apology to her. Lent wrote the following:

Dear Rebecca,
    I am very sorry for what I did to you. It was a scary, awful experience for me as I'm sure it was for you. I can only hope you can try to understand that I really cannot understand my own feelings but I really do care about how you can try to live a happy life without worry about such things hurting your feelings and changing you somehow in some bad way. I wish it had never happened and that you can try to leave it in the past somehow. I don't expect you to forgive me.
    Lew Lent

The letter was never sent, but it would later be used as State's evidence.

The New York detectives, following Lent's lead, began questioning the suspect about the incident the previous day. At first, Lent continued to deny his knowledge of the

---

20. **King, Suzanne. (January 16, 1994). Lewis Lent Jr. A Man Full of Contradictions.** *Observer-Dispatch.*

kidnapping. Although he did not actually get Rebecca into the truck, the act of holding a gun to her, walking her up to the corner, and having her temporarily in his custody constituted a kidnapping charge.

As evidence strongly corroborated the attempted abduction, Lent resorted to his Plan B: his evil alter ego "Stephen," who appeared during Lent's supposed blackouts, overpowered his positive personality, forcing him to do evil things. With his multiple personalities, he had difficulty recalling details during these spells. He attributed his actions to intense headaches, resulting in blackout spells and "fright experiences," during which he could not remember whole chunks of time. During these blackouts, his evil split personality "Stephen" took over. He was unaware of his alter ego's actions.

As Murray and Ayling chipped away at Lent for hours, often asking "what if" questions, he eventually began to speculate about what happened, speaking in the third person. If this was I, this is what I would have done. He hit the mark exactly. Lent related events only known to the police and the perpetrator. At about 3:35 PM, Lent asked to speak to Pittsfield Police Detective Gary Danford. With Ayling and Murray present, he related the events of the previous day as they really happened. He signed a written confession for the attempted abduction of Rebecca Savarese. In his attempt to flaunt his intelligence, Lent checked Investigator Murray's written statement thoroughly for accuracy in content and spelling, making the necessary corrections. He cooperatively provided samples of head and pubic hair as requested and signed consent forms both for New York and Massachusetts to search his apartment and his van.

Search, Seizure, and the Media

Lent's van, Shallies's 1975 GMC pickup truck, and Forfa's 1983 Delta 88 Oldsmobile remained under observation to ensure that no one tampered with the vehicles. By Saturday, the police had the written authority to search Lent's vehicle. They still had to obtain Phil Shallies's and Chester Forfa's permission to search their vehicles. In order to search the vehicles, the van, truck, and car had to be transported to the police garage. Phil recalls, "At night they came and were going to take my truck. Well, nobody comes to the door, so my aunt looked out and saw all these people standing around my truck in the lower driveway. So, she said, 'Somebody is out there at your truck.' I went out to the driveway to enquire about what was happening. Told that the truck was going to be hauled to the police garage, one of the cops sarcastically asked me, 'Well, what does a blind guy need with a truck?'

That incident was just one of the many indignities that the Shallies family would encounter from law enforcement and the media over the course of the case. With the necessary consent forms signed, the police towed the truck. A few days later, Chester Forfa signed a consent form, and his car was impounded by the police as well.

Phil Shallies expressed concern about the length of time that they would be without a vehicle. There were no guarantees once the police took possession of the vehicle when the owner would get it back. The truck remained in the police garage for seven months. Phil explained, "I didn't know when I would get it back or even if I would. I kept contacting the DA's office." On May 11, 1994, Shallies sent a letter to DA Downing:

Dear Mr. Downing,

Since January 7th, 1994 my family and I have been a victim in the Lewis Lent case.

My truck was impounded on January 7th and to this day is still impounded.

We have cooperated fully with the FBI and the Task Force. Our lives have been totally disrupted we feel violated.

I was told by the Task Force two months ago that you had released my truck to Lewis Lent's lawyer. I in turn contacted Mr. LeBlanc who told me he would get in touch with me in a few days. After waiting one week I contacted him again and he told me he would get back to me "in good time."

A lawyer friend of mine contacted Mr. LeBlanc and he was informed that the truck had not been released by you.

Richard Vinette has contacted your office twice and asked to speak to Ann Kendall and she has not returned either call. This has been over a 3 week period.

A comment has been made by a detective on the Pittsfield Police force and a member of your staff saying, "What does a blind man need of a truck." Is this the consensus of your office? If so, I will consider this remark DISCRIMINATION against the blind. After all judge Hanna was blind.

I have many jobs to do around our house but I cannot do them without my truck. I have been needlessly paying auto insurance since my truck was impounded. I would like to know how much longer you are going to keep my truck so I will know if I should cancel my insurance or not.

Your prompt reply will be greatly appreciated.

Sincerely,

Phillip Shallies

Written by Janie Ray

A letter of response was sent to the Pittsfield Police Department on July 28, 1994:

ATTENTION: Investigators James Winn and Bruce Eaton
Re: Property of Phillip Shallies

Dear Investigators:
This letter will authorize you to release to Phillip M. Shallies, or his designee, that property of his, more specifically a pickup truck, which has been at the Pittsfield Police Department with the Shallies' permission since January 1994. I have confirmed with Attorney LeBlanc of the Committee for Public Counsel Services, attorney for Lewis S. Lent, that he has no objection to the release of this property to its rightful owner.
I have informed Mr. Shallies that he is to contact either of you between the hours of 8:00 a.m. and 3:00 p.m., Mondays through Fridays, to obtain his property.
Thank you for your cooperation in this matter.
Very truly yours,
Gerard D. Downing
District Attorney

"Finally, the Commission for the Blind helped me get hold of State Senator Jane Swift, who intervened on my behalf. With the help of Officer Kim Bertelli, who contacted Chief Gerald Lee, I finally got my truck back in August."

Janie Ray added, "We went down to get the truck and it wouldn't start. They had left the key in it and the battery was dead."

Confiscation of his possessions and intrusion by the police just added to the distress foisted on these innocent victims as events continued to unfold. This was just the beginning for the ordeal facing the Shallies family.

Then came the reporters. "When it first hit the news media, they were relentless. All this affected Phil's mother and aunt terribly. His aunt and I were afraid his mother would have a heart attack with all the people coming to the door wanting to talk to them with cameras. Phil's mother

Sally finally said, 'Leave us alone!' and slammed the door. Albany news, everyone, they all came up to the door. I told them, 'You can't come here and tape. You can't be on this property. It's against the law.' I made them go out into the road," recalled Phil Shallies's girlfriend Janie Ray.

"It was like living in a fishbowl. I remember the first morning after all this hit, there were phones ringing, people knocking on the door. It was just an unbelievable barrage from newspapers, radio, and TV stations. And then, of course, there was the police. The news media was relentless. One day, we were going to a birthday party. As we walked out of the house, the media camped across the street came racing over wanting to interview us. This upset my mother so much she cried, 'The hell with the party.' We ended up turning around and coming back, holing up in the house," lamented Phil Shallies.

Evidence

By 6:15 Saturday evening, Lent's van arrived at the police garage. With Detectives Bowler and Collias present, Investigator Winn searched the vehicle. The van contained the following:

- Item #1 – Light colored canvas bag with green handles, found under the right side of the right rear seat.

CONTAINED IN THE ABOVE-MENTIONED CANVAS BAG WERE ITEMS 2 THROUGH 25:

- Item #2 – .22 cal revolver, "High Standard" fully loaded 9 shot, Ser # 1354332
- Item #3 – Black holster for the above revolver
- Item #4 – One roll of "Manco" duct tape, 2 in. by 60 yds.

- Item #5 – One roll of Johnson & Johnson waterproof tape, one half inch x 180 in.
- Item #6 – One roll "CVS" waterproof tape, one in. by 108 in.
- Item #7 – One "Buck" knife with sheath, 6 in. blade
- Item #8 – One latex rubber mask
- Item #9 – One bottle "TUMS" antacid tablets
- Item #10 – One bottle "RITE-AID" Ibuprofen caplets, 200 count
- Item #11 – One "DURACELL" Durabeam flashlight
- Item #12 – One "RAY-O-VAC" Roughneck flashlight
- Item #13 – One brown leather belt, 2 in. wide by 40.5 in. long
- Item #14 – One plastic "CVS" pharmacy bag
- Item #15 – One large "HERSHEY'S" chocolate bar from inside item #14
- Item #16 – One CVS pharmacy cash register receipt for purchase of item #15, this was also contained inside the CVS bag Item #14
- Item #17 – One pack book of matches
- Item #18 – One left hand men's glove with knit cuff
- Item #19 – One right hand men's glove with knit cuff
- Item #20 – One plastic "CVS" bag, larger than bag mentioned in item #14
- Item #21 – One "EQUITY" battery operated alarm running with the correct time. This was found inside item #20
- Item #22 – One of "TOP CARE" sheer strip band-aids, 30 count 1 in. by 3 in. This was found inside item #20
- Item #23 – Three "PAPERMATE" pens, found inside item #20
- Item #24 – One pair of florescent orange kid's sunglasses, this found inside item #20
- Item #25 – One pair of prescription sunglasses

- Item #26 – One purple "LL BEAN" school bag, found under the left side rear seat.

CONTAINED IN THE ABOVE-MENTIONED SCHOOL BAG WERE ITEMS 27 THROUGH 31:

- Item #27 – One "FIVE-STAR" notebook, found inside item #26
- Item #28 – One "LITERATURE" book found inside item #26
- Item #29 – One book "THE SECRET STORM" found inside item #26
- Item #30 – Key chain with keys and assorted charms found inside item #26
- Item #31 – Assorted pens and pencils
- Item #32 – One dark blue knit hat, found on a mattress in the rear of the vehicle
- Item #33 – One black knit hat found on a mattress in the rear of the vehicle
- Item #34 – One yellow long sleeve pullover shirt found on the floor of the vehicle's rear passenger area

The van was then roped off and the items seized were stored safely for evidence.

Master Plan

Finishing the written statement, which he signed, Lewis Lent again wanted to talk with New York State Police investigators Ayling and Murray. He admitted to stalking Rebecca as well as other girls as they walked the same route to school. He chose Rebecca because she was the first of the girls that he saw that day.[21] After giving his statement, Lent told Murray he felt relieved to have unburdened himself.

---

21. **Pittsfield Police Department, Detective Gary W. Danford Investigation Report, 1/18/94.**

Shortly after the confession, Lent hit his interviewers with another shocking confession. Again, speaking in the third person throughout his discussions, he revealed his "master plan":

1. It was Lent's intention to build a small area in his bedroom by separating it with a wall. This was to keep any other people away and give him privacy. He intended to build shelf-like boxes along one wall that he could use to store his victims. They were to be like bunk beds with a door he could close and secure. He wanted to keep victims in these beds "AT ALL TIMES" so that he could take them out when he needed to use them for sex. To this end, he began construction of this wall in his bedroom in North Adams, sometime within the last few weeks. He described putting females in these lockers, two to each locker with heads at opposite ends. This way, their legs could be intertwined.

2. Lent would go out on hunting trips, looking for vulnerable victims. He would go out on "PLEASANT" days, but overcast was acceptable. He wouldn't go out when it was raining. He wanted to be sure that kids would be out and available. He described his victims as "ACCEPTABLE VULNERABLE VICTIMS"; by this he meant young girls who looked to be between the ages of 12-17 years old. He felt that girls lost their attractiveness after the age of 22. The girls would have to be between a certain height and size. He was looking for slim young girls who were just beginning to develop. He wasn't interested in heavy girls. He liked long hair and color didn't matter.

3. Lent indicated that no matter who he was with or where he went, he was always looking for acceptable, vulnerable victims. He would make mental notes of

their locations, as well as notations on maps of these locations.

4. He would range great distances on his trips; most times he would have a cover for his trips. He would drive in a direction where, if stopped, he could say that he was going to visit friends or family or would travel areas that he knew. He always carried his snatch bag with him.

5. Basically, you cannot limit the distance he would travel.

6. THE THINGS HE WOULD LOOK FOR WHILE HUNTING WERE:

   a Liked rural areas because people in rural areas are less security minded.

   b Liked pleasant weather because kids would not normally be out in the rain.

   c Would look for tents, tree houses, or playhouses that were away from the main house where parents would be.

7. He would leave so that he would be in desired area when the kids were out and involved in their activities.

8. If he located a potential victim, he would stalk that victim.

9. All conditions had to be in what he perceived to be in his favor, or he would not make an attempt. All conditions had to be exactly what he wanted.

10. He would take no notice of clothing, only the underpants, which caused him to get sexually aroused.

11. The master plan was still in the works and not complete, so to satisfy his sexual desires he would pick girls up for "QUICKIES."

12. Probably didn't have intercourse with all his victims. He indicated that he had "FINGERED" others.

13. Lent indicated that he had done reading on various sexual activities and that he had read that males had difficulty having sexual intercourse face to face and had tried to disprove this theory.
14. He was afraid of being caught by trace evidence and took great steps to destroy any type of evidence.
15. ALTHOUGH THIS IS THE TYPE OF PEOPLE THAT HE WOULD BE MOST INTERESTED IN HE MAY BE DRIVEN TO OTHERS IF THE CONDITIONS WERE RIGHT AND HIS SEXUAL URGES WERE OVERWHELMING.[22]

Father and Daughter

Owen Boyington worked continuously until he finally arrived home on Saturday afternoon exhausted, but still revved up from all that he had dealt with in the last more than twenty-four hours. For the first time since he became embroiled in the Rebecca Savarese case, he had the chance to sit down with Amy to hear about her adventure the previous day at the Girls' Club. As she unfolded the story to her father, she had his full attention. He felt somewhat disappointed in himself for not being there for her as her adrenaline-pumping event occurred.

"Amy, I'm so proud of you."

As he gave her a hug, Amy felt the moment was perfect. "Dad, I have something to tell you. By the way, I got a tattoo."

---

22. As appears as Addendum "C in Judge Daniel Ford's Commonwealth v. Lewis Lent, Jr., Superior Court No. 94-0083 & 0084, MEMORANDUM OF DECISION ON DEFENDANT'S MOTION TO RECUSE, October 11, 1994, & Commonwealth v. Lewis Lent, Jr. MEMORANDUM OF DECISION ON DEFENDANT'S MOTION IN LIMINEREFERENCES TO OTHER CRIMES OR BAD ACTS, May 29, 1996.

Judy, quietly observing this whole scene, watched as her husband's face instantly changed from pure joy to a crestfallen "what were you thinking?" look. Yet children know their parents. Timing is everything.

The next day, Amy reported to the police station, where Owen took her formal statements about the event at the Girls' Club.

CHAPTER 7

THE SPILL

Sunday at the Station, January 9, 1994

Having unburdened himself with his confession about Rebecca Savarese and his master plan the previous day, Lent prepared himself to finally share with Detectives Ayling and Murray details about Jimmy Bernardo.

I am here at the Pittsfield Police Dept. talking with Inv. John Murray and Inv. James Ayling of the New York State Police. I am talking with them of my own free will and I want to talk to them about Jimmy Bernardo. He is the boy who was missing from the city of Pittsfield, Mass. And was found murdered in the town of Newfield, N.Y.

During October 1990 I was employed at the Cinema Center at West Pittsfield Plaza Rt. 20 City of Pittsfield, Mass. I usually worked from Wednesday night at 12 midnight, until 7AM each night through Sunday night. I had Monday and Tuesday nights off. Instead of working Sunday night for October 22, 1990 I went to work starting at 12 noon.

I was working cleaning and at about 5:30 PM on Monday, October 22, 1990. I was walking out to my van to leave. I saw a boy ride up to the front of the movie theater on a small wheel bike, color blue/green. The boy got off of the

bike and was standing looking in the doors of the theater.
At this time I had an overwhelming desire to have sex with
somebody and he looked vulnerable to me. I approached
him and asked him if he would like to make $5.00 by helping
me move chairs in the movie theater. He said "yes." He did
and I then realized I had nothing to tie him up with, so I told
him I had to get something out of my van.

He waited in front of the theater, so I went to my van and
got a white canvas bag which I carried items I used for the
purpose of kidnapping people with. I know that inside the
bag had duct tape, white tape, a hunting knife, and rope. I
also carried some medicine in the bag. I know I bought the
duct tape at Carr Hardware as well as the rope. I bought the
hunting knife at a sporting goods store on Fenn St. and paid
between 50 and 60 dollars for it. I bought this knife when I
first moved to Pittsfield. I bought the rope and tape about
one month before I met Jimmy Bernardo.

After getting the bag from my van I went back to where
Jimmy was waiting and I used my key and we went in the
front door of the theater. Once inside we went down the hall
to theater 6 and we went in the theater and walked to the
front and went into a storage room. I took the knife out of
my canvas bag held it to him and told him to lie face down
on the floor and put his hands behind his back which he did.
I then took duct tape from my bag and wrapped his hands
together behind his back. We then walked from theater 6 to
theater 7. I had him on the floor inside theater 7 against the
wall. Then went out front and brought his bicycle inside. I
rode the bicycle back to theater 7 where Jimmy was and I
left it near the exit door at the end of the hall. I then ran to
my van and drove it around the back to the exit door.[23]

---

23. The Cinema Center consists of 11 separate theaters divided down the
middle by a large hall, with doors at the end that exit to the rear of the
plaza. To the back of each theater there is a hall area that also exits to the
rear of the plaza.

I took the bike out and put it in the back of the van and covered it up. I would like to add that before leaving Jimmy in theater 7 I used the duct tape to tape his feet together. I then went back in and used my knife to cut the tape on Jimmy's feet and I made him walk and get into the front passenger side of the van. His hands were still together in the back. Before getting in the van Jimmy asked not to take him. He said his mother would miss him. So I had to tell him that if he did not get into the van I would take him into the bushes behind the theater and kill him with my knife. Once inside the van I drove to my apartment at 304 Tyler St., Pittsfield, Mass. I lived upstairs and lived alone. Downstairs was an old man who lived alone and was the owner of the building.

After arriving at 304 Tyler St. I pulled into the driveway and took a pull over shirt and put it on Jimmy to hide the fact that his hands were tied together. I also put a baseball type cap on his head to hide his haircut, and put sunglasses on him. The sunglasses are orange and I had them in my canvas bag. In fact the sunglasses are still in my canvas bag. I made him walk in the front door up the stairs to my apartment. Once inside the apartment we went to my bedroom and I used my knife to cut the tape and removed his clothes. He had on white Jocky type underpants. And nothing else. I then had him lay on his back on the bed and I used the duct tape to tape his legs and arms to the bed. I taped his right wrist and right ankle to the right bed rail and his left wrist to the left bed rail. I then taped his mouth with duct tape. I waited a few hours until he fell asleep and I took a razor blade to cut the under pants. While I was cutting the pants off he woke up. I told him not to move because I did not want to cut him. Even though I knew I may have to kill him.

Jimmy was tied spread-eagle in a prone position on the bed. In his research, Lent had read that males had difficulty having anal intercourse face to face. This was his chance to try to test out the theory. This position proved unfulfilling leaving the kidnapper with the only option he felt he had.

It was at this time I knew he had to die. I went into the living room and slept on the floor. I got up at about 5:00AM, cut Jimmy loose and told him to get dressed. I gave him a pair of my underpants to wear. They were white Jocky style underpants, size 30-33. I taped his hands in front of him with white tape. I moved the tape from his mouth and I saw that the tape had left a rash. I retaped his mouth this time with white tape so it would not leave a rash. I put the pull over shirt, hat, and sunglasses back on him and we went out and got into my van. I told Jimmy I had to go to see a man to pick up a paycheck and this man lived a long way away. I had him sit in the back of the van on the floor so nobody could see him.

Once outside the city of Pittsfield I let him move and sit in the passenger seat front. I drove directly from Pittsfield to Ithaca, N.Y. This is the area in which I grew up and where my parents still lived. My idea was to visit my parents after I killed Jimmy but I knew that my parents would know that I worked at the Cinema and they may have put this together and called the police. As I came through Ithaca and approached Rt. 13 to Newfield, N.Y. and I turned right onto a side road across from the firehouse. I drove about one mile and took a left turn onto a dirt road and drove past a few houses on my left side. I drove this dirt road until I past[sic] what looked like a wide graded area that was to be a new Road. I drove past this new road and it was very muddy. I told Jimmy that we would have to take a path through the woods to the back of the man's house. I told Jimmy that the man we were going to see required any persons coming to his house be blindfolded. I then put some kind of pad between his eyes and the tape. I then put white tape across his mouth. I also changed his hands from the front to the back using tape. We then started walking into the woods from the drivers' side of the van. I took a length of rope from my van and brought it into the woods with me. The rope was about 3 or 4 feet long and was a clothesline type rope. We walked 200 or 300 feet into the woods. The lim[sic] of a tree hit Jimmy in the face and he stopped walking.

At this time I made a loop in the rope like a half knot. I was standing behind Jimmy at this time. I told him I had to move near him and he should stand still. While he was standing there I placed the loop of the rope over his head and around his neck.

I pulled the knot tight by using both hands and pulling in opposite directions. He stiffened up and I pulled him back and he fell to the ground on his side. I placed my knee on the middle of his back and continued to pull on the rope. After a short time he stopped struggling but I could hear him breathing through his nose, so I pinched his nose closed with my fingers. He stopped breathing and moving. I looked around and saw a tree with a lim [sic] about 3 to 4 feet from the ground. I tied the rope around the lim[sic] in such a way that Jimmy's body was suspended from the ground keeping weight on the end of the rope around his neck. The reason I did this was because I was not sure he was dead and I wanted to keep pressure on his neck so he couldn't get any air. I pulled his pants and underpants off and used my knife to cut his shirt off. I cut the shirt off in such a way so I could remove it without untying him or removing the rope from around his neck. I also removed his shoes and socks. I took all his clothes off for a reason. I did it so that if he was still alive because of the cold rain he would die of hypothermia and if the body was found they wouldn't know it was Jimmy. I then took all of the clothes and started to run through the woods. I was taking the clothes because I did not want to leave any trace evidence that could link me to the crime.

As I was running through the woods I found a puddle of water so I put the clothes in this puddle and I stepped on them hoping to wash away any evidence. I left the clothes and continued to run and came out of the woods at the new road. I fell down in the mud and then realized I had been running in the wrong direction. After seeing where I was I made my way back to the van got in and drove off. This all took place between 12 noon and 12:30 PM on October 23, 1990. I drove directly back to my apartment only stopping for gas at exit 15 off I88 in Oneonta, N.Y. at the Red Barrel gas station. The van I was driving that day was a 1980 Ford 15 passenger light blue van with a wide white stripe on the side. The interior was blue with blue seats and blue carpet on the floor. This van I sold to a man in W. Sand Lake, N.Y. shortly after this. I did this to get rid of the van so I couldn't be linked to this murder.

I am giving this statement to Inv. Murray and Inv. Ayling on my own free will. They have not promised me anything in return and I give this statement without any duress or threats. I have had this statement read to me and I do not want to make any changes at this time.

Lewis Lent.

At the scene of the murder, next to where Jimmy lay, detectives found a broken lavender colored button, the type found on a lavender dress shirt. The button did not come from Jimmy's clothes. No underpants were found among the clothes.

Sara Anne Wood

While they were still reeling from the "master plan" and the Jimmy Bernardo confession, Lent hit Detectives Ayling and Murray with yet another shocker.

On August 18, 1993, twelve-year-old Sara Anne Wood left Vacation Bible School at Norwich Corners Presbyterian Church in Frankfort, New York, a small community fifty-five miles east of Syracuse. Riding her pink and white, ten-speed mountain bike while balancing poster boards, transparencies, and a church song book, she took off for her one-mile ride home. Last seen pedaling up a steep hill four-tenths of a mile from her house on Hacadam Road, she vanished. By that evening, her bike was found off the road up against a tree in overgrown brush a football field's distance from the road where she had last been seen.

In this quiet, Upstate New York community of about 7500 residents, everyone knew each other. Sara Anne's father Robert Wood, the pastor of the Norwich Corners Presbyterian Church, was the spiritual leader for many in the community. The community embraced the Wood family and adopted the beloved Sara as its own. The police and the community wasted no time jumping into action. Hundreds of volunteers joined the police in searching first in the vicinity where she had disappeared, then spreading out for miles looking for any clue to the child's whereabouts. The Sara Anne Wood Rescue Center, manned by volunteers, took calls and did whatever they could to help find Sara. The search continued wholeheartedly for five months with no break in the case. Sara Anne's story appeared on TV's *48 Hours* and *America's Most Wanted*.

Nearly five months after her disappearance, Pittsfield Police contacted Herkimer County District Attorney Michael E. Daley to inform him that they held a suspect in Sara Anne's disappearance. That afternoon, Lewis Lent recounted what had happened that fateful day. He laid out details that only the perpetrator and the police knew:

I went out for a drive in my 1983 Ford Econoline... I would often take a drive in my van for the purpose to locate vulnerable girls between the ages of 14 and 17 years old. If I found a vulnerable girl, a girl that looked older than 10 years old, my intention would be to kidnap her and use her for sex. On this day, I remember driving west on Rt. 20 in New York State.

I remember going through several small towns. I carried maps and on these maps I sometimes made notations of locations of possible future victims. I remember that I saw road signs that said Utica. As I was travelling this side road I saw a young girl having trouble balancing packages and pushing a bicycle up a hill. I knew that she was vulnerable and sexually arousing to me. As I approached her I picked up my hunting knife from the floor of the van. I had previously removed it from the sheath and had it available. I pulled the van up, on the roadway, slightly ahead of her. This would give me the opportunity to get out as she approached. She was on the driver's side of the van.

I jumped out and had the knife in my left hand. She panicked and dropped her bike and packages, turned and started running down the side of the road away from me. She only got a few steps before I caught up to her. I grabbed her, tripped her up and she fell to the ground. I threatened her with the knife. I forced her up and into the van thru the side door. Once inside of the van I taped her hands cross ways in front of her. I knew that I had to do it quickly, because I couldn't stay there long with my van in the middle of the road and the bicycle and papers laying alongside.

I threatened her again and forced her to lay face down in the open area of the van. I told her not to move and I jumped out and threw the bike in the woods and kicked packages into the area alongside of the road. I jumped back in the van and quickly took off. She was pleading with me saying Please over and over and Please don't kill me. Finally I had enough and told her to shut up....

After a time I found a road that was acceptable to me. It was a dirt road in a very remote area. This road was like a logging road. I stopped and threatened her again with the knife. I got into the back of the van with her. I told her that if she didn't cooperate with me that she would die.

I saw that she was crying. This was when I really got my first good look at her. I could see that she was very pretty even though she was crying. I knew then that she was younger than I thought she was. She had curly wavy brown hair. I put a piece of white tape across her mouth so that she couldn't talk to me.

He then stripped her and raped her. Forcing her out of the van, he made her walk about 100 feet into the woods.

I came to a place in the woods where I told her to stop. I picked up a large tree lim [sic] and gripped it with both hands. I struck her in the back of the head and she fell immediately to the ground. She didn't move, so I went back to the van. I got a shovel and pick that I brought with me that I had purchased a short time before this. I bought the shovel and pick for the expressed purpose of burying a victim. I went back to where the girl was lying in the woods and dug a shallow grave. I rolled her into the grave, face down and covered her with dirt. I didn't check her to see if she was breathing because I don't like to touch dead bodies. After covering her with dirt, I covered her with leaves, twigs and branches. I went back to the van, with the shovel and pick. Leaving the branch I used to hit her with lying close to the grave. I wiped off all the dirt from the pick and shovel with on old tee shirt that I had in the van. I shook out the tee shirt to remove the dirt. I put the tee shirt with the girl's underpants, shorts and shoes in a plastic bag that I left in the van until later. I got back into the van, pulled out into the dirt road and drove back down in the direction I came.

I drove until I saw a large shopping plaza. I drove behind the stores and threw the bag with the clothes into a dumpster and drove to my apartment in North Adams, Mass.

The next morning I disassembled the shovel and pick by breaking the shovel handle and knocking the head off of the pick. I bagged the metal heads of the shovel and pick in a dark garbage bag, tied it tight and disposed of it at Vicom,

Pittfield, Mass., in the non-burnable section. I threw the handles of both in the burnable section there.

I would like to add that since talking to the State Police Investigators tonight I learned that this girls name was SARA ANN WOOD.

I have been speaking with Investigators MURRAY, LAWRENCE and AYLING of my own free will. At no time did any one promise me anything or threaten me in any way. The fore going is the truth to the best of my knowledge.

Lewis S. Lent

Sunday Night

January 9, 1994

Captain Pace received regular updates from Detectives Ayling and Murray that he shared with the Major Crimes Unit. By Sunday, after twenty consecutive days of snow, the precipitation was light enough that he could finally make it to Pittsfield.

Wasting no time dealing with the first break in the Sara Anne Wood case, Herkimer County DA Michael Daley and lead detective in the Sara Anne Wood case from Troop D in Herkimer County, Frank Jerome, arrived at the Pittsfield Police Station somewhere between 8:00 and 9:00 that evening.

Along with his confession, Lent drew a rough map to indicate where he had buried Sara Anne. He claimed that he had left her in a remote area of the Adirondacks near Raquette Lake. Believing they had located the vicinity off a five-mile dirt road between Rte. 28 and Sagamore Lodge, the child's parents and New York State authorities did not want to waste time getting started with the search. The New York authorities came up with a plan: They wanted to take the prisoner, via helicopter, to Raquette Lake to show them where he had buried Sara Anne. DA Downing pulled ADA Capeless aside and they agreed, "No way, we may never get him back." This was their case and they needed to deal with the alleged perpetrator here in Berkshire County. Downing simply stated to Daly, "Sorry, we can't do it." This infuriated Daley.

Thus began a campaign on the part of DA Daley and the girl's father, Reverend Wood, to get Lent over to New York to lead them to Sara Anne's remains. Angered by DA Downing's insistence that Lewis Lent's case needed to be dealt with in Massachusetts, Reverend Wood and DA Daley accused DA Downing of grandstanding for political purposes. Reverend Wood would later march, carrying a cross from his home in New York to Pittsfield, to protest what he felt was Downing's resistance to allowing Lent to come to New York to reveal where he had buried their daughter. Downing felt great sympathy for the Wood family but knew he had a strong case that would keep Lent in prison for life. He also seriously doubted that Lent would show anyone what he had done with Sara Anne's body.

Opinions varied as to why Lent would not give up this information. Some felt he had forgotten where he buried her. Some felt he was too smart to ever forget this, but he wanted to hold on to a bargaining chip that would give him some power. Others guessed that he did not want people to see what he had done to Sara Anne. Still others speculated that there might be other bodies buried along with Sara that could cause him to be given the death penalty. Lent was very afraid of dying. All these theories, however, were just speculation.

Scheduled to begin opening statements for the Wayne Lo case the next morning, DA Downing called Judge Ford before leaving the police station late Sunday night. "Dan, we just arrested the guy who murdered Jimmy Bernardo. It is a huge case. It is a big deal. I'm going to have to deal with the press and arraign this guy, so can we start Wayne Lo evidence on Tuesday?"

With the complicated logistics of the Lo trial, Judge Ford could not postpone the proceeding. He grumbled, "I'll give you until 1:00 tomorrow."

Finally, at 1:30 on Monday morning, David Capeless dropped off Gerard Downing at home. As he was getting out of his car, Downing told Capeless he needed to fill in for the prosecution's opening statements in the Wayne Lo case. Capeless had less than twelve hours to lay out for the judge and jury one of the biggest cases in the history of Berkshire County.

CHAPTER 8

THE SEARCHES

North Adams

Winding north from Pittsfield, Route 8 links Berkshire County's two cities—Pittsfield and North Adams. Topographical beauty surrounds North Adams. The town is bordered by the Hoosac Range with the Appalachian Trail passing through the city, crossing Mount Williams at the highest point in the city. The mountains surrounding the city provide an eye-catching backdrop to a depressed area.

North Adams, named for the patriot Samuel Adams, evolved as a mill town before the Revolutionary War by virtue of its location at the juncture of the two branches of the Hoosac River, providing enough waterpower to encourage the development of small industries.

Starting in the 1860s, Arnold Print Works established its reputation as a world-renowned manufacturer of printed textiles over its more than forty years in the city. Unfortunately, the booming business providing textiles during World War I went the way of many businesses during the Great Depression.

Downsizing and leaving the city would have proven devastating if not for the purchase of the factory space by the Sprague Electric Company. Sprague Electric Company, with its top-notch scientists, engineers, and technicians, proved a boom for North Adams. Holding government contracts to manufacture advanced weapons systems during World War II, the company flourished. After the war, the company transitioned to a major research and development center for the emerging technology of electricity and semi-conducting materials. Sprague products were used in the launch of the Gemini low Earth orbit missions, the precursor to the Apollo moon missions. With the growing demand for new electronic devices, Sprague's component parts contracts flourished. Unfortunately, in the 1980s, the US began outsourcing manufacturing to cheaper labor markets overseas. Sprague, which employed about one quarter of North Adams's 18,000 population, closed shop, devastating the city's economy. The great brain drain, high unemployment, and shrinking population left a depressed city.[24]

Hopes to repurpose the abandoned Arnold Print Work/ Sprague complex of industrial buildings and revive the city now hinged on the burgeoning tourist industry in the Berkshires. It would take several years until the dream of the Massachusetts Museum of Contemporary Art would reach fruition in 1999.

Meanwhile, the city showed its deterioration as neighborhoods grew shabbier. With unemployment rising, the resulting social changes became inevitable. Property values decreased, rental properties suffered neglect, and people had entirely too much unproductive time on their hands, with resulting crime and despair.

Following the divorce of his parents, teenager Jonathan Wood[25] came to live with his Uncle Lew. Jonathan was having problems at home, getting in trouble with his group of friends. His mother, deciding Jon needed to move away

---

24. http:// en.wikipedia.org/wiki/North Adams_Massachusetts.
25. No relation to Sara Anne Wood

from his peers, gave her son a choice of people with whom to live. Jon chose Uncle Lew.

Lewis Lent secured a suitable apartment in North Adams to accommodate his teenage step-nephew and himself. This two-family apartment house was located on Hudson Street, a narrow road barely wide enough for two lanes of cars to maneuver. Most of the houses on this short, tucked away block on the steep hills in the city contained multiple dwellings. Lent's gray vinyl-sided, wood-framed, two-family rental house had side-by-side entrances to #16 downstairs and #18 upstairs. The neighborhood bore the shabby, rundown look of absentee landlords either unable or unwilling to maintain their property. Despite the comings and goings of new tenants, the neighbors living in close proximity depended on each other to get them through the challenges of daily life, bonding rapidly.

Searching Lent's Apartments

Petitioning the court for search warrants, the request checked off three probable cause boxes:
1. Is intended for use or has been used as the means of committing a crime.
2. Has been concealed to prevent a crime from being discovered.
3. Is evidence of a crime or is evidence of criminal activity.

As stated in the search warrant, "You are therefore commanded within a reasonable time and in no event later than seven days from the issuance of this search warrant to search for the following property:
1. White jockey style underwear of James Bernardo.
2. Wood partition in Lewis Lent Jr.'s bedroom.
3. Duct tape and rope as shown in exhibit C in affidavit.

4. A shirt with lavender buttons.

5. Any material used to record the event of crime, i.e., news clipping/diaries/photographs.

You are authorized to conduct the search at any time during the night. You are not authorized to enter the premises without announcement. You are not commanded to search any person who may be found to have such property in his or her possession or under his or her control or to whom such property may have been delivered."

To make the case for the warrant, Pittsfield Police Detective John McGrath summarized the case against Lewis Lent Jr. and added:

"I have personal knowledge based on my training and experience that suspects who commit these types of crimes often take personal items from the victim as remembrance or collect and save items and articles which record the event.

"Furthermore, I have personal knowledge based on my experience and training that crimes of violence often involve a struggle, the use of instrumentalities, and the element of unpredictability. I also know that the person or persons participating in the commission of a violent crime are in contact with the physical surroundings in a forceful or otherwise detectable manner. Traces may be left in the form of blood, saliva, and physiological fluids and secretions, hair, fibers, fingerprints, palmprints, shoe prints, fabric wear impressions, and dirt/dust/soil, paint samples, glass, and plastic fragment and items containing traces of any of the above-mentioned articles. Many of the above-mentioned articles are minute and/or microscopic, and may require a systematic search to locate, seize, record, and process, and may also require additional specialized examination by forensic laboratory techniques.

"Finally, I have knowledge based upon my experience and training that if untrained persons are allowed into a crime scene they may unintentionally disturb, damage, or obliterate crucial evidence. Accordingly, while the crime scene search warrant is being executed, I respectfully seek the Court's authority to impound and secure the apartment and to keep out all unauthorized persons not assigned to this investigation."[26]

With search warrants in hand, the police had access to both Lent's previous apartment on Tyler Street in Pittsfield, where he allegedly took Jimmy Bernardo, and his current apartment on Hudson Street in North Adams.

A year and a half had passed since Lent lived in the Pittsfield apartment and a new tenant had moved in. Yet the detectives ascertained the condition of the apartment when Lent left.

Massachusetts State Police Lieutenant Robert Scott described Lent as very smart and savvy. "Lent was extremely aware of fine details for disposing of trace evidence as well as fingerprints. Before he moved out of the Tyler Street apartment in Pittsfield where he abducted Jimmy Bernardo, Lent left no fingerprints and polyurethaned over the floors so no hair or fibers could be detected on Tyler."

The North Adams apartment was another story. Lent shared this apartment with his nephew, whose parents had recently separated. In time, his nephew brought a friend who needed a place to crash to move in with them. Drab, thread-bare carpeting with faded beige wallpapers of varied patterns circa 1950s decorated the living room and bedrooms. The kitchen, pantry, and bathroom sported well-worn linoleum floors. Tacked up sheets and throw blankets served as makeshift curtains on all the windows. The apartment, with its filthy bathroom and kitchen, had the chaotic, grungy look of a dwelling inhabited by teenage boys and an unkempt bachelor. This scene presented no surprises for the detectives as they made their way through

---

26. **Search Warrants, Trial Court of Massachusetts, Superior Court, Pittsfield, January 9, 1994 & Trial Court of Massachusetts, District Berkshire, January 12, 1994.**

the rooms of clutter and disarray until they came to Lewis's bedroom.

When the investigators entered the room, Detective Scott's blood ran cold.

Faded chevron patterned, beige, with touches of blue, and orange wallpaper covered the plaster walls in Lewis Lent's nine-by-ten foot bedroom located off the kitchen. A single mattress and box spring lay on a metal frame screwed into a make-shift headboard of two-by-four inch boards. Behind the bed was a boarded-up window. The room also contained a built-in closet without a door, a dresser, and a table with a refrigerator resting on top. Several pieces of lumber were stacked against the walls, along with assorted tools, a circular saw, electrical cords, and screws. White map boards rested at floor level.

"Lent had screwed plywood over the only window in the bedroom. He had attached strong hasps and a padlock on his bedroom door so the boys could not enter when he was not there. He installed dead bolt locks on the other side of the door so no one could just barge in on him. Lewis had threatened to kill anyone in the house who tried to enter his room. He nailed heavy wood planks to the floor moldings to provide a solid foundation to reinforce the sheets of plywood screwed into the studs in the plaster walls. He screwed eyebolts into the makeshift sound-proof wall to attach shackles to keep his prisoners bound up. He was in the process of building wooden boxes in which to store his victims.

"I think at that moment it became real to me just how vicious, cruel, and determined Lent was to carry out his 'master plan.' When I saw the intricate maps that he made and all the planning that went into stalking his victims, I knew we had a true predator. There were maps of where his victims went, their routes of travel. He knew every school day where a particular child would be from start to finish. The combination of the sights, the smells, the emotions of seeing what that room was going to be used for just blocked out all the peripheral stuff," described Lieutenant Scott.

The detectives thoroughly combed the apartment. They made detailed charts of the contents in each room, in the basement, and in attic of the building, listing the locations of all objects in every drawer, on every shelf, on every table and entertainment center, on the floors, on the beds, and in the closets. Paint scrapings were obtained from around the vent in Lent's bedroom.

Among the books that investigators found in Lent's bedroom was a DSM, *Diagnostic and Statistical Manual of Mental Disorders,* published by the American Psychiatric Association. This book described various psychiatric disorders for diagnostic purposes, helping to craft Lewis Lent's alter ego "Stephen." His methodical planning and attention to details clued the police that Lent was a lot smarter and more cunning than they originally thought. A second search warrant was requested three days later to "obtain and document all written records including printed materials."

Up to this point, Lent had no police record known to the local police. "Yet he attempted to abduct Rebecca Savarese right out in the open. Evidence showed that he stalked her for a while. I think he felt that he almost knew her from having watched her for so long. Observing her, he thought he could control her quite easily. She was wearing the headphones and seemed distracted. Because he had gotten away with his criminal acts for such a long time, he felt more confident and invincible. I think the thrill of it became intoxicating and he was like an alcoholic who just could not control his urges," explained Lieutenant Scott.

In the attic of the apartment house, the investigators found the seats from Lent's old, discarded van that he had used when he abducted Jimmy Bernardo. The seats were sent to the FBI lab for examination, along with Jimmy's bicycle, which had been taken previously as evidence.

The Shallies House

Lent's residences were not the only targets for police searches. The invasion by the police into the Shallieses' home unnerved the older sisters, Sally and Eleanor. Phil Shallies recalls the intense scrutiny of his home by the authorities. "The night of Lent's arrest, the police returned to my house going through room by room, opening cabinets, and checking out the garage. All this occurred without a search warrant. My sister came up when she heard the news and she felt like a stranger in her own house. The investigators were here investigating my mother in one part of the house. They took my aunt to another part of the house and me to another part of the house. Everyone was being interviewed. My sister said, 'I don't know where to go in the house.'"

Phil recalled, "Lew called me from jail. The call was just small talk. I found it curious that he asked me how the ditch was doing. There is a ditch that runs down the property. He and I worked on the landscaping all along the edge that runs along the ditch. Whether he ever buried anything there, I have no idea."

The police knew about the exterior work but were more focused on the interior of the house. They wanted to bring Hannibal, the cadaver sniffing dog, into the house. "I told them they would be more likely to find something outside, but they were not the least bit interested," said Phil. The search concentrated largely on the basement of the residence. Phil and Lewis had worked extensively, rebuilding the home's foundation and reinforcing the cellar. As recalled by Phil, "The police wanted to drill holes in the floor and take the basement apart brick by brick and stone by stone, which I would not let them do. The FBI brought equipment from Quantico, VA to x-ray the floor. An FBI agent asked me about my gut feeling. I reminded them that the cement floor was poured nine to ten months before Sara Anne Wood disappeared." The police scrutiny of the Shallies family and their home lasted for about six months.

CHAPTER 9

WHO IS THIS GUY?
Cellophane, Mr. Cellophane shoulda been my name Mr.
Cellophane 'cause you can look right through me, walk
right by me and never know I'm there.
—Mr. Cellophane from Chicago: music by
John Kander, lyrics by Fred Ebb

In 1971, in Seattle, Washington, while volunteering one night a week at a suicide crisis hotline, a fortyish, divorced mother of four immediately struck up a friendship with a handsome, young University of Washington psychology work-study student. He was smart, compassionate, and astute with his callers, friendly and welcoming. He was the kind of guy mothers would hand pick for their daughters. The two volunteers clicked. Ann felt a bit maternal toward him. They struck up a platonic friendship that, despite distances and time, could be picked up where it left off.

Eventually, they each went their separate ways. Ann, a former police officer turned crime reporter, became much sought after to cover the local crime scene. Ted moved on, working for the Republican Party, then going on to law school.

As Ann covered horrific stories of young women's murders, the perpetrator remained a mystery. A few spotty clues about an attractive young man with brown hair who drove a Volkswagen bug struck a vague hint in the far recesses of her mind, but it could not be. Besides, the unspecific description could fit any number of people.

Yes, a seasoned professional could not or would not allow herself to entertain her shady suspicions, although she did later mention them to the police. After all, Ann Rule, a former police officer with a long list of family members involved with law enforcement, a psychology student, a prolific crime reporter could read people. She knew trouble when she met it. She trusted and genuinely liked her friend Ted Bundy, who eventually confessed to killing thirty people between 1974 and 1978.

Lewis Lent

"He was different. He was always nice. He came here just wanting to help, he didn't want money." – friend Phil Shallies.

"He was quiet and polite, gave unselfishly of his time— never aggressive," described friends Sally Shallies and Eleanor Turner.[27]

"He was basically a cipher. We have nothing on him." – NY State Police spokesman James Atkins.[28]

"He was a little country boy who never got into trouble." – Milford Warner, principal of Watkins Glen High School.[29]

---

27. Elfinbein, Gae. (January 11, 1994). Suspect Befriended Lanesboro Family. *The Berkshire Eagle.*

28. Campbell, Ramsey, Ritchie, Lauren. (January 12, 1994). Ramsey Campbell and Laura Ritchie. Former Lake Man May Be Serial Killer. *Orlando Sentinel.*

29. Bullard, Janice (January 13, 1994). Kids Picked on Him Because of his Glasses. *Democrat and Chronicle.*

"He's always been a good boy. He went to preacher school, Church of Christ's New England Bible School in Clifton Park, NY." – Stepfather Alfred Wood.[30]

"This is not the kind of person who is going to go out and kill a child. He was not an aggressive kind of kid." – Cousin Linda Henderson.[31]

An individual with no conscience or superego, one who cannot feel guilt has, over the years, been termed psychopath, sociopath, and more recently, antisocial personality. "To live in our world, with thoughts and actions always counter to the flow of your fellowmen, must be an awesome handicap. There are no innate guidelines to follow: the psychopath might as well be a visitor from another planet, struggling to mimic the feelings of those he encounters. It is almost impossible to pinpoint just when antisocial feelings begin, although most experts agree that emotional development has been arrested in early childhood—perhaps as early as three. Usually the inward turning of emotions results from a need for love and acceptance not filled, from deprivation and humiliation. Once the process has begun, that little child will grow tall—but will never mature emotionally," as author Ann Rule so eloquently explained in her book, *The Stranger Beside Me.*[32]

Born in the small rural upstate town of Reynoldsville, New York in 1950, near the Finger Lake National Forest, Lewis

30. **CBS News Archives, (January 28, 1994). Child Hunter: Lewis Lent.** *48 Hours.*
31. **CBS News Archives, (January 28, 1994). Child Hunter: Lewis Lent.** *48 Hours.*
32. **Rule, Ann.** *The Stranger Beside Me, pp. 427-428.*

"Little Lewie" Lent Jr. was the middle child and only son of Lois and Lewis "Big Lewie" Lent Sr. Sister Merry arrived eleven months after Lewis Jr. Shortly after Merry's birth, when Lew was just one year old, Lois and Lewis Sr. parted ways, dissolving their volatile marriage, leaving Lois to raise Sandra, Lewis, and Merry on her own.

Not long after the divorce, Lois married Alfred Wood, a friend of her ex-husband's. Together, they became a blended family with seven children—his, hers, and theirs. Lewis explained to his friend Phil how the entire clan, existing at a poverty level, lived in the cellar of their house for a year until they built the upper floors of their modest, wood-framed home.

As Lois's new life took shape, so did Lewis Sr.'s. In 1954, "Big Lewie" began a relationship with a fourteen-year-old girl named Charlene, a family friend who would live with Lewis Sr. on and off for fifteen years before he finally married her when she was twenty-nine.

Lewis Jr. began to resist his weekend visits with his father. "Little Lewis" would scream and cry, clinging to his mother, begging to stay home. The family attributed the youngster's behavior to his extreme closeness to his mother, never realizing the chaos this child had experienced with his father's tangled web of relationships and the confusing and frightening childcare he received during his weekend visits. At a young age, "Little Lewie" became lost in these confusing family dynamics. Recalling his childhood, Lewis Jr. recounted to his boss at the movie theater. "The only excitement he got in his life was when he and his father would go to the dump picking through garbage."[33]

The same year that the relationship started with Charlene, Lewis Sr. fathered a daughter, Debra, with Ellen Venetten. In 1955, when Debra turned one, Ellen and Lewis Sr. married, sending Debra and her older brother Frank to

33. Elfinbein, Gae, (January 11, 1994), Suspect Befriended Lanesboro Family. *The Berkshire Eagle*.

live with Ellen's mother. The couple subsequently had a younger son, Ronald, who remained at home with them. Lent Sr. stayed in the Reynoldsville area for about ten years before moving to Florida with Ellen. He returned to New York State often while living in Florida.

When daughter Debra's grandmother died, she and Frank returned home to their mother. Not wanting to take on the responsibilities of two more children, Lewis left Ellen in 1967. Waiting in the wings was Charlene, Lewis Sr.'s "go to" throughout his marriage to Ellen.

About this time, quiet, staying out of trouble, Lewis Jr. dropped out of Watkins Glen High School after his sophomore year. This was a boy who was floundering. The years of resentment that he felt about his parents' split had no constructive outlet. Lack of parental guidance failed him. He never knew what to expect from his mercurial father. Although his grades were not bad, he just did not fit in. Teased because of the coke-bottle, thick-lensed glasses he wore and just not interested in school, he puttered around with go nowhere jobs. In 1967, Lewis Jr. decided to head down to Florida, where his father and father's relatives lived.

In 1969, Lewis Sr. married Charlene, and they moved down to Florida. Charlene had two daughters, Patty and Pamela, from previous relationships. Together, the couple had daughter, Penny.

Lewis Jr. moved around, as did his family, living in Lake Mack and Deland, Florida.

Lake Mack and Deland are both located in the wide catchment area surrounding the Orlando, Kissimee, Sanford Metropolitan area. Lake Mack and Deland, however, lacked the excitement and glamor that attracts tourists, second homers, and retirees to living in the paradise of Florida. Many low income workers commuted from trailer parks in these small communities to work in the tourist industry or local agricultural economy. Lewis Jr., who worked picking oranges, harvesting ferns, and doing odd jobs, could not or chose not to hold on to them.

Lewis Jr. lived off and on with his cousin Rene and her family, as well as with his father and Charlene. While living with Lewis, Charlene found her stepson to be relatively easy-going and quiet. His primary interest was cars, which he and his father, a former diesel mechanic, would work on together. Unlike others who described Lewis as a loner and black sheep of the family, Charlene described him as having a good relationship with his father, having friends, and being well-liked by the neighbors. Unlike his father, Lewis was not a heavy drinker but a habitual marijuana smoker. Although he could party with his peers, his closest friends were his cousin's daughter Renee and her friends Kelly and Angel, ages twelve to thirteen. This fun "big brother" hung out with the girls, taking them swimming, to the movies or teaching them how to drive.[34]

In addition to drinking heavily, Lewis Sr. was known to be physically, emotionally, and sexually abusive. Following Lent Jr.'s arrest, relatives began to recount stories of abuse perpetrated by Lewis Sr. as well as by his brother James. It was not until the police questioned Lois Wood following her son's arrest that she revealed that her ex-husband had molested/raped one of his two daughters and probably the other. She did not say which daughter. Lewis Jr. never told his mother if his father molested him.

Cousin Linda Henderson admitted that at age seventeen, her father, James, tried to molest her. Cousin Karen Lent recalled that her mother did not permit her to be around Uncle Lewis Sr.[35] As told to Matthew Spina, reporter for the *Syracuse Herald Journal*, by Lent's cousin Carol Lisenby, "Uncle Lewis, he was something else." She heard his own

---

34. Spina, Matthew, (February 15, 1994). Lent's Long Winding Road. *Syracuse Herald Journal.*

35. Murphy, Sean P., Armstrong, David. (January 14, 1994). Abuse in the Lent Family alleged. *The Boston Globe.*

daughters were victimized. "Little Lewis had to see it. I never heard of him doing it to Little Lewis, but I wouldn't put it past him."

"The old man once locked his two daughters from his marriage to Charlene in a room rather than tend to them while babysitting," said Rene Parr. She was locked in with them. "He was supposed to be babysitting me. It scared me to death because I knew he was probably drinking and smoking cigarettes and maybe falling asleep." Lewis Lent also revealed to a friend that "a family member used to slam his head against a wall and also of being locked in a room."[36]

Charlene and Lewis Sr.'s marriage was a rocky one with Lewis frequently leaving, at which time he would often return to his New York roots. Whenever Sr. left, so did Jr. Finally, in 1979, Charlene and "Big Lewie" divorced because her husband was running around with other women.

As time went on, Lent Jr.'s teenage friends married and began families. After fifteen years in Florida, with no money in his pockets, Lewis Jr. had had enough. He made his way back to Upstate New York.

Despite all the philandering and abuse in the family, Lewis Sr.'s wives, children, and relatives comingled for years both in New York State, in Florida, and, eventually, in Massachusetts. Despite his alcoholism and abuse, his daughter Merry took him into her home and cared for him in his final years. As his father neared the end of his life, Lewis Jr. went out of his way to return to Florida, bringing along his mother, stepfather, and his friend Sue to see his dad before the old man's death in 1993.

36. Spina, Matthew (February 15, 1994). Lent's Long Winding Road. *Syracuse Herald – Journal.*

Phil Shallies

Phil Shallies's family had a long history in the small town of Lanesboro. After the Civil War, Phil's maternal great-great-grandfather, Farum, established a lime company in Cheshire, Massachusetts, just north of Lanesboro. In 1917, grandfather Thare Farum purchased the family home from Ashel Jordan's vast estate on Summer Street. Summer Street, a picturesque cut through between Rte. 7 and Rte. 8, belies these two busy main thoroughfares where its scenic rolling hills feature farmland and horse farms, lovely, widely spaced homes, and an elementary school among its wooded twists and turns.

The Farnum home sat on the Rte. 7 end of Summer Street, part way up the road's first steep incline. This proud Federal style house with its central stairway got a facelift in 1870, becoming an inn. With the addition of a porch and decorative cornices, the house took on an unconventional Victorian style with a gingerbread facade. The Summer Street residence had been the anchor and safe harbor for the family for over 100 years. The Farnum girls married and moved out. Sadly, Eleanor Turner's (nee Farnum) husband was killed in World War II. Eleanor returned to the family home and moved into the upstairs apartment. She began working at the Lanesboro post office and eventually became the small town's postmaster. Sister Sarah (Sally) married and started to raise a family. When her third child, Phillip, was born, her husband took off. Sally Shallies, a single, nearly blind mom, abandoned with three children, moved back home. Eleanor turned the apartment over to her sister's family and moved downstairs with her parents.

Phil Shallies grew up to have quite a reputation around town. He was a terrific auto mechanic who worked from the garage at his home. He inherited the condition known as Usher syndrome from his mother. He suffered vision loss known as retinitis pigmentosa due to the gradual degeneration of the retina, which usually begins in adolescence or early adulthood.[37]

At age eight, Phil's vision began to slide. First it was the loss of night vision, then peripheral vision and, eventually, all went dark.[38]

Blindness, however, never stopped Phil. A car enthusiast since childhood, he had always dreamed of being an auto mechanic. As a student at McCann Technical School, Phil excelled in his automotive technician curriculum. By his teen years his vision was narrowing, and he wore glasses with thick lenses. However, his impediment did not squelch his passion for his future profession.

Each year, Chrysler's Plymouth Motors division sponsored a national competition for mechanics to trouble shoot a hypothetical description of a car with a faulty engine and solve the challenges the competition created for the participants. Out of a class of sixty, Phil came in second, which qualified him to be part of a two-person team for the next hands-on challenge. His high school, McCann Technical School, hosted the event that provided twenty-eight teams with all the same cars rigged with the same malfunctions. The mechanics were timed to determine which team of two could get their car running first. Phil's team won, qualifying them to compete in the national engine trouble-shooting competition at the Indianapolis Speedway. The competition provided Phil with the powerful affirmation of his skills as a mechanic. It also afforded Phil and his family the rare opportunity to travel. He finished the competition in the top half. Still being able to see with thick glasses, Phil experienced the thrill of a lifetime as he drove around the Indy 500 Speedway in the Plymouth Roadrunner.

37. www.blindness.org/usher-syndrome).
38. Carroll, Felix. (October 8, 2017). For Car Enthusiast 1st, Blind Guy 2nd, Feeling is Believing." *The Berkshire Eagle.*

Following his graduation from McCann, Phil was employed for nine years as a mechanic for Lindsey Chevrolet, then Pete's Motors, then Dalton Tractor, and finally, Dalton Mobil. By then, his vision was a gray blur. Despite this visual decline, he was quite adept at feeling his way around the workings of cars. Unfortunately, his employer at Dalton Mobil worried about his being a liability and fired him. This was a harsh blow to Phil. He knew he would never again be hired to do what he still had the skills to do, so he converted the garage of the family home into Shallies Summer Street Service.

Despite being legally blind, he excelled at this craft. Working from the garage at his home, word of mouth business kept him busy. Phil recalls, "I first met Lewis a few years ago when a mutual friend who worked with Lent suggested he come to me to work on his van, which needed frequent repairs. A year later, Lewis Lent returned to have some more work done on his van."

It was at this time that Lewis saw Phil working on a huge project of rebuilding the foundation of his home. Noticing that Phil was immersed in such a major renovation on his house, Lent asked if he needed help. Surprised by the offer, Phil explained that he could not afford to pay Lent. That is when the two men decided to exchange services. Lewis would help Phil with the foundation work and, in return, Phil would work on Lewis's old van.

"I had just begun this project by digging a hole outside by the meter. This caused water to pour into the basement of this 100-plus-year-old house. A trench needed to be dug around the foundation, stones to be removed, and mortar poured around the house. The rest of the work took place inside the cellar. The wall was starting to cave in and a new concrete floor needed to be poured," described Phil. "For a year and a half, we worked together to remedy the water pouring into my basement by shoveling up the entire dirt floor and throwing it out of the basement window bucket by bucket. We then brought in sand, gravel, and cement to rebuild the foundation on the inside so a new cement foundation could be poured along with a surrounding stone wall. Lewis worked long and hard with me on this project. Who could believe anyone would do this for me? Lewis even brought his mother and stepfather over from Upstate New York to meet my family and to see the construction that we were doing on the house."

Not only did Phil feel blessed with the kindness of this good Samaritan, but so did his mother Sarah, Aunt Eleanor, and his aunt's boyfriend Chet, who lived with the family. "During that time, Lewis became like family to us. My mother and I are blind. He showed such patience with us. Sometimes with blind people you run out of patience, but not him. He would put my hand on a part of the engine and say, 'Here, feel that part.'"[39] He even offered to drive the van for the Benevolent Society for the Blind.

Occasionally, Lewis would borrow Phil's truck or Chet's car to help a friend. The family remembers one such occasion when the usually untidy Lewis returned Chet's car in spotless condition, having cleaned it thoroughly inside and out, including shampooing the carpet.

Eleanor Turner's boyfriend, Chester "Chet" Forfa, often drove Eleanor, Sally, and Phil shopping and to appointments until his eyesight and poor health no longer allowed him to do so. Lewis Lent stepped up, generously offering his time to take over transporting Chet and the Turner-Shallies family in Chet's car wherever they needed to go.

Many of Chet's appointments were in Albany, New York, at the Veterans' Hospital or at the Retina Clinic. Routinely, Lent would unload a white plastic bag with handles from his van to take on his trips over to Albany. He placed the bag on the floor against the driver's seat, behind his legs. Chet never looked in the bag, but he assumed the bag contained

39. Elfinbein, Gae. (January 11, 1994). Suspect Befriended Lanesboro Family. *The Berkshire Eagle*.

Lew's lunch. On a typical ride to Albany, Lewis would stop at the same convenience store in Nassau, NY to buy soda and chips, drinking the soda as he drove.

One time at a stop, Chet moved Lewis's bag to the passenger side of the car to give Lewis more leg room. Although he never looked in the bag, Chet noted that it was heavy. When Lewis picked up Chet, he had moved the bag back behind his legs where it remained on all subsequent trips.

Typically, Lewis would drop off Chet at his appointment and return an hour or an hour and a half later, depending on the length of the appointment, to pick him up. During the appointment time, Lewis claimed to go to a restaurant to eat. Chet wondered why he would go to a restaurant if he brought along food for lunch.

In 1993, Chet was hospitalized at the Albany VA Hospital for two months. Lewis made the hour-and-a-half trip each way almost daily, bringing Eleanor with either Sally or Phil to visit the patient. Again, he would drop them off and return at an appointed time.

As the task force later developed, following up on every lead, they had Mr. Forfa sign Authorization for Medical Records forms to corroborate the dates of his appointments in Albany to track Lewis Lent's whereabouts on a particular day.

The Shallies family, Phil's girlfriend Janie, and Chet developed a fondness for this man, although they sometimes found his thought processes a bit odd. "His problem solving was a little different than mine. I'll never forget the day he told me he overfilled his van's battery. So, what does he do? He takes a straw and sucks out the battery fluid. It burned his tongue and everything else, I would imagine," mused Phil Shallies.

Despite living on a shoestring, Lewis Lent could be extremely generous about giving or loaning a friend money. He was generous almost to a fault. Yet one day, a friend was telling Janie Ray about an incident where some guy jumped him, beat him up, and stole his paycheck. The description that the friend gave to Janie convinced her that the culprit was Lewis Lent, who happened to live just a few streets away from where this incident occurred.

In the early spring of 1991, Lewis hastily got rid of the first van Phil had worked on and got himself a replacement van at the Impact Auto in New York. The replacement van was a burned out junker. The van, another fifteen-seater, had a cracked windshield caused by a fire and needed a dashboard with wiring harness for all the gadgets. Phil wanted to help him find a replacement wire harness, but Lewis would have none of that. He insisted on devising his own unique dashboard made of a plank of wood, which he wired by himself, with the gadgets attached with glue and fiberglass. He attached all the switches and lights onto this board using the same color wire for every connection, which were all hanging and tangled. His brake lights did not go on automatically when he pressed on the brake pedal. He had to flip a switch on this dashboard to manually turn on the brake lights whenever he stopped. There was no convincing him to simplify this mess.

Lewis Lent

As he got to know Lent, Phil marveled at how this man, in the short amount of time he had lived in the Berkshires, had embedded himself in the community. Lewis Lent arrived in Pittsfield in 1986 following three years in Clifton Park, New York. In Clifton Park, he attended the Northeast School of Biblical Studies affiliated with the Church of Christ, a non-denominational evangelical church. Frank Colletta, the school's director, described Lewis as "quiet, intelligent, and unassuming. He always had his hand out to shake your hand

and if you didn't watch out, he'd give you a big bear hug."[40] Lewis never became an ordained minister. His goal was to be able to officiate at weddings and funerals.

Growing up, the Lent family attended the Church of Christ in Ithaca, New York. It was his former minister, Steve Singleton, who later taught at the school when Lewis enrolled. Despite Lewis having little money and living in extremely rustic conditions, the church embraced him and helped him along. Steve and his wife Cindy took him under their wings. Cindy explained that Lewis aspired to become a trucker to finally secure a job that paid well. Because of numerous unpaid traffic tickets his license was suspended, forcing him to ride a bike everywhere. The Singletons realized that his disorganization and forgetfulness caused his inability to achieve his goals. They coaxed and cajoled him to write things down and get his act together. Lewis accepted their suggestions graciously, but he just could not follow through.

After the school closed in1986, Lewis drifted to Pittsfield, where he embedded himself into church life at the local Church of Christ. Judy Boyington, Detective Boyington's wife and a member of that church, described her congregation as welcoming, embracing, and nonjudgmental, giving everyone a chance. Judy, however, struggled with her wish to embrace her fellow congregants, and something about Lent just made her uncomfortable. Ironically, Detective Owen Boyington never met or knew of Lewis Lent because he did not attend church with his wife and daughters.

The church reached out to the community in lower income neighborhoods, often transporting children to church sponsored events on the "joy bus." The bus was later downsized to a van, which Lewis Lent often volunteered to drive. He gravitated to single mothers, who seemed happy

40. **CBS News Archives, (January 28, 1994). Child Hunter: Lewis Lent. *48 Hours.***

to have a male role model pay attention to their children. Lent drove children on church retreats to Maine as well as taking his young friends camping in remote woods in North Adams. As reported by Susan Etkind of *The Berkshire Eagle*, "Children said Lent would send them off on a search to find a specific camping spot that apparently didn't exist, and he would go off by himself. He liked to hike and liked to hike Mount Greylock."[41]

Judy Boyington's younger daughter, Allison, explained that one Wednesday evening when she was about ten years old, she wanted to attend a church function, but her mother could not take her. She called Mrs. Moody, the minister's wife, who often picked up people who needed rides to church. Mrs. Moody suggested that Allison call Lewis Lent, who lived nearby, to pick her up. Allison just froze. The thought of riding alone in the van with Lewis Lent creeped her out. "I stood there holding the phone. I did not want to tell the minister's wife 'no,' so I told her I would think about it and call her back. I hung up the phone and thought, I just can't do it even if I will disappoint Mrs. Moody. I called her back and told her that it was OK. I just was not going to go." Mrs. Moody returned Allison's call, offering to pick her up. At a young age, Allison, the daughter of a police officer, had followed her gut instincts, avoiding an uncomfortable situation even when it meant not following the suggestion of a respected adult.

Lewis remained active with his church activities for about four years. In 1990, he abruptly stopped affiliating.

When he first arrived in Pittsfield, Lent stayed at the Stagecoach Rooming House. Shortly after, he moved to the YMCA in downtown Pittsfield. Upon the recommendation of a church member, Richard Baumann hired Lent to work part-time as a night custodian at the Pittsfield Cinema

---

41. **Etkind, Susan. (July 21, 1994) Lent Took Children of Adams Site Searched by Police.** *The Berkshire Eagle.*

Center. For six months, Lent also worked part-time as a cabulance driver.

Although he had employed Lent at the Cinema Center for seven years, Richard Baumann knew little about this strange employee. He had the following things to say about his employee:

"Lent was a quiet man who talked of involvement with a church and carried a hunting knife."[42]

"He was the kind of guy who could swim through the sea of life without attracting any attention."[43]

"He just wasn't one of those guys you could love. There was nothing about him that was personable, just one of those guys in a group that nobody would bother with."[44]

"He's the guy who walks into a group—he's noticed, but nobody wants to get next to him, and he won't say anything of significance. You'll never remember he was there—he glides through and nobody gives a damn about him."[45]

Although Lent primarily worked the night shift when the theater was empty, he had keys to the building and could come and go as he pleased. Children from his church were hired to help clean the movie theater on Saturdays. He would transport the youngsters to work and sometimes work with them. His job provided a wonderful place to bring the children to play video games and go in to see a movie.

Being in the theater at various hours, Lent had contact with some of the other employees who worked during theater

42. Campbell, Ramsey. (January 12, 1994). Former Lake Man May Be a Serial Killer. *Orlando Sentinel.*

43. Daley, Lynn A. (January 16, 1994) An Omission, Question of What If. *The Berkshire Eagle.*

44. Campbell, Ramsey, Ritchie, Lauren (January 12, 1994). Former Lake Man May Be Serial Killer. *Orlando Sentinel.*

45. Daley, Lynne A. (January 17, 1994). Any Omissions, Questions of "What if" Lingering Questions of 'What If'.) *The Berkshire Eagle.*

hours. He presented himself differently to various people at work. One of these employees, manager Richard Baumann's cousin Chad Baumann, worked as an usher and ticket seller. Lent told Chad that he was married. Lent brought a woman and two boys to watch a movie, leading Chad to believe that these people were Lent's wife and children.

Richard Baumann's daughter Heather worked at the movie theater for eight years before working with Lewis Lent. They worked together cleaning the theaters for five years. Lewis cleaned the odd numbered theaters while Heather did the evens. When she was not there, Lewis was responsible for all the theaters. In 1990, she became his supervisor.

Heather began to notice some questionable actions on the part of Lent. She remembered that Lewis always carried a hunting knife in his rear pants pocket. He said that the theater was a scary place after hours. One day, she observed Lent washing off his knife in the storage room. His unsolicited explanation when observed was that he was cleaning gum off the floor.

One night, Lent had a young friend in for a sleep-over at the movie theater. Heather caught them camping in theater 7 in front of the movie screen. As soon as she informed her father, Richard Baumann confronted Lent. Lewis explained that he had promised to take the child camping, but because of bad weather, he brought the camping trip indoors. He did not want to disappoint his young friend. Baumann thought this unorthodox. He let Lent know quite firmly that this behavior was unacceptable and would not be tolerated again.

Some other questionable things were discovered in the theaters. Baumann found a sleeping bag, blue knit blanket, and two pillows in the hall area behind theaters 3 and 4. He believed they belonged to Lent but did not ask him about them. These items were later secured and brought to the Task Force Command Center. In the summer of 1993, Baumann found two empty wallets in the dumpster behind the theater. Despite the rain the previous nights, the wallets were dry. When questioned about the wallets Lent became irate, screaming at Baumann for even asking him.

As Heather noticed more of Lent's behaviors, his relationship with her became a grudge match. She remembered Lewis coming into the theater with his nephew Jon. This went on for about two weeks. As soon as Heather started to become friendly with Jon, Lewis never brought him back.

"Lewis seemed to resent working with me. He kept leaving notes, trying to get me fired. There came a time when Lewis Lent would not even come into the theater while I was there. He would sit outside in his van until I left before entering the cinema. If I walked into the theater while Lewis was inside, he would walk away and avoid me."

In 1993, after seven years working evening maintenance at the theater, things began to change. Lent would come into work at night wearing dark glasses. His work became sloppy, partially because he could not see well with the glasses. Finally, in November 1993, after several warnings about the quality of his work, Richard Baumann fired Lent. "He was upset with me, and I was upset with him. He said if I was going to fire him, 'I know where you live and all about your family.'"[46] After the threat, Baumann attempted to call the police, but rang the wrong number. Lent left and Baumann never saw or heard from him again.

While scraping by on part-time jobs, in 1991, Lewis qualified for a State and federally funded program for unemployed and underemployed adults. The one-semester program at Berkshire Community College trained aides to work in group homes with mentally and educationally challenged residents. He did well but quit half-way through the course. His teacher, William Cavanaugh, remembered him for an unusual question he posed in class. "Lewis

---

46. King, Suzanne. (August 15, 1994). *Observer-Dispatch.*

Lent was the only one who ever asked if the class would study or talk about split or dual personality." Cavanaugh had responded, "We do not get into topics like criminal insanity."[47]

In his other part-time job as a cabulance driver, Lent befriended Ray Oschman, whom he transported to hospital appointments. Oschman owned a two-family house on Tyler Street, where he lived in the first-floor apartment. In January 1990, when the second-floor apartment became available, Lent moved in. From his second story window, Lent could look diagonally across the street from the building's back yard to Morningside Elementary School's playground.

Living next door to Williams Sewing Machine shop, Robert Johnson, owner of the shop, observed, "Lent often befriended young boys who helped him work on his van or went on bike rides or fishing trips. I've seen maybe a half dozen boys come and go, but I always thought he was being a big brother."[48]

The Tyler Street apartment also served as a gathering spot for teens. In 1990, a girl fifteen or sixteen years old, along with her boyfriend, an acquaintance of Lewis Lent's, hung out at Lent's apartment six or seven times. A runaway, heavy into cocaine and acid, she would spend entire days with other young people at the apartment drinking vodka, beer, and Southern Comfort. This weird, quiet man whose name she never knew smoked marijuana with the teens. When Lent did drink, he talked more and sometimes would just yell at the teens.

Lent lived on Tyler Street for two years, until Ray Oschmen died and his nephew Charles Potter, the landlord and maintenance man for the building, inherited the property.

---

47. O'Connor, Gerald (January 20, 1994). Lent, While at BCC Expressed Interest in Dual Personality, His Teacher Says. *The Berkshire Eagle.*

48. Sennot, Charles M., Greenwald, Michael, Ellement, John, Globe staff and freelance writers Chant, Cate, Roche, (January 12, 1994). B.J. Possible Serial Killer Probe. *Boston Globe.*

With the new landlord, Lewis stopped paying his rent the last two months that he lived in the apartment. When Lent finally moved out, Potter cleaned the property and put it on the market for sale.

In 1992, Lent moved from Pittsfield to the former mill town of North Adams. He found a second-floor apartment in a two-unit house on Hudson Street. As Lewis was moving in, the little ten-year-old from next door came out to meet his new neighbors. Stephen Domenichini helped Lewis move in and the pair became fast friends.

Stephen lived with his mother and younger sister. Linda, the single mom of two, was a bit slower to warm up to her new neighbor, but it did not take long for the families to grow close. Lewis was generous and helpful whenever Linda needed a hand with something in her apartment.

Lewis was available to pitch in and watch Stephen and even take him to an occasional doctor's appointment when Linda could not. In turn, Lewis was treated as part of the Domenichini family, spending a great deal of time at their apartment simply doing his laundry or celebrating family gatherings and holidays. In August of 1993, Linda and her family moved downstairs from Lewis.

Lewis spent most of his spare time with Stephen, often taking him along with him in his sky-blue van. According to Stephen, "I used to help Lewie clean the theater in Pittsfield. When I helped, it was usually late at night after the movies had let out and the ushers had left. Lewis would bring up the Jimmy Bernardo case and scare me. I know that the case is about a boy that was eleven or twelve and he was missing from around the theater. I know that he was killed and found in the woods. Lewie told me that a car was involved and there were two men, and the kid was hung. Lewie told me that the kid wasn't dead enough, so the killer shot or stabbed him. He told me this story many, many times. One day, he told me Jimmy was kidnapped near the road and another day he told me he was kidnapped in the woods. Lewie told me Jimmy was riding his bicycle when he was kidnapped. He also talked about Sara Anne Wood and mentioned a girl named Holly who disappeared. These stories scared me to death."[49] Lent used these stories to caution Stephen and to maintain a pseudo-parental control over the boy.

Lent took Stephen on camping trips and to New York State for overnight visits with Lent's parents. Once, when Stephen was sick and Linda had no one to watch him, Lewis took the boy along while he worked on Phil Shallies's house. Although Phil was not happy with having this kid hanging around, he tolerated it because of Lewis's generosity toward him.

Stephen asked if he could stay in the van while Lewis worked in Phil's house, to which Lewis agreed. As he was exiting the van, Lewis opened the rear doors of the vehicle and removed a canvas bag in which Stephen noticed a bottle of pills, Band-Aids, and white medical tape. Lewis pulled a black gun from the bag. He got a belt from inside the van, attaching a gun holder to the belt and inserting the gun in the holder. He warned Stephen that if Phil knew he had a gun he would be scared. Steven knew that Lewis carried a hunting knife, but this was the first time he had seen the gun.

Stephen adored his best friend Lewie, but he realized that, "Sometimes he would act like a grown-up, but sometimes he would act like a child. Lewie would flip out over little things. He blamed other people if something got lost. He just accused them of things that were not true."[50]

When interviewed by the police, Stephen insisted that Lewis never made any sexual overtures toward him. Lewis did, however, make sexual remarks about Stephen's best friend, twelve-year-old Libby, whom Stephen described as developed and having boobs.

---

49. **Supporting Deposition (CPL 100.20) The State of New York.**

50. **Hutchinson, Bill, Kennedy, Helen, Mallia, Joseph, (January 12, 1994)** *Boston Herald.*

Jonathan Wood

Following the divorce of his parents, teenager Jonathan Wood, Lewis Lent's step-nephew, moved from Upstate New York to live with Uncle Lew. He described his uncle as "a pretty weird guy sometimes, but most of the time he's quiet and stays alone a lot."

Living with his bachelor uncle, Jon Wood had few parental constraints. Jon was expected to contribute to the rent although he was still in high school. Arriving in North Adams at age sixteen, instead of matriculating as a junior, he was placed back in the freshman class. He did not last long in school, complaining that he was not learning anything. With the expectation of his contributing rent money, Jon found a job at Jaeschke's Apple Orchard, where he worked as a laborer and as a driver leading the wagon out in the orchards. His job at the orchard lasted until the first frost. He then found work in the packing room at Modern Aluminum.

Jon met Melissa Benoit, then age fifteen, at a Masonic Temple dance in North Adams. The two teens became inseparable. On weekends, Melissa would arrive at Jon's apartment at 8:00 or 9:00 in the morning and stay until 10:00 at night. On school days, she would go over after school and stay until 9:00 at night, when Jon would walk her home.

Melissa described Lewis Lent as "really secretive." He spent much of his at home time alone in his room, which he kept padlocked so no one could enter uninvited. Lent would come out to eat, watch a football game, or go to the bathroom. He shut himself in his room for considerable amounts of time with his cats, his books, and his collection of cassette recordings about the Bible. There were days at a time when he would be holed up in the room with migraines.[51] When

---

51. Ellement, John (January 12, 1994). *Boston Globe.*

these headaches came on, Lewis would not show up to work with Phil. It could be days before Phil saw his friend again.

Lent's schedule and moods were erratic. He could be nice, polite, generous, and funny, yet his mood could instantly flip to become irrational and violent. Lewis loved his two cats. Once, when one of his cats became ill, he blamed Melissa for kicking the cat, causing his pet to get sick. He told her, "It is best if you don't show your face around here again."[52] According to Melissa, "I recall one time being in the apartment when Lewis couldn't find the remote control to the television. Lewis tipped the couch over and was banging it on the floor trying to get it out. Lewis was yelling obscenities. I would say I was very scared during Lewis's fit of rage."

Lent also had an incident with a neighbor across the street regarding a barking dog. The usually mild-mannered Lewis approached the neighbor's mother and told her that "if she did not restrain her German shepherd, he would use a bat to kill the dog. If the bat didn't work, he threatened to use his pistol."[53]

Lewis left for work at the Cinema Center at 11:00 at night. Jon never knew when his uncle would return. Sometimes he stayed away all night. Sometimes he stayed away for two or three days at a time, sleeping in his van. Jon guessed that the van was parked at Phil's house, but he never knew where his uncle was sleeping or when he would return home. Heather, Lent's coworker at the cinema, often saw Lent sleeping in his van in the parking lot of the Cinema Center even on days when he did not work. As Heather drove late at night from Pittsfield to Lanesboro to pick up her husband at the Berkshire Mall, occasionally she

52. *de Bourbon, Lisi. (January 12, 1994)* **Lewis Lent Man of Contradictions.** *The Berkshire Eagle.*
53. *de Bourbon, Lisi. (January 12, 1994)* **Lewis Lent Man of Contradictions.** *The Berkshire Eagle.*

saw Lent's van parked in a lot overlooking Pontoosuc Lake, not far from Phil Shallies's home.

In the summer of 1993, Jon's friend, Roger Beaudoin, moved in with Jon and Lewis. When Roger's mother kicked him out of the house, he asked Jon if he could move in. Jon did not think that was such a good idea. Roger instead went to Lewis and asked him if he could move in, to which Lewis agreed. It is unclear what arrangement they made for Roger to contribute to the household expenses, since Roger was unemployed. Jon was taken by surprise that his uncle had agreed to this arrangement. Roger told Jon that Lewis asked him to move in. Lewis and Jon had their own bedrooms, while Roger took up residence on the couch in the living room.

Without an adult at home, the apartment became a hangout for Jon and his friends. The few occasions that Uncle Lew hung out with the teens, he joked with them and even, on occasion, furnished them with alcohol, warning them not to leave any alcohol lying around the apartment.

Yet Lewis's discipline was as erratic as his behavior and his schedule. Uncle Lew could have a *laissez-faire* attitude with his charge, but unexpectedly could come down hard on Jon about issues in the apartment. He laid down the law that he wanted everyone in the apartment by 11:00 PM. If they were not home, he would "get out my gun and shoot, and ask questions later."

Since Roger did not have a job, he hung around the apartment, sleeping a good part of the day. It is unclear when and how often Roger had access to Lewis's room. In his deposition to the New York State Police on January 9, Roger described Lewis's room. According to Roger, "Lewis built a wall in his room a short time ago, about a week and a half ago. There is only one window in his room, and it is boarded over. I thought this was strange and wondered why, but I never asked him about it. His room was always a mess. There were all kinds of things in the room such as dishes, food, clothes, gun magazines, and things like that. I saw a lot of tape in the room, duct tape, masking tape, scotch tape. They were on the dresser sometimes and other times, they were on the floor. There was a bundle of thick white rope. He had a set of encyclopedias, very neatly stacked on a shelf. About a week ago, he got up suddenly and put one of the volumes back into place and made a comment about it being out of place. He said, 'This is really pissing me off, I need to fix it!' He put the book neatly back into place and sat back down. This wall that he built, it doesn't go all the way from the floor to the ceiling. There is a space between the top of the wall and the ceiling to allow room for a light fixture."[54]

Lewis worked nights until he was fired from his job at the movie theater. According to the story he told Jon, he quit because the boss was always yelling at him. He told Roger he quit his job because his boss came in drunk and was yelling at him. Lent then got a job paying $6.00 an hour on a paper route, dropping off bundles of papers. This job lasted just a matter of weeks. One excuse for losing the job was that he did not deliver all the papers. Then he claimed that he quit because he was not paid for eighteen hours. Lent's stories often had many iterations, depending on whom he told. He subsequently supported himself by living on support money that Jon received.

Lent kept his guns in his room, but his gun magazines were strewn around the apartment. He did show the guns to Jon, Roger, and Melissa, each at separate times on the rare occasions when he invited them into his room.

On the occasions when Lent wanted to be alone, he would ask Jon and Roger to leave. Sometimes it was for one night, and sometimes for a weekend. Uncle Lew told the boys that he wanted to entertain his girlfriend Liz at the apartment and wanted privacy. On one occasion,

---

54. **Investigator Arthur Daniels, NYSP, Interview with Roger W. Beaudoin, January 9, 1994.**

when asked to leave, Jon decided to go camping. When he returned to the apartment to get his tent, Lewis asked him what he was doing there. He told his uncle about a dog he had been hiding in his room. When Lent opened the door, the dog ran out. Lewis grabbed the dog, who in turn peed on him. Becoming furious, he said, "Goodbye, Charlie," and flung the dog down the stairs. Fortunately, the dog was OK. Jon took the dog and hightailed it out of the apartment.

No one knew of this mysterious woman Liz or ever saw her. The teens did not actually believe she existed. Lent claimed that she lived in Albany and that they had been seeing each other for a year.

In fact, Lewis's relationship with women was rather awkward. He proposed to four females who were completely taken by surprise considering they were never in a romantic relationship with this man. At age seventeen, while still living in New York, the first girl he asked to marry him devastated him with her refusal. At age twenty-six, while living in Florida, out of nowhere he asked his fourteen-year-old friend Kelly to marry him. A few years later, while working on his car with his sixteen-year-old cousin Renee, he sprang the question on her. Besides never being more than friends, Renee was put off by the notion of marrying a cousin.

The last proposal occurred while Lent was attending Bible College. Brenda Muller, the daughter of one of the ministers who taught at the school, was a single mother with three children. To make ends meet, she cleaned Lewis's house once a week. They became friendly and started having dinners at each other's houses. One evening, when they were preparing dinner at his house, he asked her to marry him. "I told him I was not ready to marry anyone. It was too soon after my divorce," she reported. He became upset and she left the house with her children. Because of this seemingly out of nowhere proposal and his reaction, Brenda discussed this with her father, who agreed to have a talk with Lewis.

About a month later, Lewis sneaked up on Brenda in the school's library and confronted her. "How could you do this? I was always good to you. What kind of person are you?" A few years later, Brenda worried that Lent's killing of Sara Anne Wood, also a minister's daughter, might have been in retaliation for her rejection of him.[55]

Lewis did spend time with one female friend, Sue. She checked off the boxes as an age-appropriate woman and friend for him. Susan, who lived in the town of Schodack, New York, a town southeast of Albany, met Lewis in 1985 when he attended the New England School of Biblical Studies out of the Church of Christ in Clifton Park, NY. They went places together, often day trips usually using her car. She made several visits with him, three or four times a year, and sometimes with his young friend Stephen to see his parents in Burdett, NY. She even accompanied Lewis and his parents on a trip to Florida. He could count on Sue to loan him her car and sometimes even $20 here and there.

When Lent suddenly decided that he needed to get rid of the first van he had purchased from the church, he wanted it discreetly parked a distance away from his home where the vehicle would not be connected to him. He asked Sue if he could leave the van in her yard because the car had engine trouble. In the spring of 1991, Richard Varian saw the van parked off by a driveway as he was driving by. There was no For Sale sign on the car, but he thought the owner might be using the old van for parts. Varian decided to knock on the door and enquire about the vehicle. Sue put him in touch with Lewis, who gave Varian the vehicle. When Varian took possession of the van, Lent left behind various children's and women's clothes, some tools, and some crumbled up duct tape. Varian had the car towed and fixed it up, investing $1500. He drove it for a month or so until the motor blew. Using some parts, he chopped the rest of the van and

---

55. Spina, Matthew (February 15, 1994). Lent's Long Winding Road. *Syracuse Herald-Journal.*

scrapped it. He threw away the clothes immediately, and eventually misplaced the tools. Any evidence from the van no longer existed.

Unfortunately, despite Sue's kindness and friendship to Lewis, he put out mixed messages to her and strung her along, using her as he did others who thought they were his friends. She described their relationship as strictly platonic due to their religious beliefs. Lewis just could not relate in an appropriate or healthy manner to a woman.

Later, from prison, Lent sent the following letters to Sue.

Dear Sue:

I always considered you a friend, although you were one I had to keep my garden a secret from. The way I've always looked at pot is exactly as I've described it to you many times. First, I don't believe anyone should do anything they aren't convinced is alright to do. I'm convinced if someone believes God allows the use of many things in our lives as long as they aren't misused.

As far as burning any presents you gave me I don't remember ever burning anything you gave me. I've never been a person who collects cards or pictures of any kind, not even from my own family. I keep a very select group of pictures or cards and that's all. Most given to me are sorted out & either given to other people or file 13.

Speaking of being first on my list of prospects for marriage, you were first for consideration. I don't know what you've been told or why, but you would have had the first place of consideration, that doesn't mean I automatically decided beforehand you were right for me. I know there were a lot of differences between our ways of life and understanding.

I don't want to say how different our lives are, but it isn't necessary to describe. If I can encourage you, let it be to try and understand that whenever you befriend anyone also try to keep in mind that anyone who says they belong to Christ needs to examine their motives before they do anything. Please don't think I'm condemning you as a Christian. I'm only saying that our motives in friendships need to be as Christ's were who served & helped HIS friends without any seeking of profit for HIMSELF. The only negative thing I can say about your motives, in our friendship, was that they always looked for some profit in the future, either eventual marriage or some other return. That is only a weakness and not a condemnation on anyone's part. I realized that weakness and it didn't affect your position as the first to be considered, but I was watching to see if there would be any change.

The last nine years of friendship between us have had its ups and downs, but I've always considered us friends. Many times in my friendships with people in general I've endured times when I've felt wronged and misunderstood with no recourse but to ask God for the patience to endure. Differences of opinions, lifestyles, and background history many times cause us frustration and even unrighteous indignation with our friends. I'm not condemning any of my friends for whatever they may be thinking of me these days. Hopefully, the truth will come out at trial and I'll be set free by God's working with my lawyers to bring about justice.

All during our friendship I've tried to impress upon you that we are two different kinds of people. I'm hopeful you'll find a friend more compatible with your personality and be able to be the kind of friend our Lord is to us. Don't just read a passage of Bible before going to bed. Study the personality of our Lord and Savior and learn to imitate HIM in all things and life will be much richer than it has ever been. I hope you remain friends with my family, too, and if you wish to write again I will do my best to answer as quickly & honestly as possible.

Love in Christ
Lew

Dear Sue,

Thanks for the letter. I don't mind writing to you or anyone else as long as they don't want to know anything about what's happening in my legal problems.

First of all, about profanity, I do feel comfortable that I never used it to say I wouldn't marry you or anyone else. I would remember something like that and I don't remember ever saying anything even remotely similar to that. I've told John and others that as things stood I couldn't see any possibility of us ever marrying because of such a great difference in our lives. Like I said before I kept watching to see if certain things changed in your life, because I don't know what God may have in mind.

As for destroying plants you gave me, they died from lack of light and care, not from my wanting them dead. I also told John and others that those plants didn't have a chance from the beginning because they needed more light than they could get from my windows so I just watered them a few times until they started to die from lack of light & then I threw them out. They were nice plants from a friend and I never treat a gift from a friend with contempt or refuse a friends[sic] gift even if I know it will only die. If I had an apartment with a lot of light I would have had my apartment full like a greenhouse of not only plants you gave me but those violets I'd bought that died also and many others since I love all kinds of plants not just pot plants.

I think some people in trying to be absolutely honest are putting words in my mouth that express what they thought were my opinions. It's not unusual for people to misunderstand what I say as I've experienced the same thing many times. You know yourself how time after time I've said something to you as we were going somewhere and then I'd restate myself in other words and maybe even a third time just to make things clear. I'm sure I've never said that phrase referring to you and me and marriage, but what

I did say obviously stuck in someone's mind in those terms and that's how they remembered it.

I'm glad you'll be making yourself available for the trial. It should be very interesting. I'm going to make sure and testify myself. Talking to the police is out for now as it would take my lawyers away from working. Sometimes in the future I'd be glad to talk to them again, but not till my lawyers are ready.

I liked the article you sent. It fits right in with some study I'm doing right now. I'm doing a lot of studying of the Scriptures and books about them. All through history there have been people and groups who've tried to change the truth about Christ into a lie.

Write me again when you wish and I'll write back as soon as I can.

Love in Christ,
Lew

What's Up with Lew?

Shortly before Lent's arrest, friends noticed changes in him. Linda Domenichini and her boyfriend Rick Murdock wondered whether Lewis was having a nervous breakdown. She wondered about the mysterious hours that he was keeping. Linda often did Lewis's laundry for him in her apartment, but now he was insisting on doing his own laundry. It was around this time that Lent changed his glasses from his usual prescription dark glasses to regular glasses. A few days before his arrest, he started to wall off part of his bedroom. He told Stephen that he wanted to install an aquarium. He told Phil Shallies he was constructing boxes to grow marijuana behind the walled off area in his room. Both were plausible explanations to divert and to satisfy Stephen and Phil's curiosity.

Phil had never known Lewis to become agitated, yet quite uncharacteristically, a couple days before his arrest, as he and Phil were working on his van, "he started swearing like a trooper, cursing up a storm." For the first time, he also started making suggestive remarks about the visiting nurse who attended to Phil's tenant Chet. Lent also mentioned to Phil that he had an alter ego named Stephen. Janie Ray remarked to Phil Shallies that she also thought Lewis was having a nervous breakdown.

The morning of the attempted abduction of Rebecca Savarese, Lewis became angry about the downstairs neighbors blocking his borrowed truck in the driveway. He told Murdock that he had to leave at 5:30 in the morning to go job hunting. Also, Lewis arrived unusually early to the Shallieses' house. He got right to work shoveling the driveway. Seeing him outside in the cold, Janie invited him in, but he declined the offer continuing to shovel. A few hours later, Janie called Phil from work with breaking news. "Somebody tried to abduct a kid. I don't know why I called and told Phil, it's just that Lewis was acting weird that morning," she stated. Later, Phil jokingly asked Lewis if he had been in Pittsfield that morning, which Lent denied. When the two men decided to go to Pittsfield to get auto parts, Phil suggested they take Chet's car, stating, "There was no reason to borrow trouble."

Personality Disorder

"Antisocial personality disorder is characterized by a pattern of disregard for and violation of the rights of others... People with this illness may seem charming on the surface, but they are likely to be irritable and aggressive as well as irresponsible. They may have numerous somatic complaints and perhaps attempt suicide. Due to their manipulative tendencies, it is difficult to tell whether they are lying or telling the truth.[56]

How someone develops an antisocial behavior disorder remains unclear. Is it nature or lack of nurture? Has this person inherited a personality trait genetically or has the parental figure so abused or neglected this child that a part of the brain becomes stunted? Did the child suffer from head trauma or a seizure disorder severe enough to numb his ability to feel empathy? Does what happened in childhood affect whom this person, in turn, chooses as his victims? Do the attacks he inflicts somehow give him a feeling of being in control of a situation about which he was powerless as a child?

Lewis Stephen Lent Jr. began expressing terror of his visits with his father at a young age. The family described abuse and rumors of abuse in both Lent's father and his uncle. Lent Sr. drank heavily and ignored and allegedly molested his children. If, in fact, a family member beat Lewis Jr.'s head into a wall, might this account for his migraines and possible brain damage? Did he inherit his father's dangerous personality? Did he choose his victims unconsciously to now try to gain control of similar situations in which he was rendered powerless in his childhood or scenes of abuse that he witnessed in his childhood?

Whatever the reasons, the disclosure of his evil acts shocked those who knew him. "I thought he was a kind and helpful friend. He never gave me cause to be afraid. He never did anything to bring out a doubt." – Friend Sarah Shallies[57]

"It is impossible to square the man we know with the guy who was arrested. He was a very good friend. He was very kind to us. He was well-mannered, never aggressive.

56. (March 6, 2018). Antisocial Personality Disorder. *https://www.psychologytoday.com/us/conditions/antisocial-personalitydisorder.*
57. Wentzel, Michael. (January 13, 1994). Friends of Suspect Now Feel Betrayed. *Democrat & Chronicle.*

He was just a warm man who went out of his way to help us." – Friend Phil Shallies[58]

In her article in the *Union News* titled "Serial Killer Don't Look Like Monsters to Us," Rhonda Sevan profiles characteristics of a child serial killer. Most are white males ages twenty to thirty, with a history of being abused or neglected as a child. They choose victims who seem vulnerable and whom they can control through sexual dominance. They are aroused by children because they are unable to have a satisfying adult relationship. Yet after the attack, they must get rid of the eyewitness. Rather than feel guilt, they get a rush of excitement that becomes addictive. The act of the hunt, the killing, and the reminiscing preoccupy their lives.[59]

With Lewis Lent, the urges were becoming more desperate and bolder. His downfall was his carelessness and his choice of a victim who outsmarted him.

---

58. **January 12, 1994 Sennott, Charles M., Armstrong, David, also contributing Murphy, Sean P., John Ellement, John, Roche, B.J., Chant, Kate (January 12, 1994) Possible Serial Killings Probed. *Boston Globe*.**
59. Sevan, Rhonda (January 14, 1994) **Serial Killers Don't Look Like Monsters to Us.** *Union News.*

CHAPTER 10

D.A.R.E.

Rebecca Savarese was hailed as a hero. The media clamored to feature interviews with this shy twelve-year-old. Law enforcement and the public marveled at her composure and quick thinking, in the face of grave danger, to foil her attacker. Even the most seasoned law enforcement personnel were in awe of this child's ability to assess her situation and outsmart her kidnapper. A sly serial killer had met his match with Rebecca.

With the onslaught of media attention, attorney Paul Perachi was named Rebecca's guardian ad litem to shepherd her through this blitz. Perachi was the perfect choice. Before his career as an attorney, he had been a schoolteacher and principal. He later would be appointed as a Juvenile Court judge. He understood children and knew that Rebecca had no desire to have her life disrupted and her privacy invaded. She just wanted to get on with her life, not dwell on what could have happened to her. "What impressed me the most was she was so easy going. She was not interested in celebrity. She was asked to do a lot with the media interviews but didn't particularly have any interest in it," mused Paul Perachi.

Rebecca credits her training with the D.A.R.E. program in helping her realize that she would have been a goner if she had gotten into the van. The Drug Abuse Resistance Education program began in California and became part of the Pittsfield schools' curriculum. "The program is not about drugs. It's about life skills," explained Officer Kim Bertelli, the coordinator of the D.A.R.E. program in the schools. "Role play is important. I ask them what if he grabs you? They don't think of that. Kids need to know that if a stranger comes up to you, say 'no' and run away."[60]

Rebecca was able to think and react without mimicking the safe class role plays. Officer Bertelli realized, as did Rebecca's peers, that role play does not necessarily prepare you for the panic that sets in during crisis situations. She had not screamed but waited until she could catch her pursuer off guard. It was a brilliant strategy.

According to Perachi, "He picked the wrong person to attack. She was unflappable. She had D.A.R.E. training, but who has the presence of mind when someone is holding a gun to you to think, 'If I get in the van, I'll never see my family again'? She didn't have asthma, but she faked an asthma attack. I can't imagine anyone else thinking that quickly. It was like divine intervention that he picked Rebecca. It was his downfall."

Interviews with CNN, New England, and New York news outlets, as well as *48 Hours*, *The Today Show* in New York, and the *Leeza Gibbons* show in California highlighted Rebecca's heroism as well as the value of the D.A.R.E. program. Within days of the attempted abduction, for the benefit of New York public schools, "New York State lawmakers proposed legislation that would mandate D.A.R.E. or similar programs," reported Lynne Daley of the Berkshire Eagle.[61]

---

60. Lynne. (January 16, 1994). National D.A.R.E. Program Hailed After Near Abduction. *The Berkshire Eagle.*

61. Lynne. (January 16, 1994). National D.A.R.E. Program Hailed After Near Abduction. *The Berkshire Eagle.*

Just days after the attempted abduction, Rebecca joined Massachusetts Attorney

General Scott Harshbarger in addressing the graduating class of forty-two D.A.R.E. officers from across the state in Framingham. Lt. Edward Nolan, president of the Massachusetts D.A.R.E. Association said, "We want to recognize her efforts and she is an exemplary role model."[62] Also, Massachusetts Governor William F. Weld recognized her at the statehouse with a citation in recognition of her "courage and bravery" and her use of the skills that she had learned through the D.A.R.E. program. The governor took this opportunity to announce $5 million in grants allocated to D.A.R.E. programs across the state.[63]

Center of downtown Pittsfield, scene of abduction attempt on Rebecca Savarese
Photographer – Alan Metzger

62. Caldwell, Jean. (January 14, 1994). Heroine Asked to Address Group. *Boston Globe.*

63. Sliwa, Carol. (February 12, 1994). Weld Hails D.A.R..E's Role in Escape. *The Berkshire Eagle.*

Rebecca Savarese and her mother Christine Paoli
Photographer- Joel Librizzi/The Berkshire Eagle

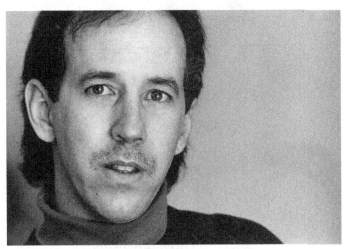

Russell Davis, eyewitness to abduction
attempt of Rebecca Savarese
Photograph – The Berkshire Eagle

Amy and Owen Boyington courtesy of Owen Boyington

Detective Owen Boyington
Photograph courtesy of Owen Boyington

*Wayne Lo(Photographer – Craig T. Walker/
The Berkshire Eagle) (left) Map of Simon's Rock
College Campus, path of Wayne Lo's rampage
Photograph – The Berkshire Eagle*

*Sites at the Pittsfield Plaza on West Housatonic
Street where James Bernardo was seen Oct. 22 are
identified by numbers. #1 is the lot in front of Wall
to Wall Billiards. Police speculate that he may have
ridden around the corner of the building there, putting
him out of sight of people in the parking lot. #2 is
roughly the last place he was seen. #3 is the Cinema
Center and #4 is Clean Machines laundromat.
Photgrapher - Joel Librizzi/The Berkshire Eagle*

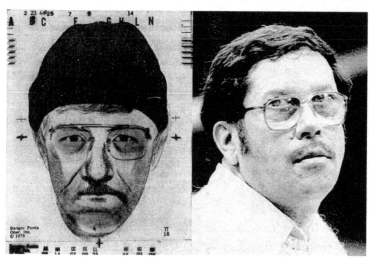

Composite sketch of kidnapping suspect,
Photograph - courtesy of the Berkshire County
DA's office / Lewis Stephen Lent, Jr.
Photograph – The Berkshire Eagle

Phillip and Sarah Shallies, friends of Lewis Lent
Photographer – Melissa Mahan/Democrat & Chronicle

Lewis Lent's Tyler Street apartment, Pittsfield
Photograph – The Berkshire Eagle

Lewis Lent's Hudson Street apartment, North Adams
as it appears today, boarded up and condemned
Photographer – Alan Metzger

Lewis Lent's bedroom, North Adams
- partition wall for "Master Plan"
Photograph courtesy of the Berkshire County DA's office

Bedroom in Lent's North Adams apartment,
partition wall and boarded up window
Photograph courtesy of the Berkshire County DA's office

Van seat in the attic of Lewis Lent's North Adams apartment
Photograph – courtesy of the Berkshire County DA's office

CHAPTER 11

COLLECTING EVIDENCE

Setting up the Task Force

With a suspect in a kidnapping and two high profile child murder cases in Massachusetts and New York locked up in the Pittsfield Police Station, news traveled fast as stunning details unfolded during that first weekend. Bulletins reached law enforcement agencies throughout the country. Calls from jurisdictions everywhere with unsolved disappearances and murders flooded the Pittsfield Police Department. "They thought he (Lewis Lent) killed everyone from Kennedy on up," remarked Massachusetts State Police Lieutenant Jack Flaherty.

Locally, some noteworthy calls came into the Pittsfield Police. Daniel E. Clukey contacted the police department to say that when he saw pictures of Lent and Savarese in the newspaper it jogged his memory. He recognized the man from an incident that had happened before Christmas. Clukey was walking back to work from the cleaners when he saw a man standing around, watching Rebecca walking from school. When Mr. Clukey made eye contact with the man, the guy acted as if he just got caught doing something suspicious. He jumped into his late model, dark-colored pickup truck and drove away. The man was Lewis Lent.

A week before the incident with Rebecca, a similar occurrence happened to a young girl at a K Mart in Bennington, Vermont, just fifteen miles from Lent's home in North Adams. While shopping with her parents, the girl, who had similar features and build as Rebecca and Sara Anne, noticed a scruffy-looking man watching her and following her around the store. She went to the ladies' room and as she exited, the man approached her, reaching out to grab her coat. She ran toward her father, who grabbed her and stepped in front of her. When the man saw the girl's father, he remarked, "I just wanted her to know that she didn't have to be afraid of me." The man walked away, and the incident was not reported until the family saw Lewis Lent's picture on TV. Recognizing him as the man at K Mart, they called the police.

Dawn Fuhlbrigge briefly worked at the Cinema Center during the time of Lent's employment. She was questioned along with all the theater's employees, although she had little or no contact with Lent and could not offer information about him or his vehicles.

Shortly after the first interview, Dawn re-contacted the task force to report an incident in 1989 or 1990. She had been followed by a van operated by a man with glasses. The van followed her each day for about a week as she walked home from the store owned by her parents, located at an intersection with Tyler Street, where Lent lived. The van would slow down to keep pace with her. On the third or fourth day, the van slowed down near her. She took off running and reported the incident to her parents. It was the last time she was followed. Her mother believes that the girl's father reported the incident to the police at the time.

Another call would come in later to the police about an attempted abduction at a Howard Johnson's on the New Jersey Turnpike. A teenage girl walked out of the restaurant to her family's car moments before the rest of her family. A man tried to grab her, but again was thwarted by her parents arriving at their car just in time. This incident went unreported until the family recognized Lewis Lent as the perpetrator while watching national news.

Shortly after his arrest, a Florida woman spotted Lewis Lent on TV and called authorities. She identified him as the man who had raped her fifteen years earlier in Casselberry, Florida, when she was only ten years old. With no leads at the time and Lent not having a criminal record, the case had been closed since 1979. However, as a result of the sighting of Lent, the case was now reopened in Florida.

Due to the inordinate number of calls regarding Lent that were coming in, Pittsfield Police Chief Jerry Lee asked the New York State Police if they would stick around to help him monitor the telephone lines. There were sightings of Lent in several New England states, Pennsylvania, Virginia, and Florida. There were even calls from as far west as New Mexico and California.

New York State Police Chief Investigator Captain Frank Pace was released to Pittsfield to help oversee this investigation. He was given the go ahead and resources to do whatever needed to be done in these proceedings. Coming from a para-military background, Pace had served as a soldier for four years and a federal agent for two years before joining the New York State Police fifteen years prior to this assignment. Being a task-oriented person, he had worked his way up the chain of command in the department. The best piece of advice he had learned when he joined the force and which guided him through his career was, when responding to a call do four things: investigate, evaluate, take action, and follow up.

Pace joined Senior Investigator Dave McElligot, one of the original New York State Police officers, to come to Pittsfield to join the Pittsfield Police Department working on the Jimmy Bernardo case. Also joining the group was Frank Jerome, the lead investigator for the Sara Anne Wood case.

According to Frank Pace, "My job was to administer the handling of evidence collected in the investigation of Lewis Lent." As a large volume of calls came in from New York State, by the following week, New York State Police investigators poured into town. Various troops providing assistance rotated in and out of the investigation so as not to deplete the workforce of any particular troop. Troopers were sent from areas where there were open homicides or child abductions. Other troopers arrived if they had a specific expertise that was needed, such as evidence handling or computer skills. They brought along computer technicians with their technology and teletype system to check listings and to run checks on people.

Massachusetts State Police commanding officer, Lieutenant Robert Scott, investigator with the major crimes unit known as CPAC (Criminal Prevention and Control) who worked out of the DA's office, was assigned immediately to the Lent case. Scott, a twenty-two-year veteran of the Massachusetts State Police, started his career doing road patrol, working all three shifts for three and a half years. While a patrolman, Scott was the first state trooper to arrive at the scene of a homicide, allowing him to be assigned to temporary duty helping with that homicide investigation. Proving his investigatory acumen and his sharp people skills, Scott became an investigator with the newly established Crime Prevention and Control Unit of the Massachusetts State Police housed in the Springfield District Attorney's satellite office in Pittsfield before Berkshire County's DA's office became a separate entity from Springfield.

Having the desire to learn the best methods for interrogating sex offenders, Scott worked with Mr. Nicholas Groch, who was located at Summer State Prison. Under Groch's tutelage, Scott learned best practices for interviewing sexual offenders. He wanted to know how offenders who confessed to crimes were interrogated. Law enforcement needed to rethink interrogation techniques, including how the offender was approached and even the room where the interview took place. Scott wanted to know what drew the perpetrator to a victim. With his training, confession rates increased 30%.

Scott's training made him a valuable member of the task force. Scott remained on the Lent case, often escorting the suspect to court, as well as on some of Lent's wild goose chases searching for the body of Sara Anne Wood.

During his first weekend in custody, Lent dropped the bombshell to investigators from the New York State Police that he held the key to the disappearance and murder of Sara Anne Wood. He drew up a rough map and directions to a site deep in the Adirondack Mountains, near Raquette Lake, where he alleged to have buried her body. The search for Sara Anne Woods began without Lent's participation. Deep in the woods with heavy underbrush, 150 New York State troopers, Forest Rangers, Air Force personnel, Army National Guard, FBI, and volunteers under the direction of Captain Ronald Tritto braved the elements to start this painstaking search.

With thirty inches of snow on the ground, temperatures dipping as low as -20° F., the searchers scoured the huge area. An area of three acres was carefully mapped out in grids. Specialized backhoes to be less destructive to potential evidence, as well as ground penetrating radar on loan from the FBI, were sent to the dig site. Unfortunately, the radar ground imaging machines just could not penetrate the rugged, steep terrain. Following the intense work of clearing snow and the use of salamander heaters to warm the frozen ground enough to break through, came the delicate digging and sifting through the earth, similar to the technique used at an archeological dig site.

Searchers worked for twenty-minute intervals, then availed themselves of a warming tent to prevent frostbite. Medical personnel graciously volunteered their time to treat frostbite cases or any other medical emergencies that might occur.

After a month of excruciatingly difficult conditions, the search for Sara Anne Wood's remains was getting nowhere. Lent finally had his opportunity to assist with locating the girl's body. Released to the custody of the New York and Massachusetts troopers, he was driven to the digging site. Lieutenant Bob Scott was flown to the site by helicopter to oversee the prisoner's aid in the search. In this rugged terrain, with no place to land the plane, the pilot finally got clearance to bring down the chopper in a nearby fenced-in school yard. The space was so tight that to take off again, the pilot had to unload enough fuel to be able to maneuver the chopper out of this spot. The day provided an outing for Lewis Lent, but it turned out to be just another one of his frustrating games of one upmanship with the authorities. The culmination of weeks of this grueling search turned up nothing.

Because the spokesperson for the DA's office was too busy handling the Wayne Lo trial in Springfield, MA, Chief Lee had to manage the media chaos at the police department. Along with Captain Frank Pace and Lieutenant Robert Scott, he appeared for daily press conferences until the DA's office assigned Frederick Lantz to handle the media.

Almost immediately after Lent's arraignment in District Court in the Savarese case, TV crews out of Albany, Springfield, and Boston flooded into downtown Pittsfield with their TV trucks, satellite dishes, and rooftop electronics.[64] Producers and reporters from *America's Most Wanted*, *48 Hours*, and *The Today Show* swarmed the basement of the Pittsfield Police Department's task force command post. Pittsfield's City Hall was not exempt from the media onslaught. City Hall sits directly across Allen Street from the police station. With limited parking, police

---

64. **Lahr, Ellen G. (January 15, 1994) A Media Circus,** *The Berkshire Eagle.*

cars parked diagonally in front of the station on this rather narrow street. "It drove Mayor Reilly nuts. You'd come down Allen Street and there were the big TV trucks blocking the road," recounted Chief Lee.

Besides running the police department, Lee was actively involved with the task force. He had an exhausting schedule. "It got so bad with the media that one evening I came home about 5:30. I was taking out the garbage cans and a big one of those trucks shows up in front of my house with a satellite dish and they wanted to interview me. I told them to get the hell out of here. I'm not interviewing now. That's how bad it was."

Jerry Lee remembered, on a more pleasant note, "I was videotaping in the police station for *48 Hours.* I get a call from my niece down in Florida, who knew nothing about what was going on in Pittsfield, that she saw me on television."

For the task force to track the comings and goings of Lent, a toll-free number was released to encourage and expedite communication from anyone who knew or had contact with him. The line was manned from 9:00 AM until midnight, seven days a week, with an answering machine to take calls during the unmanned hours.[65] The response was overwhelming.

As all these calls came in, there also arose a serious timing issue with personnel. Most of the Massachusetts State Police detectives were needed at the Wayne Lo multiple murder trial, fifty-five miles away in Springfield, leaving only four Massachusetts State Police detectives to work on the Lent case. With this investigation, no longer under their purview, the Pittsfield Police detectives needed to return to their routine duties. Chief Lee assigned Patrolman Richard "Dick" LeClair as the Pittsfield Police Department's liaison

---

65. **Gerald B. (January 27, 1994). The Police Appeal to Tourists. *The Berkshire Eagle.***

to the task force and rotated in PPD detectives when he could.

The task force began to take shape. Headquartered in the basement of the PPD, the space became the central clearinghouse and lead desk for the massive investigation that lay ahead. With no formal agreement between these agencies, feeling their way, they began by starting a timeline following Lewis Lent's whereabouts, believing he may have committed crimes up and down the East Coast. Frank Pace was running the show, yet he felt constrained. "New York State Police had no jurisdiction operating in Massachusetts. There was nothing in the Massachusetts criminal or penal law that allowed New York law enforcement to be in Massachusetts with firearms and conducting investigations. What if our men were out on an interview and something happened? The New York State troopers needed to be partnered with either a Massachusetts State trooper or a Massachusetts Police officer to do their assigned investigations," explained Captain Pace. Because New York State Police had no jurisdiction operating in Massachusetts, the task force desperately needed more help from Massachusetts. Although there was some talk about deputizing some of the New York troopers, that never happened.

Chief Lee found the lack of Massachusetts State Police troublesome. "We were going to obtain search warrants for different locations; I think Adams, North Adams, and other places where Pittsfield police had no jurisdiction. The New York Police had no jurisdiction, and the FBI did not want to make it a federal case. So finally, I remember calling the Lee barracks because I knew the lieutenant down there. I said, 'Hey, look it. We don't have anyone here from the State Police because they are all with Gerry Downing in Springfield. I need state police. We're doing search warrants.' So, he got me hooked up with a colonel in the Massachusetts State Police and the head of the detective bureau. Due to the high profile of this case both locally and nationally, the next day I had all sorts of troopers from major crime units and DAs' offices across the state. So now I had New York and Jack Flaherty, a lieutenant in the Massachusetts State Police who became a major coordinator in this whole thing," explained Chief Lee.

Lieutenant Jack Flaherty, assigned to troop headquarters in Northampton, which covered all of western Massachusetts from Sturbridge west, got the call. "I was on another assignment and got contacted by the colonel of the State Police. He said, 'We are going to send you to head up the task force,'" recalls Jack Flaherty. "Friday I'm doing something entirely different, and Saturday I came and joined the forensics people in the basement of the Pittsfield Police Department. It was quiet when I came in." Flaherty had a chance to get the lay of the land without the chaos of a full weekday crew. He added, "On Monday, the dog and pony show started. Everybody's coming and they are going to want to see the new guy in town, which is me. I said, 'This is how it's been running, let's keep doing it. We can bring in all the resources from the state.' I could bring in whatever I needed."

The FBI joined the team to assist with profiling, with out-of-state inquiries not in the jurisdiction of New York or Massachusetts, and with technical assistance. Because of the nature of the case, the FBI sent Field Agents Jerry Downs and Michael Smith from Springfield, MA. Along with him came Agent Clint Van Zandt, a profiling expert from the FBI's Behavioral Science Unit in Quantico, Virginia. Van Zandt's expertise aided in developing a scenario of how a serial killer enhances his skills with each attack. Chief Lee recounted how Van Zandt explained, "People like Lent constantly improve their ability to kidnap kids. If they find they are missing an element, they get it for the next kidnapping. For example, in Lent's van he had pieces of rope cut to size instead of the whole length of the rope which would need to be cut. He had a gun, he had candy and all kinds of stuff to enhance his ability to commit the crime. This is what Van Zandt talked about, and this is exactly what we found. We already had the evidence, but I don't know that I was that sharp to know why it was the way it was." Van Zandt then advised on specific investigative techniques and lines of questioning.[66]

The FBI clerical staff came along with computers that connected to the FBI and State databases. VICAP, the Violent Criminal Apprehension Program still in its relative infancy, was designed to linked similar crimes anywhere in the country. The FBI also introduced a new method of picking up latent fingerprints with ultraviolet lights used at night. The "War Room," transforming the PPD's basement into a mass of computers, telephones, technicians, and detectives, began to take shape.

Prior to assembling the task force, three New York State Police investigators, attempting to fast track and enhance their careers, were discovered planting crime scene evidence in various cases, one of which was the Jimmy Bernardo Case. The FBI investigated this scandal, resulting in arrests, convictions, and prison terms for these New York State policemen.

The FBI investigation left a rift between the two agencies. Although the troopers' crimes did not directly affect the Jimmy Bernardo case because fingerprints were planted before Lewis Lent became a suspect in the case, the two agencies now had to work together. Lead investigator Frank Pace and FBI lead investigator Jerome Downs had a rather chilly start. It was not until they got to talking with their distinct Brooklyn accents that they realized they had gone to the same high school. This revelation began the thaw, which led to a top-notch working relationship. When Massachusetts State Police finally arrived in earnest, Jack

66. O'Connor, Gerald B. (January 12, 1994). Lent Case Brings Separate Continuance Dates. *The Berkshire Eagle.*

Flaherty fell right in step with the workings set up by Pace and his team, which Flaherty felt was well organized and well thought through. Feeling their way without precedent or guidelines for meticulously tracking a serial killer, but with seasoned, highly intelligent leadership, this group got right down to business.

The purpose of the task force was to build a timeline of Lewis Lent's whereabouts for as far back as they could go. This would help provide accurate corroborating evidence for the district attorneys in the Bernardo and Wood cases. Lent's confession alone was not enough to build a case against him. The task force's work would have to connect Lent in time and place to other crimes or eliminate him as a potential suspect.

While living in Florida, Lent often traveled back and forth to Upstate New York. On one of his trips, he briefly settled in New Mexico. Until this point, authorities knew nothing of his arrest in Truth or Consequences, New Mexico for stealing tires from an auto repair shop. After repaying his debt, charges were dropped.[67] Lent told Phil Shallies that while in New Mexico, he worked at a gas station. After six weeks of not getting paid, he took it upon himself to use one of the station's checks to compensate himself. Upon his return to New York, the police stopped him and arrested him in Ithaca. His mother repaid the amount of the check, and he was released.

Lent made frequent trips from Pittsfield west into New York State, also wandering east along the Massachusetts Turnpike and back roads to scout neighborhoods along the way. The task force needed to check into what vehicles Lent drove and when he drove them. Not only did Lent cruise around in his van, but he was cagey for many years about borrowing friends' vehicles on many of his outings. At his workplace at the Pittsfield Cinema, various cars or a truck

---

67. Gerald B. O'Connor (January 14, 1994). Lent's Tyler Street Days. *The Berkshire Eagle.*

would be seen parked behind the movie theater during his work hours. At his residence on Tyler Street in Pittsfield, he worked on various cars in his driveway. In North Adams, neighbors recalled seeing various vehicles at Lewis's disposal. Even back in high school and in Florida, he would borrow or trade cars. Lent's friend Sue provided detailed information about the many cars that he owned during the ten years she knew him.

William O. Stanley

On February 2, 1994, a fellow inmate of Lent's at the Berkshire County House of Correction had information that he wished to share with members of the task force. House of Correction Assistant Deputy Superintendent Jack Quinn, New York State Police Investigator Arthur Daniels, and Massachusetts State Police Trooper Joseph Capillo were all present when William O. Stanley attested that he was speaking of his own free will, without the promise of leniency and without threat.

Stanley resided two cells away from Lent. Their first encounter occurred when Stanley walked past Lent's cell on his way to the phones. As he passed Lent, he thought the man in the cell might be someone he knew. He asked Lent if they knew each other. Lent replied, "No." Stanley then remembered that this was the guy he had seen on TV. When Stanley asked him, Lent just nodded yes. As the two got to talking, they realized that they knew some of the same people and had met briefly a few times on Main Street in North Adams. Stanley asked Lent if it was true about the little girl. Lent just sat down on his bunk, lowered his head, and said, "Yeah."

In a later conversation, when Stanley enquired about why Lent was in jail, Lent said that he had tried to get another girl into his car. Lent said, "She's lucky. The little bitch got away."

The men talked on four different occasions. The investigators were anxious to know if Lent talked about where he had buried Sara Anne Wood's body. Lent told him that he had spoken to investigators and had drawn a map, but that they would not find her because he lied. Lent said that she was two hundred yards away from the site he had designated in a clump of birch trees. As Stanley stood talking to Lent, a fellow inmate nearby using the phone warned Stanley that a guard was coming. Stanley kept on walking toward the back of the cell block. As he was walking away, Lent said something about "north." Since the guard was not there yet, Stanley backed up and Lent told him, "Northeast."

During another conversation, Stanley asked Lent whether or not the police would find any of the girl's clothes. Lent said that they had found one piece of clothes, but the rest he put in a green plastic bag and buried in a cellar.

The investigators wanted to know why Stanley offered to talk with them. He replied, "Because I liked to be able to help you people find that body of the little girl. I have five children of my own, and I would like to be able to see my wife-to-be and my little kids."

Stanley's attorney advised him that his conversation with members of the task force would not have an impact in court, but maybe would allow him to see his girlfriend and children. Stanley swore that all he recounted was true to the best of his knowledge and recollection.[68]

Phil Shallies

On February 10, the task force re-interviewed Phil Shallies. In this interview, Shallies offered what he knew about Lewis

68. **Sworn Testimony to Members of the Task Force, February 2, 1994.**

Lent. Much of the information was based on stories that Lent had related to Shallies. The information Phil related from Lent's stories, whether or not they had any kernel of truth, helped to roughly establish time and place of Lent's whereabouts. Some of Lent's stories were told when he was straight and some were told when he was stoned, laid back, and rambling. Marijuana seemed to be one of the recurring topics when talking about Lewis Lent.

It was well known fact among Lent's friends and Florida family members that unlike his father, Lewis was not a heavy drinker; rather, he was a habitual pot smoker. According to Lent, as told by Shallies, Lewis started growing marijuana years earlier near his parents' home. He told Phil that he was an active partner in a marijuana growing operation. Lent did not disclose to Phil names of the others involved or specific time frames.

The growing operation was located just over the Massachusetts/New York State line in the Stephentown/ Lebanon area. The partners grew a substantial amount of weed and secured a barn, which they used to dry the crop. Apparently, a friend or relative of Lent's partner stole the drying crop from the barn and took off for the Adirondacks. Finding out about the theft, Lent and his partner took off to find the culprit and the missing stash. Arriving in the Adirondacks, they learned that the person had left the area. A neighbor informed them that the man they sought had rented a van and was seen loading garbage bags into the van. Lent's partner followed the guy to Los Angeles, only to learn that the pot and the proceeds were gone.

Lent also talked to Phil about his girlfriend Liz, who would come to visit him in North Adams. Phil noticed that Lewis was happy when supposedly meeting up with Liz and down when they did not meet. Phil also noted that Lewis dressed better when he said he was going to see his girlfriend.

Lent usually shied away from large gatherings that made him feel uncomfortable. He would either remain only briefly or just not show up. This happened at a birthday party that Phil planned for Lewis on May 21, 1992. Lewis never showed and did not reappear for a few days. He made the excuse for his absence as a visit with an old friend of his father's. Lewis did, however, accept an invitation to attend a Christmas party on December 4, 1993. Finally, his friends would meet Liz. Lewis eventually showed up very late to the party, alone and dressed in sweatpants and work shoes.

Going back in time, Lent told Phil that he had a child in Virginia. Phil did not know when this occurred but speculated that it was in the '70s before Lent had moved to Florida.

Lent recounted other wild stories about living in Florida. There was one about knowing people involved in smuggling marijuana through an offshore island into Florida. As with many of his stories, there are various versions depending on whom Lent told. Another version of why he left Florida that Lewis would later spin for his friend Phil Shallies, was that when not living with relatives, he lived in a trailer with two or three other guys for a short time. These roommates were thieves. One day when he came home to the trailer, Lent walked in on one of the roommates raping a girl. He said that he grabbed a bat. He said that after that incident he quickly left Florida, moving back to New York. Quite a different story from simply running out of money.

CHAPTER 12

PROCESSING EVIDENCE

This new task force was treading in uncharted waters. Previously, much of the information accumulated was recorded in unwieldly hard copy. Dave McElligot, who was very sophisticated with computers, set up the entire network. Although national databases existed, the task force had the mission to organize all the incoming data into orderly and useable material that could easily be referenced. A new computer technology needed to be developed to process the myriad of incoming tips. Avoiding duplication of responsibilities or stepping on toes required tremendous organization and patience.

The New York State Police were the first to use the lead desk that had originated with the FBI. McElligot ran that desk, which coordinated all the leads, reading all of them and deciding if they were of any importance. Everything went into the computer database. There was an individual sheet on each interview or assignment. The information then went to the computer analysts, who would comb through the sheets thoroughly and pick out all the germane data that was retrievable to enter into the massive database. Some was valuable; some was not. From there, the decisions were made if more investigating, based on the information returned, should follow. From this data, the FBI profiler would develop ideas about what to look for next.

Because eye-witness accounts are often unreliable, the more corroborating data, the more reliable the information. According to Jack Flaherty, "Where has this man been? As far back as we can go. There were also several missing children not only in New England, but in Florida and along the East Coast. We were basically trying to put together a timeline and put his vehicle or Lent in the area. We were just trying to place him anywhere a child was missing. And, of course, most of these children were either found dead or were still missing. The purpose was to pinpoint where Lent was, especially around this area and connect him to the Jimmy Bernardo case and the Sara Anne Wood case."

The extremely tedious work of entering massive amounts of information paid off. The Massachusetts State Police brought in all their computer forensic people, who worked together with the other agencies to develop a system that could, at a click, provide needed information. Explained Flaherty, "For example, if an inquiry came in about a missing child somewhere thought to be linked to Lent, the computer folks could access their data and either place him in the vicinity at the time or say no way, we have him miles away. He is not your man. These random details were now retrievable to connect the loose pieces and provide relevant, useful evidence. This had never been done before."

Each morning, the entire task force of about seventy packed the "War Room" for a daily briefing. Chief Lee never missed a day. He remarked, "The problem I had, things were going on in the police department at the same time, but the task force was so damned interesting you got involved." Everyone received current updates from the previous day as well as their assignments for that day. All calls that came in went to a supervisor who made the decision about what to do with them. He would then punch it in with a number and code. Then Flaherty would assign investigators to do the interview. Each investigative team was given one specific task. They were to attend to that specific task and only that specific task.

"We would send a team to a location to check on an incoming tip. If they found a piece of information that would lead down the street, they were not supposed to do that. Then someone would be assigned to follow up on the new lead," explained Flaherty. This assured the team that no one went rogue.

The more leads that came in, the more there had to be verification of facts. Jack Flaherty used as an example, "If a woman said, 'I was jogging when this white van followed me early in the morning and I had an uneasy feeling. The van sped up then stopped, turned around, and went the other way.' Well, it certainly is suspicious activity, but what does this have to do with Jimmy Bernardo or Sara Anne Wood? All this is put in the database. You say wait a minute, someone else saw this car two streets over. The volume of information was just getting overwhelming. You are putting out sixty or seventy investigators and each one is investigating one individual item. The investigators return and the analyst puts their findings in the database. You bring it up and it becomes a Venn diagram that may all connect." A massive chart tracing the daily sightings of Lent hung on the wall. Frank Pace and Jack Flaherty ran a tight ship, keeping things well organized and running smoothly with no duplication of service. The professionalism from the top down allowed the various agencies involved to remain focused and highly task oriented.

Captain Pace explained, "Every day, we were sending out teletype messages basically saying we're here, this is what happened, this is what we have. Police departments were contacting us, saying, 'We have a homicide involving a child around the age of Rebecca Savarese.' It is possible Lent could be involved. We would put the timeline together of where he was living at that time. We would contact the police departments and say we can tell you that Lewis Lent was in your area at that time or close by or he was not anywhere near your locale at the time of the homicide. It was then up to the particular police departments to follow up. Some did and some did not."

The Wood family desperately wanted to find Sara Anne's body. That was the task force's mission. Lewis Lent confessed that he had buried her at Raquette Lake. A plea went out to the public asking if anyone vacationing in the vicinity of Frankfort, NY or Raquette Lake had taken photos or home movies that might have captured a glimpse of Lent's van. The investigators, trying to follow up on Lent's lead, went to where he said he had taken her at Raquette Lake. Lent said he had gone up a certain highway. A nearby bank had a drive-up window and a camera which went out into the road. Sure enough, they got his van going by on videotape. Lent, however, seeking an alibi for his whereabouts that day, had rushed back to the Berkshires to take his blind friend, Phil Shallies, to the bank so that he would be recorded on the video surveillance camera at the bank.

Jerry Lee recalls, "The FBI checked with NASA to see if they had a satellite up at Raquette Lake. They did not have any in the area at that time. The FBI thought the Russians might have had a satellite, but they thought the Russians would have told them to go to hell. So I wrote a letter to the Russian embassy. I told them what had gone on and wondered if they had taken photos of that area. The Russians responded that they don't take pictures inside the United States."

The investigations moved along smoothly until April 29, 1994, when the *Albany Times Union* got hold of Lent's five-page signed statement of how he had abducted and killed Sara Anne Wood. They featured this leaked information on the front page of the newspaper. "Everyone was having a coronary. The DA from Herkimer County thought we leaked it, but we had no contact with the *Albany Times Union*," explained Jack Flaherty. The task force had been so careful to withhold sensitive information. We felt betrayed by this breach of confidentiality. The Wood family suffered enough. Tormenting them by reading graphic details in the newspaper added to the agony of their ordeal.

The search for Sara Anne resumed at Raquette Lake in the spring during the window of opportunity between the warming temperatures after the snow melted and before the black fly season. Scores of State troopers and Forest Rangers gathered to comb the acreage. "The police were determined to continue until they were satisfied that every square inch of the forest bordering the dirt road into the woods off Route 28 had been examined," reported Lewis Cuyler.[69] Ground sniffing dogs, a high-tech global positioning system, followed by digging and sifting again came up empty.

The task force investigators, nonetheless, doggedly pressed on, leaving no stone unturned. The task force's intense research provided sufficiently incriminating evidence in both the Bernardo and Wood cases to arm the prosecutors for a strong court battle.

Yet there were others. Joanne Conners-Wade, in her book *No Tomorrows,* noted a cluster of unresolved cases in Western Massachusetts including twelve-year-old Jimmy Bernardo (Pittsfield, October 1990), twenty-four-year-old Lisa Ziegert (Agawam, April 1992), sixteen-year-old Jamie Lusher (Westfield, November 1992), and ten-year-old Holly Piirainen (Sturbridge, August 1993).[70]

Other unsolved cases included ten-year-old Sarah Pryor (Wayland, eastern MA, 1985), twelve-year-old Sara Anne Wood (Litchfield, NY, August 1993), fifteen-year-old Robert Gutkaiss (Stephentown, NY, 1983), fifteen-year-old Sean Googin (Cazenovia, NY, 1992), twenty-two-year-old

69. Lewis C. (May 4, 1994). The Freshing Adirondack Spring, Police Search for Elusive Grave. *The Berkshire Eagle.*

70. Conners-Wade, Joanne. (2006). No Tomorrows. *Author House,* P.165.

Karen Wilson (Clifton Park, NY, 1985), sixteen-year-old Angela Ramsey (Deland, FL, 1977) and fourteen-year-old Gordon Eyerly (Deland, FL, 1981). The bodies of Lisa, Jimmy, Holly, Robert, Sean, and Gordon were found slain, but Sarah, Jamie, Sara Anne, Karen, and Angela simply disappeared.[71] These were just some of the cases that begged consideration. This is where the FBI, under the skilled leadership of Jerry Downs, stepped in to track down out of state leads.

Of all the inquiries that came in, three popped out as having Lewis Lent's signature. On Sunday, November 8, 1992, James Lusher Sr. arrived at the Westfield Police Department to report his sixteen-year-old son Jamie missing.

Jamie Lusher

Jamie Lusher desperately wanted his father to drive him from Westfield, Massachusetts to a bicycle race in Blandford, Massachusetts that was to be held on Sunday November 8, 1992. Prior to the race, Jamie hoped to spend the weekend with his maternal grandmother in Blandford, which he often did. He became quite angry with his father when Mr. Lusher, not knowing his former mother-in-law's plans for the weekend, refused to take him.

When Mr. Lusher returned from work on that Friday, November 6, Jamie was not home.

Lusher Sr. figured he had just taken off on his bike to his grandmother's. Finally, on that Sunday morning, James Lusher reached his mother-in-law, only to discover that Jamie had never arrived at her house. Quite alarmed, James immediately drove to the bike race in Blandford looking for Jamie. No one had seen the boy at the event. By 4:00

---

71. **Lahr, Ellen. (January 19, 1994). So Far No Evidence Lent's a Serial Killer.** *The Berkshire Eagle.*

on Sunday afternoon, James Lusher went to the Westfield Police Department to report his son missing. At 7:00 that night, Mr. Lusher confirmed to the police that Jamie had not returned home.

Jamie looked younger than his sixteen years. Small in stature as well as emotionally and intellectually immature, he functioned as a twelve-year-old. His father described the boy as "extremely hyperactive and loud, friendly and would go anywhere with anyone if asked." Jamie attended the Westfield Alternative School, surrounded by students who carried baggage. Being impressionable, Jamie learned from some tough peers. He could be a handful as well as quite naïve and impressionable. Although he was old enough to get a driver's license, his father could not trust him in a car. Instead, he received a bicycle for his sixteenth birthday.

The father was waffling between wanting help and thinking he should go out and continue looking for his son on his own. He wondered if Jamie had gotten into a fight with other kids. When the detectives went to the Lusher home, the family's emotions were running high. Mr. Lusher reacted by arguing with the police as well as the family arguing among themselves. The police had to navigate around this distraught family's ambiguous calls for help. The Lushers' anxiety and concerns manifested themselves in confusing requests for help from the police. The push and pull of wanting help and wanting to handle Jamie's disappearance on their own in the hopes of minimizing the potential for heartbreaking news gave mixed messages. The family's bickering and erratic cooperation with each other and with the police made law enforcement's involvement in the case difficult. The police thought that with a three-day lead, the boy could have gone anywhere.

It became a missing person case in earnest when Mr. Lusher finally came into the station to file a missing person report. When the family formally signed off on the report, it was entered into the computer database and the information was circulated. Detective Michael McCabe was one of the officers assigned to the case. The police department proceeded with a search of the neighborhood at the onset. The sector cars looked for the boy, but nobody had seen him.

On November 12, just six days after Jamie had been seen last, his mountain bicycle was discovered by a hunter in a field near a pond at the end of a dead-end road. It was then that an exhaustive search began. Field, grid, and helicopter searches ensued. Ponds were drained and riverbeds searched. The Westfield Police came up with nothing. Shortly after Jamie disappeared, the case was entered into a national computer network of missing people but yielded no leads.

Police originally said they thought Jamie was a runaway. The parents wanted to believe that their son had run away but would come to his senses and return to them. James Lusher and Jamie's mother, Joanne Levakis, hired a psychic to help locate their son. The psychic believed that Jamie had been abducted. But the parents decided to wait until after Christmas, hoping their son would return home to be with his family for the holiday he loved.

When the holiday passed without Jamie, Joanne Levakis, who was divorced from Jamie's father, decided she had to do more. She needed to get Jamie featured on *America's Most Wanted* and *Unsolved Mysteries*. The Westfield Police chief agreed. "Any help that we got was always positive."

The case went cold until Lent's arrest for the attempted abduction of Rebecca Savarese.

This scenario looked eerily similar to Jimmy Bernardo's. After two years working on Jimmy's case with no credible leads, the Pittsfield Police thought there might be some connection between both boys' disappearances. The Pittsfield Police approached the Westfield Police Department, but it was not until Lent was in custody that the two cases were officially linked.

When the task force began to pursue leads on Jamie Lusher, the FBI used the Cellmark lab to test DNA samples.

This was new for Massachusetts. The investigators took hair samples from a brush and blood samples from both of Jamie's parents in case his body was found.

The detectives began collecting timelines with Lent sightings in the area corresponding to Jamie's disappearance. Pittsfield Police Officer Richard LeClair and Massachusetts State Trooper Gene Baker made several inquiries following up on a lead of a supposed sighting of Jamie at a Friendly's restaurant near the Massachusetts Turnpike Exit 3. No one at the restaurant could remember if he was with anyone at the time or even if the sighting was on the day of his disappearance. Questioning school mates and faculty also came up empty.

Lent worked in nearby Holyoke as a courier delivering circulars. It was his unique van that caught the eye of witnesses. On March 5, 1994, Officer LeClair and Trooper Baker called upon Terrance Regan at his home in Westfield, where he identified Lent's van from a van photo array. A few days later, Regan appeared at the Westfield Police Department to give a statement to Westfield Police Detective Joseph Maxton, Pittsfield's Officer LeClair, and Trooper Baker. Mr. Regan had a keen interest in the history of automobiles and car maintenance and racing. He worked in New Jersey and commuted home to Westfield on weekends. In the fall of 1992, while driving from his home located on the road where Jamie's bike was discovered, he noticed an older model Ford van backed in about thirty or forty-five feet off the road on the property of a vacant farmhouse and open fields. Being a car buff, Mr. Regan provided a vivid picture of the van, which he described as dirty white or gray with a distinctive dark blue stripe. The van stuck in his mind because it was unlike any Ford van resembling that model. He observed the van several times in about a one-month period in the same location.

Other witnesses picked out Lent's van from a line-up of sorts with other similar vehicles. The unusual lights on the back of the van stood out for the eyewitnesses. An engineer who worked as a quality control specialist for a gun manufacturer and a retired high school principal each saw the vehicle in separate locations in the area at the time of Jamie's disappearance. A house-to-house inquiry on the street where Jamie's bike was found turned up a potential witness. A woman acknowledged that her husband might have some information, but he was a pilot out of Bradley International Airport and would not be home for a few days. When he returned, he remembered seeing a funny-looking van with a guy in it on the street. The time and place fit, and the witness seemed reliable. Another woman said that she saw this van driving around where the bicycle was found. This bothered her immensely. This woman also seemed to be a credible witness.

Leads began to add up. Interstate Rte. 90, the thruway in NY and the Mass. Pike in Massachusetts, runs straight from Glens Falls, NY to Monson, MA. This is the corridor that the task force established where Lent often cruised. It was near Exit 3 of Rte. 90 aka the Mass. Pike, not far from his home, where it was believed that Jamie was abducted.

Holly Piirainen

On August 5, 1993, Holly Piirainen vanished. The ten-year-old, vacationing with her father and two younger brothers at her grandparents' vacation cottage on South Pond in Sturbridge, MA, went down a quiet dirt road to the end of the street to see a litter of puppies on the porch of a nearby cottage, her five-year-old brother in tow. Mr. Piirainen, who had vacationed here with his family growing up, had no worries about the children's safety. Holly knew not to wander past their road.

A short time later Zachary, the five-year old, returned without his sister. He told his father that the puppies were not on the porch and that Holly wanted to wait to see them. Mr. Piirainen sent Zachary and his eight-year-old brother Andrew to go get Holly. The boys returned with one of Holly's sneakers found in the road. They told their father that she was no longer at the house. There were no puppies on the porch and no sign of Holly.

Mr. Piirainen knew that his daughter would not have strayed. He sensed real danger and contacted the Sturbridge Police. He immediately got in his car with the boys looking for her, but no one had seen her. Holly's grandmother, trusting no one, went on a search of every neighbor's house and car. The names of anyone who did not cooperate with her were turned over to the police. Holly's disappearance shook the once safe community.

The police took immediate action, doing a land, air, and lake search. The search for Holly went full steam. Law enforcement along with local and bussed in volunteers conducted exhaustive searches. Holly's information was entered into a national network of missing children. Her disappearance was featured on *America's Most Wanted* and *48 Hours* along with Sara Anne Wood, missing since August 18, 1993.

On October 23, 1993, Holly's remains were found covered by leaves in a heavily wooded area off Bridge Road in Brimfield, just five miles from where Holly had been seen last. Locals believe that a stranger would never have known about this deserted road used by hunters and anglers. In the summer, it was especially overgrown and difficult to find.

Since Holly disappeared in Sturbridge, but her body was found in the Springfield area, the Springfield DA and their state police took over. At first, the State Police believed the members of a motorcycle gang, who found the body committed the crime, which later proved wrong. The investigators placed Lewis Lent in Sturbridge on the day

Holly disappeared. Although Lent denied his involvement, he could not account for his whereabouts that day. Two days later, Lent bought a pick and shovel at Central Tractor in Pittsfield, which the investigators believe he planned to use to go back to bury Holly.[72]

A Massachusetts State trooper interviewed a witness living in the Bridge Road vicinity who had seen Lent's van on TV and recalled that same van go by his house the previous summer while he was home recuperating from a motorcycle accident. Himself the owner of a 1985 Ford van, the witness pointed out on his own van that the taillights on the light blue van he had seen did not come standard on that type of vehicle. The lights located outside the van's back doors were replacements.

Although the man could not identify the face of the driver from an array of photos shown to him by the trooper, he described the van's driver as white, between the ages of forty and fifty, and wearing glasses.

Lent admitted in his interviews during his first weekend in custody that in the summertime, he liked to cruise through neighborhoods in Sturbridge where children might be sleeping out. He had a way of disconnecting his brake lights so if people were sitting on their front porches at night, they would not see his brake lights going down the street. Phil Shallies remarked on Lewis's odd or "half-assed" way of doing things when he rigged the dashboard of his refurbished, previously burned out, van. What Phil believed to be merely Lewis's quirkiness was just another tool to enhance Lent's stalking prowess.

Buried in paperwork sent from Sturbridge to Springfield was a report of a twenty-year-old woman, who looked much younger than her age, out jogging when a van pulled up alongside her. The guy looked at her and drove slowly alongside her as she ran. She flipped the guy the bird and

72. Stein, Theo. (December 28, 1996). Lee Holds Firm on Lent Allegations. *TheBerkshire Eagle.*

he took off. When he stopped at a stop sign, no brake lights went on. She reported her unsettling encounter to the Sturbridge police who filed a brief report, but nobody followed up on it. The task force contacted the jogger and showed her Lent's vehicles. She picked out the van as the one that had followed her.

Gordon Eyerly

Rene Parr, a neighbor of the Eyerlys, recalled the Easter Sunday in 1981 when Gordon Eyerly was found by his best friend Jeff Robinson, hanging by his neck from a rope to a treehouse in the woods nearby his home in Lake Mack, Florida. Gordon was the handsome, fourteen-year-old son of Harry and Nancy Eyerly, owners of the Lake Mack convenience store. Gordon had been good student, not involved with drugs or alcohol, who had a girlfriend from school. Upon discovering his friend, Robinson ran for help. Harry Eyerly cut down Gordon and rushed him to the hospital.

Theories swirled that the boy had accidently fallen into the tree house ropes, or maybe someone had hung him, or maybe he had hung himself. However, Rene Parr believed that Gordon's death had not been an accident and certainly not suicide. Investigators found a necklace belonging to Gordon, given to him by his mother, at the location of the boy's death. Gordon was never known to take off the necklace. It was placed neatly on the ground as if someone had put it there purposely.

At the time, a Lake Mack resident named John McWilliams was suspected of being involved, but that theory never panned out. Lewis Lent lived with Parr and her husband at the time. Parr's trailer was across the street from the scene of the crime. Cousin Rene reluctantly believed that if Lewis was capable of the alleged criminal activities in Massachusetts, then it could not be ruled out that he could have had something to do with the death of Gordon Eyerly. When the FBI followed up this lead years later, there were only a few short sentences noted in the records of the local police.

Task Force

Running seven days a week, twenty-four hours a day put a severe strain on budgets of the agencies involved. Bob Scott got on the phone to businesses, food vendors, and local organizations for things that the task force needed to run its operation. The community rallied behind the task force by providing meals during the weeks and months of exceedingly long work hours. Pittsfield High School students made lunches. The American Legion and area restaurants sent food. Berkshire Medical Center's recreation association raised money to buy meals prepared at Berkshire Medical Center. AT&T and NYNEX provided free phone lines and two 800 numbers. The Berkshire Hilton provided discounted accommodations.[73] The members of the task force gave back to the hospital by having their own blood donor day.[74]

After about six months of 24/7 vigilance, the task force began to wind down as calls, tips, and inquiries slowed to a trickle. This case proved unique in its meticulous tracking and logging huge amounts of information for useable applications. The task force originated a system of tracking an alleged child serial killer with retrievable information, which had never been done before. Computer programs

---

73. **Lahr, Ellen. June 9, 1994).** *The Berkshire Eagle.*
74. **Bahlman, D.R. (March 3, 1994). Lent Task Force Soak Up Local Hospitality.** *The Berkshire Eagle.*

in each state were made more compatible to aid in solving abductions. The Lent investigation was the most extensive and comprehensive in the history of Berkshire County.

As the troopers departed, they reflected on their time in Pittsfield working on the Lewis Lent investigation as the best assignment they had ever had. Frank Pace remembers the large billboard on Rte. 20 on the Massachusetts/New York border thanking the New York and Massachusetts State Police, the Pittsfield Police Department, and the FBI. Pace was touched by the gratitude of the locals. "I never had anything like that in my entire career where a whole group gets together and puts up a billboard thanking the police for the work they did," he remarked. To this day, he has a postcard of the billboard sign that he keeps as a memento of his work on the Lent task force.

FBI Agent Mike Smith said that Janet Reno, the attorney general, expressed an interest in how the task force was operating because the Justice Department wanted to set up a national model. However, a meeting with her never took place.

Because of his work on the Lewis Lent task force, Agent Jerome Downs was assigned to the FBI Academy in Quantico, Virginia. Not long after the task force dismantled, the FBI held a think tank symposium in San Antonio, Texas to establish best practices for handling cases of serial killings. For a week, Captain Frank Pace, along with Agent Jerome Downs and about 100 of the best minds from around the country who had worked serial murder cases, collaborated with the FBI to gather and exchange ideas regarding task force development and investigative techniques. Detectives, professors, forensic specialists, and computer technicians brainstormed to develop the "how to" book on pursuing serial killers. This became the prototype for how the FBI currently handles serial killer investigations. Downs subsequently led a full-time division devoted to child serial killings.

(from left to right) Massachusetts State Police
Lt. Robert Scott, Pittsfield Police Department
Chief Gerald Lee, & New York State Police
Captain Frank Pace give a news update
Photographer – Joel Librizzi/The Berkshire Eagle

Massachusetts State Police Sgt Patti Driscoll
and Massachusetts State Police Lt. John
Flaherty in the task force command post
Photographer – Craig T. Walker/The Berkshire Eagle

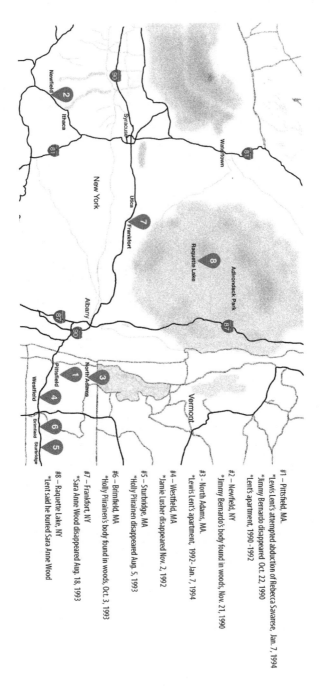

#1 – Pittsfield, MA.
*Lewis Lent's attempted abduction of Rebecca Savarese, Jan. 7, 1994

#2 – Newfield, NY
*Jimmy Bernardo disappeared Oct. 22, 1990
*Lent's apartment, 1990 - 1992

#3 - North Adams, MA.
*Jimmy Bernardo's body found in woods, Nov. 21, 1990
*Lewis Lent's apartment, 1992 - Jan. 7, 1994

#4 – Westfield, MA
*Jamie Lusher disappeared Nov. 2, 1992

#5 – Sturbridge, MA
*Holly Piirainen disappeared Aug. 5, 1993

#6 – Brimfield, MA
*Holly Piirainen's body found in woods, Oct. 3, 1993

#7 – Frankfort, NY
*Sara Anne Wood disappeared Aug. 18, 1993

#8 – Raquette Lake, NY
*Lent said he buried Sara Anne Wood

Map of Lent's path of mayhem

Billboard in Pittsfield/The Berkshire Eagle

CHAPTER 13

COURT PROCEEDINGS – THE ARRAIGNMENT

January 10, 1994

ADA Ann Kendall temporarily represented the prosecution of the Rebecca Savarese case while DA Gerard Downing and ADA David Capeless immersed themselves in the high-profile trial of Wayne Lo in Springfield. On Monday morning, the press waited at the Hampden County Courthouse in Springfield for the opening arguments in the Wayne Lo trial. This cold-blooded, unprovoked act of terror had not yet become a haunting, all too familiar scenario in the United States. The reporters, photographers, and camera crews came to cover one of the biggest and most sensational cases in the history of Berkshire County—and certainly in the career of DA Downing.

An even bigger story was unfolding at the Berkshire County Superior Court. Newspaper and TV reporters and camera crews had picked up the scent of a sensational news item. Reporters and TV crews from Albany, Springfield, Boston, and New York City followed their noses to the Lewis Lent Jr. arraignment in Pittsfield. Lent was not just a suspect in the failed abduction of twelve-year-old Rebecca Savarese, but also a suspect in the 1990 abduction and murder of James Bernardo and the 1993 disappearance of

Sara Anne Wood. Some of the reporters and crew raced out of Hampden County Court to get a sensational scoop at the courtroom action unfolding to the west.

The media swarmed the courthouse, the Pittsfield Police Department, the DA's office, and the Committee for Public Counsel office, as well as the Shallieses' home. Rebecca Savarese became an instant celebrity, sought after for interviews and TV appearances. There was no escaping the media frenzy.

The morning of January 10, 1994, Lewis Stephen Lent Jr. arrived at Berkshire County District Court for his arraignment hearing escorted on both sides by armed officers and wearing a bulletproof vest. Assigned to his case, Richard D. LeBlanc and Imelda LaMountain appeared as his court-appointed public defenders. Multiple charges lodged against Lent in the Rebecca Savarese case included assault with a deadly weapon (pointing a gun in her ribs), kidnapping (grabbing her and forcing her to walk with him to his truck), and armed robbery (walking away with her backpack). New York State's fugitive from justice charge for the second-degree murder of Jimmy Bernardo was also lodged.

Richard D. LeBlanc entered not guilty pleas on all counts for his client, who was not present in the courtroom. Lent was held on $200,000 bail for the Savarese case, but without bail for the Bernardo case with a pre-trial conference scheduled for January 20. Lent was then moved from the Pittsfield Police Department's lockup to the Berkshire County House of Correction.

The office of Attorney Richard LeBlanc was bombarded with phone calls requesting information. On Wednesday, as LeBlanc was leaving district court, he was mobbed by reporters. According to LeBlanc, "They swept us out onto the front steps, and I told them, 'I can't comment about the

case, I can't comment on the rumors. I can't say anything.' "
Of course, rumors did fly.[75]

Meanwhile, Lent's jailhouse confession of his knowledge of the missing Sara Anne Wood brought a mixed blessing to the child's desperate parents, using every ounce of their devout faith to shore themselves up. Acknowledging no hope of finding their beloved daughter alive, they just wanted to give her a Christian burial. A small contingent of investigators based at the Raquette Lake Fire Department received close to one hundred leads, all of which needed checking. They contacted hundreds of people registered at nearby campsites on August 18, the day Sara disappeared. The information they pieced together convinced the investigators that indeed Lent was in the area that day.[76] Armed with this information, the Wood family felt compelled, at all costs, to pursue a thorough search of the area to find their daughter. New York State was trying to negotiate a transfer of the prisoner to guide them in their search for Sara's body in the Adirondack Forest Preserve, some two hours away from where she had disappeared. Lent admitted that he had buried Sara's body off a dead-end road, and he drew a crude map to locate the site. Now that Lent was lawyered up, the defense did not want him speaking with anyone.

On January 20, in Berkshire County Superior Court, the grand jury indicted Lewis Lent on four counts, adding assault and battery to the already existing charges of kidnapping, assault with a deadly weapon, and armed robbery in the Rebecca Savarese case. Continuances were issued in the Savarese case until January 28 as well as in the fugitive from justice case regarding Jimmy Bernardo until February 8. Both continuances fulfilled Massachusetts laws

---

75. **Lahr, Ellen G. (January 15, 1994). A Media Circus.** *The Berkshire Eagle.*

76. **Gramza, Janet (February 11, 1994) Official: Lent's Letters 'A Ploy."** *Syracuse Post Standard.*

pertaining to the rights of a prisoner held without bail and to the transfer of a fugitive from state to state.

As a result of the onslaught of publicity surrounding Lewis Lent's case, on January 27, Judge Francis Spina imposed a gag order. The order was imposed "in order to insure that Lent's rights to a fair trial were preserved with the intent that inflammatory and inaccurate information not be disseminated."[77]

The defense filed a motion to have the murder indictment dismissed on the grounds that Massachusetts did not have jurisdiction over the murder of Jimmy Bernardo, since the actual murder occurred in New York State. New York contended that they had jurisdiction in the Jimmy Bernardo case. ADA Kendall's research countered with the notion of "continuing crime for jurisdictional purposes." Although the murder occurred in New York State, the charges constituted one continuous crime that originated in Massachusetts. The case could legally become Massachusetts' jurisdiction. However, there was no clear precedent for the continuous crime argument in Massachusetts.

As Judge Ford explained, "The issue was the perpetrator kidnapped Jimmy Bernardo in Massachusetts. Lent sexually abused Jimmy in Massachusetts, but that did not cause the death. The cause of death was the hanging, which occurred in New York State. So the issue was, does the injury inflicted in Massachusetts have to be the proximate, or primary, cause of the death in New York State? I ruled it did not have to be the proximate cause, it had to be the 'but for' cause. The connection between the violence or injury and the ensuing death means that 'but for' the injury in Massachusetts, the death would not have occurred."

Judge Ford denied the motion to move the trial, thus establishing jurisdiction to try Jimmy Bernardo's case in Massachusetts. "However, since I am in doubt as to the

---

77. **Press release issued by Gerard D. Downing March 1, 1996.**

correctness of this ruling, it is my intention to make an interlocutory report of the question to the Appeals Court," wrote Judge Ford.[78]

From the very beginning, Judge Ford understood that, "Having a case reversed on appeal is the worst thing that can happen for everybody; for the victim's family, for the prosecution, and for the defendant too." Every step of the way, Judge Ford meticulously followed the letter of the law so that his rulings would not be overturned on technicalities.

With the continuance, Kendall's findings and the judge's ruling, this allowed Berkshire County District Attorney Gerard Downing and Tompkins County New York District Attorney George Dentes time to confer on how the Bernardo trial would proceed.

---

78. **Commonwealth vs. Lewis Lent, Jr. – Memorandum of Decision of Defendant's Motion to Dismiss for Lack of Jurisdictional – Superior Court #940083 – 11/1/94).**

CHAPTER 14

THE HOUSE OF CORRECTION

Once at the Berkshire County House of Correction, Lent occupied his own cell, where he spent twenty-three hours a day. He was allowed outside for one hour in a fenced-in recreation area or inside with the other inmates in the TV room.[79]

The news of Lewis Lent's arrest shocked his friends and acquaintances. Frank Coletta, a minister for the Church of Christ in Rotterdam, NY, had taught Lewis at the School for Biblical Studies in Clifton Park, NY. He did not recall anything negative about his student. After seeing the news reports on television about Lewis's arrest, friends asked the minister to visit Lent in jail. He visited the jail twice, each time spending the full fifty minutes allowed per visit.

Lent immediately told Coletta that he was innocent. Elaborating, he described how he was interviewed for thirty-six hours with a lot of "what if" questions. The interviewers placed a statement in front of him, which he signed. The interviewers then placed paper in front of him, requesting him to draw a map, "because that is what they wanted me to do." Lent continued, "Why don't they just dig up the whole Raquette Lake area because I camped all over the

79. Suzanne King (August 15, 1994). Lent Spends 23 Hours a Day Alone in his Cell. *Observer-Dispatch.*

area?" He went on to say that when the attempted abduction occurred in Pittsfield, he was on his way to visit a friend, but the interviewers said that he still had time to attempt the abduction. Lent also told him that on the day of Sara Anne Wood's abduction, he had been cashing a check for a friend at a bank. He did not know the name of the friend or the name of the bank. He said that his attorney was working on getting this information. Most of the remainder of their visits, they talked about the Bible and Lent's personal well-being.

With plenty of time to process his situation Lent reached out to his friends. To Janie Ray, he wrote:

Dear Janie,

I am real sorry for all the trouble I've brought on everybody. You can tell Phil, Sara, Eleanor, & Chet that I didn't kill any kids and I can't say anything else until after my trial. When the time is right, though, I'm going to ask you for a video interview, but not till after the trials. I hope they can get some consolation from the pain.

Sincerely,

Lew

To neighbor Linda Domenichini he wrote:

Dear Linda and Family,

I would like it very much if you wanted to write me and let me know how you're doing. I heard you were on 48 Hours. I don't blame you or have any bad feelings toward you at all. I know it had to be quite a shock to hear all those awful things they were saying about me. I want you to know, though, that it's all lies, every word about my kidnapping and killing kids. I've always cared very much about kids well-fare [sic] and that they have as good a chance as possible of enjoying life as much as any kids do.

This place is not the most interesting place to live so I would like writing back and forth if you want to. I've always considered us good friends and I always will no matter what happens to me.

Sincerely,

Lew

Sitting in jail for a month, Lent had a change of heart. An episode of the TV show *48 Hours* titled "Child Hunter" aired on January 26, 1994. Through interviews with relatives, friends, victims' relatives, and law enforcement, the show laid out a chilling profile of a serial killer who preyed on children. Being portrayed as a "cold and unemotional serial killer" did not sit well with Lent. He was now on a mission to proclaim his innocence. He began by writing a letter to Matthew Spina, a reporter for the *Syracuse Herald-Journal*.

Dear Mr. Spina,

You are correct in saying my lawyers advise against any contact with anyone other than saying thank you for your interest. As you know I haven't had my day in court yet and that is when my lawyers and myself want to address my innocence.

I will acknowledge your ability, or that of your staff, to accurately gather facts. There will always be appreciation, on my part, for those who wish to report true facts to the public as opposed to those who exaggerate or twist facts to sensationalize a story in order to increase profits. The news media, in my case, generally, has made great efforts to portray me as something directly opposed to the kind of life I've lived. Even though I have no direct knowledge of what the media is saying, so I can't refute any particular stories, I know, by reports, that the majority is outright lies.

If you want to know what kind of person I am talk to people who have known me one year or longer. You've done good so far, but there's a lot more to my life than what you've stated. I'm sure you'd like me to quote facts from my life but I can't at this time. Try looking at my life from

1983 to present for an accurate picture of how I've lived. People from before that time as well as after will tell you the same thing. My life has always been lived as an open book. Anyone who cared to examine it was welcome to do so. You are included.

Sincerely,

Lewis S. Lent Jr.

He followed up with a letter to the Schenectady TV station WRGB. He wrote:

Dear Sirs:

You at WRGB have asked to hear from me so I've decided to say something which only I alone know to be true with no intention of expecting those who don't know me to believe. I'm afraid if I were someone else I to would not believe it because most people in our society today accept lying, for whatever reason, to be an acceptable practice in everyday life.

I am a person who believes in God and that Christ is the only Savior of the world who gives Eternal Life to those who believe in Him.

I am a person who has made mistakes in judgement in my life. None of which were ever concerning kidnapping or murder of children or adults. Never in my life have I ever kidnapped or killed anyone.

I realize that the first concern of media coverage of any story is to sensationalize it as much as possible for the greatest effect, but sometimes the media goes too far. Your station and others in Albany, I noticed over the years, even though competitors are often much more factual and so I write to you.

The facts I will talk about are the fact that because of my arrest one murderer has already confessed and if the law enforcement community keeps active it will hopefully catch even more murderers. These are things that thrill me to no end. I love seeing some injustice bringing about justice in other areas.

I heard that a psychologist said that I have no feelings. To this I say, first of all, "He never met me or talked to me in any way." If he is going on evidence of brutal murders committed by brutal people then he is applying their personalities to me. That is obviously wrong. I refer the psychologist and anyone who wants to know what kind of person I've always been to my friends who've known me for at least a year. They're all over the place where I've lived go ask them. I wrote a letter to Matthew Spina of the Syracuse Newspapers showing how I have in past cared for people through my actions and I continue to care for my friends as I wrote now.

Sincerely,
Lewis S Lent Jr.

A similar letter went out to the *Syracuse Post-Standard* again professing his innocence.

Then finally, in a general letter to society, he pleaded his case:

To Society,
This is Lewis Lent Jr. I sit behind bars an innocent man. I sit behind bars condemned by public opinion. I sit behind bars condemned of murder of innocent children. I sit behind bars condemned by a psychologist who has never met me, of being an "unfeeling animal.!" I sit behind bars listening to all they say about me on the outside and ask my Lord "why!"

As I lived my life I know "unfeeling" is one thing I never was. Four times I asked women I was very much emotionally involved with to marry me. Every friend I ever made, more than 100, have all known me to be a caring person who was quick to offer help of any kind. Upon receiving a deeper knowledge of how my Lord would have me live I dedicated my life and possessions to doing HIS will and service in my life. I have spent money entrusted to my stewardship on 2 refrigerators for those who had none and had no one to help them get any.

Obviously I was no "unfeeling animal." I have distributed clothes to organizations that help the poor several times. I have taken peoples to doctors many miles from their homes, many times at my expense. Of course this also were acts of an "unfeeling animal?" I have spent a year of my life helping a blind man rebuild the foundation of his home, remove 2 ft. of dirt from his entire basement floor and pour new foundations under the walls and a new cement floor, all without anything but his and his family's great appreciation. Obviously only an "unfeeling" person would do such a thing. I left the local congregation of the church I love when I had asked for assistance in helping the poor and got no response. Obviously, I didn't care about the need of others.

The reason the media has an awful time with finding people they want to interview regarding myself is that they don't want to hear what people who knew me have to say.

As a child I played with the kids of the neighborhood. I played cards with others on the way to school on the bus.

When I got older I found people's appreciation for helping them was worth more to me than money. Consequently I found myself fixing peoples cars, washing their homes, moving yards and helping in whatever ways I could, usually either for a small some [sic] or nothing except their appreciation.

If you think this kind of person is an "unfeeling" animal talk to my friend and see if you agree.

Lewis S. Lent Jr.

Hoping to win over his family, Lent wrote to them:

Dear Merry, Tim & Family,

I hope you are all doing fine. T.J. should find being able to control his body movements very boosting to his self-assurance. Knowing how to move in any situation is handy, especially along a road or anywhere some car might swerve or pull out suddenly. I've always watched out for kids when driving because sometimes they don't know how to stop or jump out of the way.

My lawyers were by a couple of days ago. They had some information I can't help but think of as good. The police sent over the evidence they have from the Boy's murder case. The lawyers said they had two hairs and some blue carpet fibers. To me it sounds like good news if they do honest tests between that hair & mine. If the carpet fibers come from a Ford it was probably put in cars, trucks, and vans. If that's all they got and my lawyers, with Gods help, can nullify what happened the weekend of my arrest, my case shouldn't be too tough. I'm not going to leave anything to chance if I can help it. With God anything is possible, even beating the police when they try to make someone a scapegoat for cases they can't solve. No matter what they do God can melt it away with the Truth.

Of much more concern to me is what that psychologist is doing. He's supposed to be completing the results of my physical tests & psychological tests to try & determine what's happening inside my head physically. Lately I've been having bad headaches every couple of days but motrin gets rid of them after awhile.

This last Saturday I got a visit from Mark, Carol, Amanda, George, & John. Ma & Pa and others came over last weekend. They switch, some come onetime and others another. People tell me the phase my lawyers are in now, the Pre-Trial Conference phases can take up to 8 mo. If all goes well I should be done with this trial by the end of 9 mo. from now. By then I should know if the cases they want to put against me will go ahead or drop their charges.

I'll keep you up to date as I learn what's happening. Right now I just read a lot and visit with certain people here. If I weren't here for such serious charges I would enjoy myself in here. They just brought a guy in the cell next to me who spends time here over & over again for hanging out with the wrong crowd. This time he stood watch while a friend of his tried to break into a restaurant next to the Police station. They looked out the window of the Police station and saw them. So here he is again. These guys in here do such stupid things it's hilarious to hear their stories. They pick on each other at night when its quiet and I laugh almost to the point of crying.

I still need prayers as we don't know how things would go without God's help so keep it up and write me when you can and let me know how everybody's doing.

Your brother

Lew

Dear Merry and Family,

I'm glad you don't believe the crap the media is spreading. I'm doing all right where I'm staying. I've got good books and my bible to keep my mind busy. God is with me and comforting me and I trust HIM completely to do the best thing for me. I want to be a good servant of His so I'm hoping He'll put me in the best environment to do that. I was an emotional wreck for quite some time, but with everyone's prayers with mine God couldn't ignore me as I know He cares for His own. My hope is that God will let me live with Pa & Ma and study & work for Him from there. Please ask for everyone to pray for this for me if it might be God's will for me. I believe God has given me the best lawyers possible and that they will bring about the outcome He wants for me. These lawyers have a business devoted to the defense of people. It is called Committee for Public Counsel Services – Public Counsel Division 139 North Str., Pittsfield, MA 01201 Richard LeBlanc or Imelda LaMountain.

These are two of my lawyers, but I've got one or two more who will be joining us as a team shortly. They are all specialists in different fields and they have their own investigator.

Mr. Robert Szukala at the same address is interested in anything my friends might want to say. Any letters already sent to my lawyers he will read.

They know better than I do how the case looks, but from what I do know I'm hopeful. The biggest help I could receive is that from all my friends who can show through my lawyers what kind of person I am.

If everything is completely neutralized I will stay with Pa & Ma for some time before making a trip to Florida, but I very much miss everyone and wish I could see everyone right now.

I will try and arrange to call when your [sic] home, but it might take a few days as I have to clear it directly through the big shots here to get at a phone at that time of day. My one hour is between 10:30 and 11:30 AM. Write as often as you can and I'll write back.

Love you all,

Lew

P.S. Give T.J. a hug for me.

Dear Merry, Tim, T.J., Wendy,

I haven't received any literature that you planned to send me yet. Whenever you sent it it will take at last a week to get here. I'm going to have to let them know out front to look for it since they stop anything that's not expected just so it won't upset me. They care about keeping me calm and at ease as much as possible. They are all very good people here.

Sometime around March 26 I expect my lawyers to start attending a pre-trial conference. That's where a lot of things that were done wrong will be straightened out. It is the most important time as it is when everything that is critical to the other side can be neutralized so they can't put it in the court records and used against me. Pray for me that everything is done according to God's Will for me and if possible I could serve HIM without Prison walls around me.

I plan on writing a book that will include all that happens and my impressions as to what reforms should be made in the law enforcement officers as they do their jobs. I feel if certain things were done I wouldn't be here now and the police agencies would be looking for the real murderer(s) of the kids they're trying to blame on me. My feeling is that God is going to use my book to possible do three things:

1. change police tactics regarding handling of suspects

2. make people aware of the injustice done anyone suspected of major crimes by the press

3. bring money to be used for God's purposes

I see the book as possible serving those interests anyway.

My psychologist hasn't been back to see me yet. That probably means either the tests done at the hospital are complicated to figure out or he doesn't have any time just now to see me.

My lawyers should be here to see me this week since they didn't come last week. They said they'd be here as soon as they could coordinate Alan Rubin's coming up from Boston with their schedules.

The lawyers [sic] investigator has been very busy and has a lot to cover. I've given him about everything I can think of to check on & the lawyers are having him do whatever they think is important too.

I'll wait again after talking to my lawyers so I'll have some more news for you. Pray for me.

Always yours

Lew

Dear Merry and Family,

Things here get along as slow as a snail but I keep thinking about things and telling my lawyers what I remember. Today I remembered something very significant. Don't tell anyone but the police actually kidnapped me from my friend Phil's house the day they took me to the police station for questioning. I told them three times I didn't want to go with them and they didn't have enough cause to. The lawyers say it'll be a tough one to prove but it's worth a shot. They did a lot wrong that weekend of questioning.

Basically, what I want to do is show everybody all the things the police did wrong and hope God will work in the hearts of the Judge and Jury to right the wrongs done in my case. That alone would completely free me.

My lawyers have a third lawyer joining our team from Boston who is the head of their Boston office. He's been called the best in the State, we'll see.

I haven't talked to our psychologist again yet but I know he wants to see me as soon as he can. I hope he's evaluated my MRI and the test with patches on my head.

I want to find out if there's anything physical wrong or if it's psychological. At the same time I'm going to see what he thinks about hypnotism and my Alien encounter.

All the staff here are the very best guys you could possibly expect. More than one are Christians. We talk briefly all the time, they're too busy to stand around talking.

I keep praying more than ever for others as well as myself. I've given five Bibles to guys in my section and asked officers and their bosses to give them to people who they know want them when they see them.

I don't know & don't care what the Media is saying about me. I feel bad for the Sara Woods' [sic] family because they think I killed their little girl and know where her body is, but I didn't and I don't. Their D.A. was told that by my lawyers, but they don't believe he told the Woods[sic] family.

Whatever happens I'm already living a better life than I was because I've seen where I was drifting away from God and now love HIM and let HIM know more everyday. Bye for Now.

Love You all,
Lew

As mentioned in his letter to Merry's family, Lent mingled with and listened to the banter at the jail with a smug air of detachment. He felt compelled to pass along information from one conversation to Kurt Kramer, the director of the Pittsfield YMCA. Unaware that Kurt no longer worked at the Pittsfield Y, the letter was intercepted by the new director, Marie Miszewski, and forwarded to Pittsfield Police Chief Lee.

Dear Kurt,
This letter is to warn you about an aids [sic] infested man who may try contacting a woman in her 40's who is staying at the Y. A friend of hers here at BCHC gave Thomas James[80] her name and address at the Y. She doesn't know Thomas or that he has aids [sic] or that he's coming to see her for unprotected sex. She needs to be warned.

He is supposed to be going to BMC for evaluation and to await an opening in the V.A. Hospital. He may come to the Y if he does please don't have him arrested, but taken back to BMC. He has infected some inmates here already.

---

80. Not his real name.

CHAPTER 15

NY VS. MA

Extradition

In February 1994, an Extradition Request for Lewis S. Lent Jr. by of Herkimer County District Attorney Michael Daley's office was sent to Massachusetts Governor William F. Weld. The request included New York Governor Mario Cuomo's rendition request.[81]

Daley's office received a response from Brackett B. Denniston III, the Massachusetts governor's chief legal counsel, in early April. The letter informed DA Daley that Governor Weld had decided to defer the request pending the trial of Lewis Lent Jr. in Massachusetts for the kidnapping of Rebecca Savarese and the murder of Jimmy Bernardo.

Expressing the governor's sympathy and understanding of the pain and frustration felt by the Wood family, his first obligation was to the safety and well-being of the citizens of Massachusetts. Since Lewis Lent had been arraigned in Massachusetts, in accordance with Massachusetts Speedy

---

81. Wikipedia definition – "surrender" or "handing over" of persons or property, particularly from one jurisdiction to another. For criminal suspects, extradition is the most common type of rendition. Rendition can also be seen as the act of handing over, after the request for extradition has taken place.)

Rules, rendition to New York would hinder this process. The governor wanted District Attorney Downing to have the unimpeded ability to prosecute Lent to the fullest extent. To that end, if convicted, Mr. Lent would serve numerous life sentences with no chance of parole. In New York, if convicted of the murder of Sara Anne Wood, he would face the maximum sentence of twenty-five years with the possibility of an early parole.

The letter expressed Massachusetts' willingness to work with New York authorities to search for Sara Anne Wood's body. If Mr. Lent willingly chose to cooperate with New York authorities, DA Downing would give them full access to the prisoner.

Another Indictment

On February 14, 1994, three and a half years after the murder of Jimmy Bernardo, the Berkshire County Grand Jury indicted Lewis Stephen Lent Jr. for kidnapping and murdering Jimmy Bernardo. Appearing in the courtroom for the first time, the defendant listened as the charges were read aloud in court as per legal mandate.[82] At this point Alan Rubin, the regional supervisor of the state committee for Public Counsel in Northampton, became the lead defense attorney. Richard LeBlanc and Imelda LaMountain would continue with the Rebecca Savarese case, while Rubin would handle Lent's murder defense with the assistance of the Pittsfield team.

It was now up to the district attorneys of Oneida County, New York and Berkshire County, Massachusetts to sort out where the defendant would be housed, would be tried, and if fugitive charges still pertained. The DAs decided to allow

---

82. O'Connor. Gerald B. (February 15, 1994). Lewis Lent arraignment Came Quickly. *The Berkshire Eagle.*

Massachusetts to proceed with the case against Lent for several reasons.

In New York State, Lent could only be charged with second-degree murder. First-degree murder charges were reserved only for the killing of a law enforcement or a correctional officer. In New York, a second-degree murder conviction carried a twenty-five-years to life sentence with a chance for parole. In Massachusetts, Lent would be charged with first-degree murder, which carried a life sentence with no chance of parole.

Administratively and financially, a trial in Massachusetts made sense. One prosecutor handling the case lessened the complications and the financial burdens of duplicating responsibilities of two DAs' offices. Logistically, a trial in Massachusetts made sense because of the preponderance of family, friends, and witnesses who lived nearby.[83]

Finally, in New York State, once arrested, counsel must be attached. Once cuffs are put on and a person's freedom is restricted, counsel attaches. The defendant cannot waive the right to counsel. Oneida County District Attorney Dente showed prudence in his thinking that since Lent had been detained and questioned for a full weekend before attaching counsel, New York could throw out the case on a technicality.

Herkimer County DA and Sara Anne Wood's parents still held out hope that if they could get Lent back to New York, he would lead them to Sara. As the pressure was mounting for Lewis Lent in Pittsfield, his help locating Sara's body was not looking promising. Frances and Robert Wood's *raison d'être* focused on finding their daughter no matter what. Their grief, anger, and frustration zeroed in on Gerard Downing, whom they believed to be showboating to curry political favor. Yet politics had nothing to do with Downing's shrewd handling of the cases against Lent. He

---

83. O'Connor, Gerald B. (February 15, 1994). **Lewis Lent arraignment Came Quickly.** *The Berkshire Eagle.*

was the best hope for assuring that Lent serve out the rest of his life in prison. As a father, the suffering of Sara's parents was not lost on him. It was just that pain that propelled him through the arduous task of keeping Lent from ever harming another child.

DA Downing, after a long period of silence, responded to the highly emotional vitriolic charges against him in the following letter published in *The Berkshire Eagle* on February 24, 1994.

Downing's Statement

"During the past several weeks, there have been numerous public allegations made to the effect that my prosecution of Lewis S. Lent Jr. for the crimes that he has committed within my jurisdiction, including the kidnap and murder of Jimmy Bernardo and the kidnapping of Rebecca Savarese, has somehow impeded New York state investigators in their search for the body of Sara Anne Wood. Although I am constrained by ethical rules and the standards applicable to professional prosecution, I find it necessary nonetheless to publicly respond to those limitations. It is important that people of Berkshire County, the state of New York and all others concerned understand the true nature of the situation regarding Mr. Lent.

"From the beginning, I have been, and remain, sympathetic to the pain and anguish of the family of Sara Anne Wood. Their frustration is evident and understandable. However, it is incorrect to portray me, or anyone associated with this investigation, as blocking the cooperation of Lent in the search for the body of Sara Anne Wood. To the contrary, my office has done all it could reasonably and legally to attempt to secure Lent's cooperation. In fact, at the direct request of staff members of Attorney General

Janet Reno, I personally made inquiry of Lent's attorneys and was told that his status remained unchanged in terms of his ability and willingness to cooperate or to provide further information.

"There have been statements made to the media that there was a so-called 'federal plan' by which Lent's return to New York and cooperation could be achieved. That information is not correct. There have been extensive discussions with all appropriate federal and state authorities to see if there was a way to accomplish this goal. However, as U.S. Attorney (Massachusetts) Donald Stern told a Pittsfield radio station (WBRK) on Friday, Feb.18, no viable legal plan was ever proposed, much less authorized by his office.

"There have also been circulated in the media reports that myself and my office did not cooperate with grand jury proceedings in New York state. That information is incorrect. In a published report in the Berkshire Eagle on Wednesday, Feb. 16, Chief Gerald Lee of the Pittsfield Police Department specifically addressed those issues, noting that my office did fully cooperate. My office has consistently provided legal and personal assistance to New York authorities in their investigation into the Sara Anne Wood matter, as well as the overall investigation of Lent.

"There have been public accusations that I have somehow sought political gain in my handling of this matter. That charge is, on the face, ridiculous. Unlike other prosecutors and elected officials who have made statements to the media and conducted press conferences, I have followed, and will continue to follow, a nonpolitical route to maintaining a posture which enhances the eventual successful prosecution of Lewis S. Lent Jr. and the ongoing efforts of the multi-jurisdictional task force investigating all possible criminal activity of Lent.

"I hold a public trust and responsibility to the citizens of Berkshire County to vigorously and professionally prosecute all those who violate the laws of the commonwealth within *this jurisdiction. That responsibilities considered no less compelling in regard to the kidnap and murder of Jimmy Bernardo and the kidnap of Rebecca Savarese, I will continue to uphold the public duty professional vigor and attention to the laws and constitution of both this commonwealth and of the United States. My office has a reputation for honesty and integrity in all its dealings with victims, attorneys, investigators, defendants, and the public. I flatly reject the notion that anything done by, or on behalf of, this office has been done for supposed 'political advantage.'*

"According to media reports of Rev. Wood's account of the meeting with Attorney General Janet Reno, there is no reason to believe that the course of action I have followed has been but proper and appropriate. I willingly and freely provided to the attorney general's representatives any and all information which they sought. At no time was there any suggestion that anything else which I, or anyone else, could do or could have done would have altered the current state of this matter. I have received no suggestions, guidance or advice which is in opposition to the course of action taken regarding Lent since his arrest on Jan. 7.

"We will continue to proceed in the prosecution of Lewis S. Lent Jr. for the kidnap and murder of Jimmy Bernardo and the kidnap of Rebecca Savarese. If any change occurs in the posture of Lent's willingness or ability to cooperate with the investigators in the matter of Sara Anne Wood, or any other ongoing investigation, we stand ready to do all that we can to assist."[84]

---

84. **(February 24, 1994).** *The Berkshire Eagle.*

CHAPTER 16

THE JANUARY 7, 1994 TRIALS

Defense Strategies

At his pretrial hearing in early October, Lent's defense team presented a tenacious effort fighting for their client. They used every possible angle and loophole to defend Lent against very damming evidence, both in the Savarese kidnapping case and the pending Bernardo murder case.

First, the defense tried to have Judge Daniel Ford recuse himself from the case. They argued that by granting a search warrant for Lent's apartment and van issued by Pittsfield Police officers who would most likely be testifying at the trial, the judge implicitly compromised his neutrality.

According to Judge Ford's ruling, "Ordinarily, the question of disqualification is left to the discretion of the trial judge."[85] "When a judge is faced with a question as to his impartiality, he must consult first his own emotions and conscience. If he passes the internal test of freedom from disabling prejudice, he must next attempt an objective appraisal of whether this is a proceeding in which his

---

85. Commonwealth v. Gogan 389 Mass. 255, 259 1983.

impartiality might reasonably be questioned."[86] "Having consulted my own emotions and conscience, I can say unequivocally that I am free from disabling prejudice." He considered this charge frivolous and ill-timed. Judge Ford denied the motion.

The defense questioned the procedures used to obtaining the witnesses' identifying their client through the photo array. The attorneys contended that because Rebecca and Russell sat in the same room during the identification process, they may have influenced each other. Judge Ford ruled that the witnesses were far enough away from each other to independently make their own identification. The defense also questioned that the composition of the photo array might, in some way, have singled out Lent's appearance to make him standout from the others in the array. The judge also ruled that the photo array was "fair and entirely nonsuggestive."

Hoping to have the confessions Lent made during his first weekend in lockup ruled inadmissible, the defense attorneys lodged the following charges: The defendant faced persistent intimidation, sleep deprivation, coercion, and unlawful interrogation without being mirandized. All these allegations proved unsubstantiated because of the thorough, by the book procedures of the Pittsfield police.[87]

Lead Defense Attorney Alan Rubin alleged that officers preyed on an unstable man, suggesting Lewis Lent was a victim of battery when one police officer repeatedly patted him on the shoulder. As a matter of semantics, the police called this touching consoling, while the defense called it intimidation.[88] New York State Police Senior Investigator

---

86. **Commonwealth** v. **Dane Entertainment Services, Inc.,** 18 Mass. App. Ct. 446, 449 – 1984, quoting **Lena** v. **Commonwealth,** 369 Mass. 571, 575 – 1976

87. **Pratt, Abby. (October 6, 1994). Police Testify on Statements Made by Lent.** *The Berkshire Eagle.*

88. **Donn, Jeff. (October 13, 1994). Lent Lawyers End Bid to Bar Confession.** *Union-News.*

James G. Ayling's and NYSP Investigator John F. Murray's testimonies were so strong and straight forward that the defense's arguments just could not hold up.[89] [90]

As the defense prepped for the Savarese case in November, they represented Lent at his evidentiary hearing in the Bernardo case. In this pretrial hearing, they hoped to convince Superior Court Judge Richard F. Connon to suppress physical evidence that they contended was illegally obtained. They contended that officers searched the attic of Lent's apartment house that was shared space and not within the purview of the search warrant. They also charged that search and seizure of his van was illegal. The prosecution defended their procedures used to obtain evidence. The judge would issue a ruling in the future.[91]

With the Rebecca Savarese trial approaching, Lewis Lent again resumed his campaign of denial and reproach of law enforcement's handling his arrest and first weekend of detainment. In a letter to reporter Joe Mahoney of the *Albany Times Union*, he wrote:

Dear Joe:

My civil rights guaranteed by our Constitution are supposed to be inalienable. Mine were alienated from me by Pittsfield Police Detectives & 3 New York State Investigators.

I was put in custody at a friend's home after a Pittsfield detective had probable cause. He called for a second car and two more Detectives, who secured both my arms and took me, against my will, to the police station. They then

---

89. Gentile, Derek. (October 8, 1994). Lent has "Master Plan. *The Berkshire Eagle.*

90. The defense then worked the mental incompetency angle. This involved Lent's "alter ego" Stephen, who took over his mind along with blackout periods and "fright experiences" caused by extraterrestrial beings.

91. Etkind, Susan. (November 2, 1994). Lent Confession Admissible. *The Berkshire Eagle.*

confined me in the Detective Bureau until they were ready to interrogate me. Then they interrogated me without giving me my rights called "Miranda." A Pittsfield detective testified to that under oath at my pretrial evidentiary hearing.

The last two months I've spent reading up on Federal statutes concerning what constitutes "in custody" and when your "Miranda" rights warnings are required to be given by law enforcement personnel. I was deprived of my rights approximately 15 times over 2&1/2 days of interrogation.

The Federal statutes also explain that a second law enforcement agency "cannot" come to a police station where a suspect has been interrogated and immediately upon the ending of the first interrogation begin another interrogation by the second police agency without moving the suspect into another environment and thereby reducing the pressure of the first interrogation. New York State Investigators didn't move me from that environment and began their interrogation immediately following the first.

There are people who want to rewrite the Constitution. Is this the part you'd like rewritten? That weekend culminated in false statements full of lies, manufactured by police personnel. If this is allowed to continue, the book "1984" will soon enough become reality.

Sincerely,
Lewis S. Lent, Jr.[92]

Nicholas F. Mangiardi Jr.

Meanwhile, court proceedings were moving forward for the perpetrator of the incident at the Girls' Club. In April 1,1994, Nicholas Mangiardi pleaded guilty to a charge of Lewd and Lascivious Behavior for exposing himself in

---

92. (January 6, 1995). *The Berkshire Eagle.*

the locker room of the Girls' Club. He was sentenced to six months in the Berkshire County House of Corrections and the court's recommendation that he attend an alcohol treatment program.

Just short of a year after the incident at the Girls' Club, on December 22, 1995, Mangiardi struck again. Two girls, one a high school student and the other a fourteen-year-old middle school student, were headed toward Reid Middle School, cutting through Springside Park, which lies just south and adjacent to the middle school. Mangiardi jumped out at them and tackled the older girl to the ground. The younger girl ran for help. The perpetrator pinned the girl down, removed her underpants, and got on top of her, attempting to have intercourse with her. She struggled and screamed for her attacker to stop. Unsuccessful at penetrating the girl, the attacker masturbated as he held her down.

Lawrence Daoust, retired from GE, was taking his daily walk through the park when he heard the screams. He followed the sounds and witnessed the attack in progress. Mr. Daoust yelled at the attacker, who took off running. Unable to catch the assailant, Mr. Daoust returned to the victim to try to calm her. The girl was not badly hurt, but very shaken. The police arrived shortly after and were provided with a description of the attacker.

Within half an hour, Mangiardi was arrested and charged with assault and battery, assault with intent to commit rape, indecent assault and battery, and open and gross lewdness.

At his arraignment, his court-appointed attorney, Richard LeBlanc, requested an evaluation to determine his competence to stand trial. At his trial on July 31, 1995, Nicolas Mangiardi pleaded guilty to all counts. He was sentenced to two to three years at MCI Cedar Junction

Prison, with credit for time served plus $50 victim witness fee.[93]

Rebecca Savarese Trial

Just prior to his day in court, Lewis Lent sent the following letter to the Berkshire County DA's office:

Dear Sirs:

I have been informed by the duty officer of the Attorney General's office for Massachusetts that if I've got a complaint about my civil rights being violated I'm to inform you as the first step.

Consider this my official complaint to you. It will be copied for my lawsuit later so your office won't be able to claim ignorance of my complaint. I've also notified the media.

The evidence is clear. Federal statutes describe when someone must be considered "in custody." I was taken into custody at my friends' home in Lanesborough, MA. A Pittsfield detective was drawn to my friends' home by a pick-up truck similar to one they were looking for. After speaking to my friends and myself the detective produced a composite picture of a suspect they were looking for and said it looked like me. That produced probable cause and they call for another car and two more detectives to take me to the Pittsfield police station for questioning. The detectives arrived took hold of both my arms, restraining me and forcing me to accompany them to the station. At the station they secured my arms again and took me in the station where my freedom was restrained in a very significant manner by putting me in a chair where I was not only guarded, but I had to ask permission to use the bathroom and was only

93. Etkind, Susan. Man Accused of Springside Assault Ordered to Undergo Sanity Check. (December 24, 1994). *The Berkshire Eagle.*

allowed to after a discussion amongst themselves to decide which bathroom was suitable and escorted by two detectives to it and back to the chair.

Before questioning the first time I wasn't given my "Miranda" rights. According to the U.S. Supreme Court it is mandatory that those or an equivalent be given to me and a guarantee that I will be able to use them at any time during questioning. I received nothing.

A Pittsfield detective testified at my pre-trial evidentiary hearing that I wasn't read/given my rights that first questioning session at the Pittsfield police dept. My written statement shows I met Federal statute requirements for being "In custody."

Pittsfield detectives testified at my pre-trial evidentiary hearings that they considered me a good suspect at my friend's home.

Therefore, according to Federal law I was in custody when my rights weren't given to me before questioning began.

This complaint is also to inform you that other violations of law occurred throughout that weekend. Most have been hidden by officers lying under oath as to what happened.

Federal law states that all evidence and statements that come from an illegal questioning are inadmissible in court. That whole weekend came from that first questioning which was illegal.

You and Judge Ford will be held accountable for illegal prosecution eventually.

Sincerely,
Lewis S. Lent Jr.

One year after the alleged kidnapping and robbery of Rebecca Savarese, Lent's trial was set for January 1995. The prosecution scored some pretrial victories. First, the defense wanted the trial moved to Springfield because of too much pretrial publicity. Judge Ford ruled that the trial would remain in Berkshire County with a jury pool selected from Hampden County despite the defense's call for a change of venue.

Second, the defense argued that because Rebecca Savarese and Russell Davis were in the same room while making their photo recognition IDs, they could have influenced each other. Judge Ford ruled that Rebecca Savarese's and Russell Davis's photo identifications of Lent at the Pittsfield Police Department were admissible evidence because the two were nowhere near each other in the room, therefore could not see or hear what the other had chosen. The motion to suppress was denied.

Third, the defense tried to have the charge of robbery dismissed since Lent had not intended to steal Rebecca's backpack. Judge Ford ruled that there was evidence that Lent had Rebecca's backpack and the charge of robbery would go forward.[94]

The defense petitioned the court not to include Lent's confession about his "master plan." The defense feared that this information could be highly prejudicial and could bring up other bad acts committed by the defendant not relevant to the Savarese case. The criteria for admitting this evidence would establish intent. Rebecca fit the description of the type of victim he described as "acceptable." The evidence was relevant in terms of proximity of time and place since this incident took place not far from his home and close to when he started to implement his "master plan." Lent clearly did not intend to "visit" with the young girl as he stated to the Pittsfield police, but to hold her against her will.

Although the judge deemed the "master plan" highly relevant, he had to weigh the probative value versus the prejudicial impact. For this reason, he ruled that much of the "master plan" was not relevant and too prejudicial. He allowed only #1, 2, 3, and 11.

---

94. **Elfenbein, Gae. (October 26, 1994). Lent Trial Slated for Pittsfield.** *The Berkshire Eagle.*

1. It was Lent's intention to build a small area in his bedroom by separating it with a wall. This was to keep any other people away and give him privacy. He intended to build shelf-like boxes along one wall that he could use to store his victims. They were to be like bunk beds with a door he could close and secure. He wanted to keep victims in these beds "AT ALL TIMES" so that he could take them out when he needed to use them for sex. To this end he began construction of this wall in his bedroom, in North Adams, sometime within the last few weeks. He described putting females in these lockers, two to each locker with heads at opposite ends. This way their legs could be intertwined.

2. Lent would go out on hunting trips, looking for vulnerable victims. He would go out on "PLEASANT" days, but overcast was acceptable, he wouldn't go out when it was raining. He wanted to be sure that kids would be out and available. He described his victims as "ACCEPTABLE VULNERABLE VICTIMS," by this he meant young girls who looked to be between the ages of 12-17 years old. He felt that girls lost their attractiveness after the age of 22. The girls would have to be between a certain height and size. He was looking for slim young girls, who were just beginning to develop. He wasn't interested in heavy girls. He liked long hair and color didn't matter.

3. Lent indicated that no matter who he was with or where he went, he was always looking for acceptable, vulnerable victims. He would make mental notes of their locations, as well as notations on maps of these locations.

11. The master plan was still in the works and not complete, so to satisfy his sexual desires he would pick girls up for "QUICKIES."[95]

On Friday, January 6, 1995, just one day less than a year after Lewis Stephen Lent Jr. was arrested, the jury selection of thirteen Hampden County residents began in the kidnapping trial of Rebecca Savarese. Information regarding the two murder charges against the defendant were not disclosed to the jury. They were also asked not to speculate on the New York detectives' involvement with Lent.[96]

After a four-day trial, the jury found Lewis Lent guilty of kidnapping, assault and battery, and assault with a dangerous weapon. The most serious charge of armed robbery, which could hold a life sentence, was dismissed. "One of the essential elements of armed robbery is a specific intent to steal property of the victim."[97] "Moreover, the intent to steal must coincide with the force or threats against the victim. Therefore, it is not robbery if a person sets out to commit an assault, and then as an afterthought commits a theft."[98] Although there was sufficient evidence in the grand jury hearing establishing probable cause, at the actual trial the evidence proved insufficient to warrant an indictment on the armed robbery charge. Lent's intent was to kidnap Rebecca, not to steal her backpack. Judge Daniel Ford sentenced Lent to seventeen and a half to twenty years maximum in state prison at Cedar Junction in the eastern

95. (Commonwealth of Massachusetts vs. Lewis Lent, Jr. MEMORANDUM OF DECISION ON DEFENDANT'S MOTION IN LIMINE, Trial Court of the Comm., Superior Court Department, Berkshire Division 940044, 0046-47, 0703 – December 29, 1994.

96. Etkind, Susan. (January 12, 1995). Lent Was Building Boxes in Apartment, Investigator Testifies. *The Berkshire Eagle.*

97. Commonwealth v. Novicki 324 Mass 461, 464 (1949) Commonwealth v. Weiner 255 Mass. 506, 509 (1926).

98. Commonwealth v. Moran 387 Mass. 644, 646(1982).

part of Massachusetts. With Lent locked away, the district attorney now had to make the case to put this dangerous person away for life, unable to harm any more children.

CHAPTER 17

LIFE BEHIND BARS

MCI Cedar Junction is one of two maximum security prisons for men in Massachusetts. Lewis Lent, remanded to state prison, found life there particularly harsh. Prisoners do not take kindly to pedophiles. As difficult as life behind bars can be, Lent became a target of harassment and beatings by fellow inmates. Knowing what his fate would be if found guilty at his murder trial in Massachusetts and fearing retribution from fellow inmates, Lent began to decompensate. Both out of fear and self-preservation, he refused to leave his cell. Cringing in the fetal position under his bed, guards had to drag him out for meals and showers. This led to suicide threats, resulting in his transfer to Bridgewater State Prison, a maximum-security psychiatric facility on May 22, 1995, for a thirty-day evaluation. The State Department of Corrections then petitioned to have him committed as a sexually dangerous person, not to exceed six months, fearing his depressed state and potential for suicide, thus delaying his murder trial.

In July 1995, the Supreme Judicial Court upheld Judge Ford's ruling, allowing Lent to be tried for the murder of Jimmy Bernardo in Massachusetts. The SJC concurred that the kidnapping in Massachusetts and the murder in New York State did indeed constitute a continuous crime.

Massachusetts General Law, Chapter 277, Section 62, unchanged since 1882 states, "If a mortal wound is given, or if other violence or injury is inflicted, or if poison is administered, in any county of the Commonwealth, by means whereof death ensues without the Commonwealth, the homicide may be prosecuted and punished in the county where the act was committed."

In the case of Jimmy Bernardo, neither a mortal wound nor poison administered in Massachusetts led to his death. Taking into consideration causes other than deadly injury or violence, Chapter 62 further concludes that "causal connection between violence or injury and death need not be direct or proximate." Without the violence perpetrated in Massachusetts, death would not have occurred in New York, aka "but for" an act that led to a fatal consequence. Lent assaulted the boy, controlling him by threat with a hunting knife. By his own admission in his confession to the police, Lent said that because Jimmy was not an adequate sex partner, he needed to die. Lent's intentions were no longer implied or speculated but clearly articulated, justifying Judge Ford's ruling to proceed refusing the defense request for trying the case in New York.

Yet again delaying the trial proceedings, in January 1996, the Department of Corrections requested the extension of Lent's stay at Bridgewater State Prison for one more year. With the extension of Lent's stay at Bridgewater, the grueling wait for justice to take its course preyed on the Bernardos and the Woods. The Wood family's prolonged anguish regarding the handling of the case in Massachusetts delaying New York's involvement provided the perfect storm for the flourishing of media disinformation leaked from sources not connected with the prosecution or the defense.

On February 26, 1996, a hearing was held in Springfield before Judge Daniel Ford of the Berkshire Superior Court regarding matters in the case of the Commonwealth v. Lewis

Lent. As a result of the hearing, Judge Ford lifted the gag order at the request of both the prosecution and the defense. They needed to set the record straight with the public.

In his press release, DA Downing summarized the events that took place leading to the arrest of Mr. Lent and the legal steps that had taken place. He explained the legal issues that needed to be reviewed by the Supreme Judicial Court before a trial could begin. He also explained the further delay pending results of testing of Lewis Lent's mental status to determine his competency to stand trial. He ended his press release with the following comments:

"I have great sympathy for the families of Jimmy Bernardo and Sara Anne Wood and regret the delays in the process. My office has been in constant contact with the Bernardo family throughout this prosecution. I have also been in direct contact with Herkimer County District Attorney Michael Daly on several occasions.

"I have learned through media reports of Robert Wood's plan to be in Pittsfield on March 4, 1996, and have cleared my schedule in order for Mr. Wood to meet with me or any members of my staff, should he wish to do so."

Finally, in May 1996, the pretrial hearing to determine the defendant's ability to understand the proceedings and assist in his own defense gave the defense attorneys the chance to present their claim of Lent's incompetency. With testimony from expert witnesses, the defense laid out the scenario of Lent's mental deterioration since his incarceration. Dr. Paul M. Hardy, a behavioral neurologist, testified that as a result of three electroencephalograms administered in 1994, 1995, and 1996, the defendant had suffered a serious brain disease of the frontal lobe known as FIRDA (frontal intermittent rhythmic delta activity), characterized by psychosis and dementia. Dr. Paul Spiers, a clinical neuropsychologist, found that the defendant suffered from dementia of unknown etiology.

ADA David Capeless challenged the experts' findings. Among his witnesses were Bridgewater State Hospital's Dr. John Janko and Dr. Donna LoBiondo, both staff psychologists, and Dr. Stephen DeLisi, forensic psychologist. Each of these psychologists had worked with the defendant at length at the hospital. Each found the defendant showed no signs of psychosis or dementia. The anxiety and depression he experienced appeared to be situational. Once the stress of incarceration at Cedar Junction eased, he communicated and interacted normally. It was not until Lent was faced with competency evaluations that he began to deteriorate. In fact, his deterioration happened so quickly and so dramatically that Dr. DeLisi believed his actions to be contrived to avoid leaving the hospital and standing trial.

In one encounter with Lent, Dr. LoBiondo discussed the possibility of his returning to Cedar Junction. "He sat straight up, looked her in the eye, and said that he intended to 'beat her at her game.' He stated that his lawyers would make sure he stayed at Bridgewater State Hospital. At the end of the meeting, he said that he was lost, did not know how to get back to his room, and she had better call a guard to help him. Dr. LoBiondo responded by telling him to 'knock it off' and 'cut the crap.' The defendant immediately got up and walked to where he was supposed to without any apparent difficulty," as reported in Judge Daniel Fords decision.[99]

Other compelling testimony presented by the prosecution included local Pittsfield neurologist Dr. Jay Ellis. Dr. Ellis challenged the conclusions drawn by Drs. Hardy and Spiers. These doctors had spent a minimal amount of time with the defendant and did not know all the facts surrounding the EEG results. There were technical difficulties with the EEG administered at Lemuel Shattuck Hospital in 1995. At that

---

99. **Commonwealth of Massachusetts vs. Lewis S. Lent, Jr. Memorandum of Decision re: Competency) – Superior Court Criminal Action No. 940083 & 0084).**

time, it was unknown to those administering the test that the defendant was taking medication. The slowing noted in the exam could have been caused by medication and drowsiness. No notation was made of any side-to-side eye movement, which can produce a result looking like FIRDA. An EEG administered at Berkshire Medical Center in 1996 showed no FIRDA.

After almost a year, when the defendant returned to the Berkshire County House of Correction for his hearing in court, Lent remembered Mark Massaro, a counselor at the Berkshire County House of Correction. His memory was crystal clear. Mr. Massaro testified to Lent's excellent recall of names and events.

In court, Lent's demeanor was appropriate. When Dr. Hardy took the stand, he testified that the defendant suffered from myoclonic jerks. When brought to the judge's attention, the judge carefully observed the defendant. These jerks occurred on a number of occasions when the doctor mentioned them. Amazingly, these movements no longer appeared when Dr. Hardy left the witness stand.

"For a criminal defendant to be competent to stand trial, the judge hearing the competency issue must find that the Commonwealth has shown by a preponderance of the evidence that the defendant has sufficient present ability to consult with his lawyer with a reasonable degree of rational as well as factual understanding of the proceedings against him."[100]

"I rule that the Commonwealth has met its burden. I have weighed the credibility of the expert testimony presented to me, and I find that the experts called by the Commonwealth are simply more credible and more persuasive than those called by the defense. Accordingly, I rule that the defendant is competent to stand trial," ruled Judge Ford.[101]

---

100. **Commonwealth** v. **Prater**, 420 Mass. 569, 573-574 (1995).
101. MEMORANDUM OF DECISION RE: COMPETENCY.

Another issue facing the judge was the defense counsel's desire to withdraw from the case. The basis for this motion occurred in a note in the medical records of Dr. Janko. Lent told the doctor that his lawyers had told him to exaggerate his symptoms because it would help his case.

Judge Ford wanted to wait until after the competency hearing on April 29, 1996, to deal with this matter, but a Supreme Court justice ordered Judge Ford to conduct a hearing and issue a ruling on April 24 on the Motion to Withdraw and the Motion for the Appointment of Substitute Counsel filed by the defense. "Defense counsel argued that Lent's purported allegations, which accused counsel of serious professional misconduct, create a conflict of interest requiring their withdrawal."[102] It was never suggested that Lent's allegations about his attorneys were true. Based on prior experiences, Judge Ford had no reason to question the defense's credibility. Although the defendant expressed concern that the statement in Dr. Janko's report might prejudice his case, the judge saw no reason that the statement made by Lent to Dr. Janko need to be admitted into evidence in the trial.

Judge Ford understood the awkwardness and unpleasantness of this incident for the defense counsel, but he had great faith that Attorney Rubin could rise above it and provide fair and unbiased counsel for his client without any compromise of his integrity. With the countless hours already spent on this case, to reassign a new attorney would delay proceedings at least four to six months. Expediency not being enough reason to deny the motion, the judge and the defense counsel agreed that counsel's reputation would not be an issue and that he could continue to provide an unbiased defense. The motion to withdraw was denied. Alan Rubin would continue with the case.

---

102. **Commonwealth vs. Lewis Lent MEMORANDUM OF DECISION ON DEFENSE COUNSEL'S MOTION TO WITHDRAW No. 94-008340084.**

The defense then claimed that evidence tampering on the part of the New York State troopers unfairly tainted the case against their client. However, the troopers accused of lifting fingerprints from Jimmy Bernardo's body at his autopsy to plant evidence for a future murder suspect were already in jail before Lent became a suspect in the case. That argument did not hold up.[103]

103. Lahr, Ellen G. (April 6, 1996). Lent Wins Another Round on Doctored Evidence. *The Berkshire Eagle.*

CHAPTER 18

JUSTICE FOR JIMMY

The defense motions denied, the way was now cleared for Judge Ford to set the trial date for June 4, 1996. Five years and eight months after Jimmy Bernardo's murder, Lewis Lent would have to face the kidnapping and murder charges in court.

The defense insisted that Lewis S. Lent Jr. could not get a fair trial in Berkshire County.

Judge Ford agreed. The media coverage, both locally and in New York State, was enormous. Most of Berkshire County news came from Albany, New York TV stations. Residents of Berkshire County were obsessed with the frightening and sensational reporting. Judge Ford decided that since the trial could take weeks, it was not fair to sequester jurors from Hampden County in Berkshire County so far from home. The trial would take place in Hampden County. Matters needed to be handled as expediently and efficiently as possible.

Starting ten days before the scheduled trial, on Saturday and Sunday, in conference with Herkimer County's DA Daley, DA Downing was on the phone with Attorney General Janet Reno to work out a plan to have Lent serve his time in a federal penitentiary. The attorney general heads the Department of Justice, which presides over the federal prison system. They needed her OK to make this happen. A letter was also secured from Massachusetts Governor Weld that he would go along with Lent's transfer to federal prison. In the plea deal, Lent would agree to plead guilty to the first-degree murder and kidnapping of Jimmy Bernardo and go back to New York to plead guilty to second-degree murder for Sara Anne Wood. He would also help locate Sara Anne Wood. The agreement did not say that he had to find the body but that he had to convincingly show that he was making a credible effort to help locate Sara Anne Wood. In return, he would be incarcerated in a federal prison instead of the Massachusetts state facility at Cedar Junction, where he feared for his life.

On June 5, 1996, Peter M. Carlson, assistant director of the US Department of Justice's Federal Bureau of Prisons, sent a letter to Gerard Downing stating that Lewis Lent would be accepted in a federal prison on the conditions that DAs Downing and Daley agree that Lent had complied with his plea agreement. He asked to include in the plea agreement:

"Service of sentence in a federal institution will be approved upon the Commonwealth of Massachusetts referring Defendant pursuant to intergovernmental agreement and subject to all requirements of this agreement. The Defendant agrees to conduct himself in a responsible manner; prison misconduct may result in his return to Massachusetts custody."

The Saturday before the trial was to begin, Judge Ford received a telephone call from Clerk of Court Deborah Capeless, asking him to convene an emergency session of the Court. At 10:00 that morning, DA Gerard Downing, First Assistant DA David Capeless, Defense Attorney Richard Leblanc, court-appointed defense attorney for the Sara Anne Wood case Frank Blando, and Jack Quinn, assistant superintendent of the Berkshire County Sheriff's Department representing Sheriff Massimiano, who was unavailable, met with Judge Ford. As a result of the prior ten days of discussions and negotiations, Mr. Lent agreed to cooperate in helping to locate the body of Sara Anne Wood in exchange for pleading guilty to murder charges in Massachusetts and New York and to being transferred from the Massachusetts State Prison to a federal penitentiary.

The attorneys were now asking the judge to sign off on allowing Lent to be escorted to New York State to lead them to the remains of Sara Anne Wood. Lent alleged that she was buried no more than thirty to forty miles past the Massachusetts border. Judge Ford's court order read as follows: "After hearing, it is the ORDER of this court that the Defendant shall be turned over by the Berkshire County Sheriff's Department to Detective Lt. Robert Scott, Trooper Steven DelNegro, Trooper George Hamilton, and Trooper Travis McCarthy of the Massachusetts State Police. Those officers are hereby authorized to transport the Defendant to New York State for purposes of assisting New York authorities in certain matters pending there. The Defendant shall remain in the custody of Massachusetts officials at all times (Massachusetts State Police and Berkshire Sheriff's deputies who shall accompany the state police) and shall not be turned over to the custody of any other agency or department, specifically including the New York State Police and the Herkimer County district attorney. The Defendant shall be returned to the custody of the Berkshire County Sheriff by 9:00 PM on June 1, 1996."

The Massachusetts State troopers were met by five New York State troopers as they now entered their jurisdiction. Lent said that he remembered one of the roads in New Lebanon, New York. Lieutenant Scott, tasked with escorting Lent on this adventure, marveled at Lent's memory. It had been a long time since the two had had a previous encounter. Lent recognized Scott immediately and had a remarkable recall of their conversation more than a year before. Lent remembered Scott's full name. In their previous encounters,

Lent had asked numerous questions about the kinds of weapons that the troopers carried, showing particular interest in handguns. Lent had total recall of his earlier probing questions. Scott remarked, "I remember feeling a bit of a chill at how good his memory was and how he took such careful note. He was so meticulous and observant of things like that."

Judge Ford made it absolutely clear to Lieutenant Scott that he wanted the prisoner returned to the Berkshire County Jail by 9:00 PM. Although Scott was friends with the judge, he knew that if he did not get the prisoner back in time, the judge would have no qualms about holding the officer in contempt. Judge Ford knew how much New York wanted custody of Lewis Lent. He trusted Detective Scott to be sure that New York law enforcement did not try anything.

Lent again led his entourage through trails and woods, coming up with nothing. The prisoner, however, was treated to lunch, got some nice, fresh air, and even got some snacks from a local general store before having to return to Massachusetts. As time was running out for Lieutenant Scott to return Lent at the hour designated by Judge Ford, Lent suddenly thought of another road that may have been where he buried the body. New York State Police did not want to give up the search. Scott knew that Lent was taking them on a wild goose chase and that Lent was too smart to forget where he had buried the body. He knew Lent's game. Against the insistence of the New York State Police, the Massachusetts troopers called it a day and returned the prisoner back to jail on time. Unfortunately, nothing panned out from the search for Sara Anne's body except another day's outing for this manipulative prisoner.

On June 3, 1996, the day before jury selection was to begin in Hampden County, Judge Ford met with the attorneys, with Lewis Lent, and with Jimmy Bernardo's family in his chambers in Pittsfield. Lewis Stephen Lent Jr. pleaded guilty to first-degree murder. For the first time in the history of Berkshire County and only the third time in the history of Commonwealth of Massachusetts, a defendant pleaded guilty to a first-degree murder charge. This plea insured life imprisonment with no chance of parole.

Now Jimmy's parents and his brother Robert had the opportunity to express themselves in impact letters to the man who murdered their brother and son:

Mr. Lent –

On October 22, 1990, it was like any other day. My brother and I like always hung out together. Me like always being the tag along. It was supper time and my brother after finished eating was planning on going down to the Cinema Center to meet a friend and hang out. He asked me if I wanted to go with him, and I said no because I had some homework to finish. Well he finished eating and left. He left without me being able to say good-bye. I didn't even know that I would not be able to see him ever again. That was the last time and last second that I ever spent with my brother and I will remember it for the rest of my life. You do not even know how it feels to in one minute have a brother, to another minute not even know where he is. If you only knew what it was like you could see the pain that my whole family and I have gone through, you would want to relive those couple of minutes or hours in which you made a decision to do what you did, and change time.

Because of you I have never had a big brother to guide me and make sure that I don't get into trouble. I will never know what it is like to have an older brother graduate from high school. For the last 5 and a half years I have lived with pain. I have also had to live with people saying bad things about my family that aren't true. During this time people thought that Jimmy ran away, but really he didn't. He was going to have fun with his friend not even knowing what could happen. Because of you my families and my life have been a living hell.

It seems today that parents cannot even let their children run and play in the backyard let alone down at the movies, because they have to think mostly about people like you doing something to their children like you did to my brother.

My brother had almost everything going for him. He had many friends in school, he was popular, a great personality, and a great mind. He may not of [sic] been the greatest at school, but to me he was the smartest friend I knew. My brother and I had everything going for us, great parents, a good life, and you came along and took that away from him, me and my family. My brother can finally rest in peace in heaven, but you have to live in jail for the rest of your life, and live in fear. I hope that my letter has showed you how I feel towards you and towards my brother. I hope that you have to live with this letter being in your mind every time you look in the mirror. I hope that your life is as hard as it possibly can be because you still don't even deserve to live a life. But that would be the easy way out of life, you have to rot in jail and live with it for the rest of your life.

Mr. Lent,

I have been given the opportunity to let you know just what your terrible crime has done to me and my family.

You took from us, and this world, a beautiful young man. Jimmy was so full of life and was the life in our home, now our home is quiet. He had so much to offer this world with his sensitiveness and loving way and you robbed everyone of this.

We feel angry that we thought our child could go out with his friends and play but because of you, no child was safe. We only hope that with you behind bars our children are a little safer.

Every day for the past 5 ½ years and for the rest of our lives there will be a void. To me it feels like someone ripped my heart out and tore it in two. Jimmy's brother has had to grow up like an only child because you took his brother from him. He has felt lonely, confused, and angry that he missed out on so much.

I only hope that you suffer, with what you have done, every day for the rest of your life. I also hope you feel the pain and agony that you caused my Jimmy and his family.

In an interview with Kevin Moran, a newspaper reporter for *The North Adams Transcript*, DA Downing spoke from the heart about Lewis Lent. "Fear, fear was the initial reaction. I think in part because I'm not just a prosecutor, I'm a parent and the realization that someone like this was about, abroad in our community.

"Becky Savarese happened to be a classmate of one of my children. So, the reality—not that it doesn't always— but it had a particularly close-to-home feeling. Jimmy Bernardo was twelve, and I have children around that age. I think on a personal level, the quick reaction was absolute fear and the realization that there was nothing that couldn't happen in Berkshire County. If Wayne Lo and Lewis Lent can happen, there isn't much else on the spectrum that could be any worse.

"Still one of the biggest questions that will remain about the Bernardo case is how Lent was missed during the 1990 police investigation... Lewis Lent had somehow fallen through the cracks in an otherwise meticulous police investigation."[104]

With Lent a permanent ward of the State of Massachusetts, New York was now seeking temporary custody to return him to the Herkimer County Jail to await his trial for the kidnapping and murder of Sara Anne Wood. Although his plea deal in Massachusetts called for his assistance in locating the girl's body, he could not be forced to do so. He had the constitutional right against self-incrimination. Again, here was yet another stalling tactic to

---

104. **Moran, Kevin. (June 4, 1996). D.A. Downing: Plea Came After Tumultuous Weekend in Pittsfield in 1994.** *The Transcript.*

keep himself out of Cedar Junction. He could be awaiting trial in a New York county jail for up to six months.

CHAPTER 19

NEW YORK'S CASE

Four months after being transferred to jail in Herkimer County, Lent finally agreed in October to plead guilty to the murder of Sara Anne Wood. Before the much-anticipated trial, he wanted to talk to FBI agent Jerry Downs.

Downs, the lead FBI agent in the case assigned to the task force, had built a rapport with Lent from the very beginning. The two corresponded while Lent resided at Cedar Junction. Downs, who had since returned to FBI headquarters in Quantico, Virginia, drove to Upstate New York upon Lent's request, to talk with the defendant. He hoped that Lent trusted him enough to give up information about the location of Sara Anne's body. When Downs got all the way up to the Herkimer County Jail, DA Michael Daley would not let him meet with the prisoner for fear that Lent would back off on his guilty plea.

That is just what happened. Lent, who had informed his lawyer that he wanted to confess, arrived in court and changed his mind. Sara's parents, sitting in the courtroom, expected to hear Lent confess to the murder of their daughter. Again, Lent piled more disappointment and torment on the Wood family. As a result of Daley's decision not to allow Lent to speak to Downs, Lent no longer had any interest in talking to anybody. It was over.

Nine days later, on October 25, 1996, Lewis Stephen Lent Jr. finally pleaded guilty to the murder of Sara Anne Wood. However, in another crushing blow to the Wood family, he refused to reveal where he buried the body. As Judge Ford explained, "The level of cooperation Lewis Lent gave in finding Sara Anne Wood's body was not deemed to be sufficient to bring the deal to fruition."

No more plea bargaining. The murderer took his secrets with him to life incarceration at MCI Cedar Junction State Prison. He was once again back at this maximum security facility that he so feared.

Search for Sara

The search for Sara Anne's body continued, with investigators following numerous leads of possible sightings of Lewis Lent and/or possible locations of camp sites linked to Lewis Lent. Massachusetts State Troopers' reports describe the witness accounts. In May 1996, a call came into the State Police from a man who had seen footage of Lent's van on the TV news. The man remembered having seen a vehicle that matched the description of Lent's van on his large tract of land in West Stockbridge, MA. In a small town of about 1500, it raised this man's curiosity seeing an unfamiliar vehicle on a small rural road near his property. As the man approached the van to get a better look and to get the license number, the van driver sped off.

A week or two later, the property owner began to notice an awful stench coming from the nearby wooded area. The odor lasted for about a month. Being a veteran of WWII, he said that he knew the smell of decaying human flesh and of decaying animals. He believed the smell to be from a human. Massachusetts State Trooper Chet Warawka and his certified K-9 sniffing dog searched the area. No human remains were found.

A more convoluted story came through to the police in November 1996. A man reported that he had overheard his hospital roommate talking in his sleep about Lewis Lent. When the man awoke from his sleep at 4:00 AM, his roommate related what he had heard the man saying in his sleep. The sleep talker now related to his roommate that he had seen a man hanging out in a field by a barn. When the man noticed that he was being watched, he returned the stare with a mean look.

The barn subsequently collapsed and was buried prior to Lent's arrest. From the media coverage, the patient recognized the man at the barn as Lewis Lent. Continuing with his story, he recounted that he knew two associates of Lent's implicated in stealing a baby. Any time Lent was mentioned by the media, one or both of his associates would leave the area, traveling to Canada for a while. The man's story about Lent's suspicious behavior may have had some connection to stories that Lewis Lent told Phil Shallies about his involvement in a marijuana growing operation.

Trying to follow up with the story presented some challenges. The storyteller did not want police showing up at his house. When they tried to reach him by telephone, a recorded message from the telephone company stated that the number was no longer in service for incoming calls.

In December 1996, Detective Robert Scott received a letter at the district attorney's office from a North Adams man. While this man was fishing in the Hoosac River during the last week of November, he looked for an out-of-the-way spot to relieve himself. As he started down an old embankment, about twelve to fifteen inches below, he almost stepped down on a camp's roof. This spot was not visible from the river or railroad embankment. He found the spot only by chance and probably would not have seen it if he were looking for it. He specified, "The camp has a black plastic type tarp draped over a wood frame. From appearance the camp looks more like an adult made it, instead of kids." The fisherman drew a rough map of area, included his telephone number, and offered to show the investigator the area.

Following up on the fisherman's information, Trooper Warawka and K-9 Altos searched the area. They found no human remains or evidence of human remains.

In February 1997, a call came in from a man in Williamstown, MA. In the early fall of 1993 or 1994, he and his wife were walking on an abandoned road starting south of the North Adams reservoir and south in Adams around Greylock Glen. Greylock Glen stretches over 1000+ acres of scenic trails, fields, streams, ponds, and a waterfall. As they strolled, his wife walked ahead, savoring the beautiful surrounding, singing and whistling as she went. The man ambled along, taking in his surroundings with his wife now out of hearing range. As he looked down an embankment, he noticed a man standing "frozen" about fifty to seventy-five feet lower on the embankment. As he continued staring, the man slowly started moving backwards. He described the man as about forty-five years old and somewhat out of shape, with dark hair and a dark complexion, wearing thick glasses "like old fashioned coke bottles." Fearing that the man was stalking his wife, the husband hurried along the road to catch up with her.

This information was passed along to Sgt. Steven DelNegro, a member of the task force. DelNegro advised that as a result of a number of leads generated by the task force regarding this area, it had already been thoroughly searched on numerous occasions by members of the New York State Police (including K-9s), Connecticut State Police (including K-9s), and local police and FBI agents. This information was relayed to the informant, and he was thanked for his information.

In June 1997, a tip came in from a hunter about a possible sighting of Lewis Lent in Chesterfield, MA. Chesterfield, a rural hill town with a population of about 1000, is located twenty-six miles east of Pittsfield and ninety miles west of Boston. While deer hunting in 1993, the man forgot something and had to return to his car. When walking back, about 800 feet into the woods, he observed a man about 200-300 feet off to his left crouched over. Making eye contact, the man yelled, "Don't shoot."

The hunter replied, "Don't worry, I won't." He did not see the man's face but noted that the man was not wearing the required "hunter orange" clothing used for deer hunting. As he watched the news, the hunter began thinking that the man he saw might have been Lent from Massachusetts.

The following month, Troopers Hamilton and McCarthy accompanied the hunter to the area in the woods. The informant again stated that he had not observed any facial features of the person and did not see any other vehicles except his and his fellow hunters. No further investigation was conducted.

A thorough report of sightings by Trooper George Hamilton was presented to his commanding officer, Detective Lieutenant Robert G. Scott, and then forwarded to New York State Investigator Stan Weidman. Hamilton added that, "If further investigation was desired by the New York State Police, I would be willing to assist."

For years, Lent toyed with authorities about where he had left Sara's body. Trips and searches were made just over the border of Massachusetts in New York and in the Mount Greylock region in Massachusetts. Again, each search provided the prisoner with a day's outing with searchers no closer to finding Sara.

News Media frenzy
Photograph – The Berkshire Eagle

Robert Wood and his wife, Frances, talk to reporters in
Pittsfield yesterday. They, too, were critical of District

Rev. and Mrs. Wood were critical of
District Attorney Downing
Photographer Joel Librizzi/The Berkshire Eagle

Berkshire County District Attorney Gerard Downing
(in foreground) and Spokesman Frederick Lantz
Photograph – The Berkshire Eagle

Mary and Ronald Bernardo with their
son Robert at Jimmy's funeral
Photographer – Joel Librizzi/The Berkshire Eagle

Lewis Lent being lead out of the courtroom
after sentencing to life in prison
Photographer – Craig T. Walker/The Berkshire Eagle

CHAPTER 20

OPEN CASE

Once an inmate is incarcerated, the Department of Corrections has the jurisdiction to decide where the inmate should be housed. It is the DOC's responsibility to maintain the safety of its charges. Residing at MCI Cedar Junction prison terrified Lent. A pedophile wears a virtual bullseye on his back targeting him to the general inmate population, as Lent experienced when first placed in that facility. Back in the setting he feared the most, Lent again acted with regressive behavior to finagle his way back to Bridgewater State Hospital. His manipulation worked. Back at Bridgewater, his attending psychiatrist told him that the only way he could help him was if he was hearing voices. Lent promptly started hearing voices.

Michael McCabe, one of the first detectives on the Westfield Police Force to be assigned to the Jamie Lusher case in 1992, had risen through the ranks from detective to captain, staying active with the Lusher case. After the task force discovered significant credible information linking Lewis Lent to the disappearance of Jamie Lusher, Massachusetts State Trooper Stephen Griffin, working in the Hampden County district attorney's office in Springfield, was assigned to assist the Westfield Police Department. Griffin had also risen through the ranks, becoming a sergeant, then a lieutenant. He held onto his unsolved cases throughout his career, assuring continuity. Together, the two officers maintained a twenty-one-year relationship with Lewis Lent, visiting him about two to three times a year, keeping the case alive and always respectfully building trust with the prisoner.

With the Lusher and the Wood bodies not located, as well as other missing and murdered child cases still unsolved, a long-term ad hoc task force took shape. Active duty and retired law enforcement personnel represented by the New York State Police, the Massachusetts State Police, the Westfield Police Department, the Pittsfield Police Department, and the FBI formed an unofficial task force to continue to investigate cold cases and to locate the bodies of known and suspected victims of Lewis Lent. The group met every two to three weeks to teleconference with the FBI Analytic Unit, aka profilers, as well as to hear from retired investigators.

Griffin and McCabe followed Lent from confinement to confinement. When the detectives visited him at Bridgewater, they described him as so drugged that he could barely talk to them. Eventually, his game was up. Tasked to protect its prisoners from undue harm, the Department of Corrections sent Lent to MCI Concord, a medium security prison where he would be in a secure setting with like-minded offenders keeping pedophiles, the most vulnerable prey, away from the general prison population. Lent settled into life at Concord much less stressed.

There were, however, a few incidents that shook Lent's equilibrium. It was rumored that the state planned to close his unit at Concord and that he would possibly be sent to Souza- Baranowski Correctional Center, the other maximum-security prison in Massachusetts. That facility also had a unit for sexually dangerous men. Change rattled Lent. He would often contact Griffin and McCabe when he feared for his own safety.

In 2002, Father John Joseph Geoghan, a defrocked priest, was sentenced to nine to ten years at MCI Concord for sexually abusing more than 130 boys during his thirty-year career in six different parishes. Lent, who was "born again," resided on the same unit as Geoghan, and the two struck up a friendship. Geoghan feared his stay at Concord, not because of his fellow prisoners but rather, because of the prison guards who showed him no mercy.

In 2003, Geoghan got himself transferred to Souza-Baranowski Maximum Security Correctional Center, a new, state-of-the-art facility where he felt he would be safer. Joseph Druce, an inmate incarcerated for life for murder, resided in an adjacent cell. Why the two men were put on the same unit for protective custody remains unclear. Druce harbored a deep hatred for the evil that Geoghan represented to him. Befriending the prisoner in the adjacent cell while secretly planning his revenge, Druce entered Geoghan's cell and brutally murdered the former priest.[105]

With rumors that he might be transferred from MCI Concord, the fear of being relocated to Souza-Baranowski, in what was also supposed to be a secure setting, terrified Lent. He led a crusade of sorts to protest subjecting inmates to another unsafe environment. The Department of Corrections did not want the responsibility of another murder, so again Lent dodged a bullet, next being transferred to Old Colony Correctional Center in Bridgewater. The Bridgewater complex houses psychiatric patients on one side run by the Department of Mental Health and the correctional inmates on the other side run by the Department of Corrections. Lent occupied a cell on the DOC side.

Lent settled in comfortably in this new secure setting until 2012. Stephen Griffin explained, "Out of the blue one day I get a call from the FBI. We're getting inquiries from a sheriff's department in Florida about Lewis Lent. They ran

105. Wikipedia - en.wikipedia.org/John_Geoghan).

their database and Steve Griffin's name kept popping up as the guy to contact. Would I be willing to talk to these guys in Florida?

Absolutely! I called two investigators from the Seminole County Sheriff's Department, and they latched onto it. They eventually developed enough information that they wanted to come up and talk to Lent. They felt they had enough that they were going to go ahead and charge him with something in Florida." Lent got shook up when he perceived the threat of his equilibrium being disturbed. Again, he summoned Griffin and McCabe, the trusted officers who had consistently been his touchstone.

McCabe and Griffin, together with the New York State Police, decided the time was right to confront Lewis Lent. Lent was a survivor doing what he needed to control his environment and protect himself. Still holding some bargaining chips, he was ready to talk. At first, he admitted that he was involved with the abduction of Jamie Lusher, saying that he gave the boy to someone else who brought Jamie down to New York for slave trade. He did not remember the guy's name. He only remembered him as "Bulldog."

According to McCabe, "We go back to Pittsfield, banging on doors looking for this guy "Bulldog." We eventually end up at the Pittsfield Police Department with the troopers from the Berkshire DA's office who are helping us."

Asking these guys if anyone knew a guy named "Bulldog," the response was, "Yeah, that was the mailman, Larry Bulldog, who handled the route where Lewis Lent lived." Lewis Lent adopted this character because conjuring up a real person made his description more plausible.

In 1993, confronted with this revelation about Bulldog, Lent finally confessed to the abduction and murder of Jamie Lusher. He was not sentenced for Lusher's murder since he already was serving a life sentence. He gave the investigators just enough information that only the police and the perpetrator could have known, but not all the information about the abduction. To verify the confession, McCabe and Griffin were able to get Lent out of the state prison to show them the route he had taken with Jamie after the abduction.

According to Captain McCabe, "He stayed pretty much on point for the first half hour, then got a little creative. On this particular field trip, he brought me directly to Nowheresville and told me this is where he got rid of the bike. There was only one way he would know this. This was not common knowledge to anyone. That's where the bike was found in Blandford. After Blandford, none of where he led me or told me factually made sense, but the beginning portion of our outing, all of it made perfect sense. I realized Lent gave up just enough information to satisfy what he needed to do and was unwilling to do any more."

Lent admitted that he had deposited Jamie's body in Greenwater Pond. A massive search ensued with the New York and the Massachusetts State Police and a dive team thoroughly combing the pond, coming up with nothing. "The whole Greenwater Pond was nonsensical. The time didn't match. The weather didn't match. There were no currents in the pond. The lists just kept going on and on and on," explained Captain McCabe. The dive team decided to practice their diving exercises for the next three months at Greenwater Pond so as not to waste their resources while following up on this lead. Just as Lent had led the New York State Police to Raquette Lake and several other locations in New York State and Massachusetts in search of Sara Anne Wood's body, the search for Jamie's body also proved unfounded.

Jamie's father, who always had a twinge of doubt about his son's abduction and murder, now resigned himself to the truth. With the confession to Jamie's murder, Mr. Lusher finally believed that his son had died at the hands of Lewis Lent. The truth about his son's disappearance remained small consolation to the Lusher family. Unfortunately, Jamie's mother did not live to learn the news. The haunting torment of not having the body to lay to rest perpetuated the murderer's cruelty.

Search at Notch Rd., Adams, MA for
Sara Anne Wood's body
Photographer – Leslie Noyes/The Berkshire Eagle

Search of Greenwater Pond for body of Jamie Lusher
Photographer – Ben Garver/The Berkshire Eagle

EPILOGUE

January 7, 1994, marked the day the vortex of the riptide of change roared into the Berkshires. As first steps in the Wayne Lo trial commenced, an incredibly brave and savvy young girl kept her head above water to thwart a kidnapper trying to drag her under into his riptide of mayhem.

On that day, Detective Owen Boyington not only tracked down the kidnapper, but he linked this suspect to the baffling murder of Jimmy Bernardo, occurring three years previously. As Boyington set the wheels in motion for the confluence of events that led to the capture of a serial killer, his daughter Amy displayed her heroics capturing a sexual predator as his behavior was beginning to escalate.

The haunting question remains: how did Lewis Lent get away with his stalking and killing spree for so long? What were the signs? Why didn't anyone see them? How could acts that seemed so selfless also be so opportunistic? How could such a friendly, helpful, religious, unassuming guy outsmart the law and fool so many people for so many years? How did he slip through the cracks? He was good at what he did until he got careless. His escalating urges trumped his caution. Also, he tried to mess with the wrong young lady.

A person with an antisocial personality disorder behaves like a chameleon, morphing his behavior to suit the situation making for some of the most convincing con artists. Friend Phil Shallies could not believe the charges against his friend until he learned that Lent possessed a gun and the evidence became overwhelming.

Yet why would anyone who knew Lewis Lent think in terms of their friend, acquaintance, relative, or employee being a serial killer? These thoughts were totally out of their frame of reference. Folks were more sheltered and naïve in the "good old days." In the 1990s, people were not bombarded with the media broadcasting ghastly news items 24/7. Serious criminal activities happened in large cities, not in safe bedroom communities where neighbors trusted and looked out for each other. It never occurred to people to look for hints of or suspect someone they knew of such evil deeds. Thinking of others in terms of this degree of depravity cannot be chalked up simply to naiveté. Thinking of this degree of depravity was not on most people's radar. This behavior was just too deviant for most people to fathom.

This is the legacy left behind by Lewis Stephen Lent Jr. The guilt he was incapable of feeling, he left for all those touched by his actions to feel. Lent left behind devastated parents and families who will forever grieve the loss of their children. He left behind parents who rue the day they left their children alone with this man, wondering what could have happened.

He left behind Richard Baumann, the manager of the Pittsfield Cinema Center, carrying the burden of not putting Lewis Lent's name on his employee list requested after the disappearance of Jimmy Bernardo. Baumann was haunted by the "What if?" Could he have prevented Lent from killing any more children?

Minister's daughter Brenda Mueller wondered if there was a connection between her rejection of Lewis Lent and his killing another minister's daughter, Sara Anne Wood. He left his friend Susan wondering what went wrong. He led her on, then, in his letters from prison, blamed her for not being religious enough for him.

He left behind the Shallies family to deal with years of interference and disruption in their lives by the media and by law enforcement. This warm, embracing, and upstanding family would have to deal with scrutiny of all their moves and motives. The betrayal by a trusted friend left behind emotional scars and trust issues. Lent also left behind his own family, who tried their best to deny Lewis's guilt. They fought for him and believed in him but would have to eventually live with the reality of his actions. No matter how seasoned law enforcement personnel appeared, no one working on Lent's case was unmoved by the actions of this man whom many referred to as a monster.

Wayne Lo left behind a trail of murder and mayhem. His defense tried to portray him as a paranoid schizophrenic, therefore opting for an insanity defense. The prosecution's psychiatrist labeled Lo a narcissistic personality disorder. The jury ruled in favor of the prosecution. Lo was found guilty on seventeen counts and sentenced to two consecutive life sentences with no chance of parole. He served nine months at Walpole State Prison, aka MCI Cedar Junction, a maximum security facility in Massachusetts. He was then transferred to MCI Norfolk, a medium security prison, also in Massachusetts. In a 2007 interview with *Newsweek*, Wayne Lo said, "The fact that I was able to buy a rifle in fifteen minutes, that's absurd. I was eighteen. I couldn't have rented a car to drive home from school, yet I could purchase a rifle. Obviously, a waiting period would be great. Personally, I only had five days left of school before winter break… If I had a two-week waiting period for the gun, I wouldn't have done it."[106]

During Lo's time as a prisoner, he has become an accomplished artist whose works, signed SkidLo, include drawings, paintings, and embroidered pictures. He and a

---

106. **bing.com/news.**

friend created a website, skidlo.net, featuring his work. His art has been displayed at the Hyaena Gallery in California.

After twenty-five years in prison, Wayne Lo met with Gregory Gibson, father of Galen Gibson, one of the victims that Lo killed, to apologize for his rampage. Wayne Lo felt true remorse for what he had done to his victims and their families. He made no excuses and did not beg for forgiveness. He has donated all the proceeds from the sale of his art to the Galen Gibson Fund. He owns up to his culpability.

Lewis Lent found solace in rediscovering religion. He wrote:

There may be many reasons why some people would want to study the Bible for two years, but my reasons are few.

First, the Lord, upon my acceptance of his salvation opened my eyes both physically & spiritually so that I could discern easily between the way of the world & what is right.

Even at times when I found myself in unsavory situations where I knew that I was doing wrong I could see it was and would do my best to correct everything with the Lords help. Through the Lords grace I have overcome many trials & tribulations that the community-at large accepted as everyday life. My acceptance of the Lord has shown me that in order to be a Christian it was necessary to be completely and irrevocably against satan and what the world considers normal.

Second, the Lord, or his Spirit, has taught me that without sufficient knowledge of the Lord and his purpose for us that we cannot prosper and grow in the Lord, but merely exist and eventually fall into backsliding and ruin. Therefore, I feel in order for me to be a Christian I must. I can only compare my situation to that of a high school graduate. Upon graduation you reflect on all you've learned and that reveals just how much you haven't learned. So my little bit of knowledge has revealed my ignorance and created my desire to know what is yet unrevealed to me.

Third, the Lord has moved my heart to be & live a Christian life. I have lived my life, so far, for the benefit of myself even though I am aware a Christian lives for the edification of the church and not themselves. Now, with the help of the Lord I intend to be a Christian.

Lewis Lent, unlike Wayne Lo, has felt no remorse for his actions. He has wheeled and dealed to get himself out of MCI Cedar Junction maximum security prison. He eventually ended up at Old Colony Correctional Center at Bridgewater State Hospital, on the unit for sexually dangerous predators. Judiciously guarding information, he doles hints and clues bit by bit as he sees fit when he deems it necessary to protect his own hide. There remains a fine line between what is true and what is convenient, a survival mechanism which have served him his whole life. To this day his case remains open, and he has not revealed the whereabouts of his missing victims.

Nicholas Mangiardi remains on Massachusetts' sex offender list. Although his sexual criminal behavior escalated from the incident at the Girls' Club to the incident in the park, the author is unaware of any further arrests since the last incident.

The Sara Anne Wood case remains open with the hope of finding the child's body. The Wood family founded The Sara Anne Wood Rescue Center, later renamed The Mohawk Valley Branch of the National Center for Missing and Exploited Children. Each year in Sara Anne's memory, thousands of people join the 50-100-mile Ride for Missing Children to raise money, to educate, and to bring awareness of missing and exploited children. Many of the riders wear shirts designed with Sara Anne's favorite colors of pink and teal.

Since 1995, the annual motorcycle Jimmy Bernardo Memorial Ride has raised thousands of dollars for the Berkshire County Kids' Place, Inc. which provides intervention, prevention, and treatment services for victims of child abuse and domestic violence in Berkshire County.

New Realities

The D.A.R.E. program added some changes resulting from Rebecca Savarese's kidnapping. Unfortunately, a new reality caused the D.A.R.E. officers to suggest adding to the program what to do if confronted by a gun. Parents play an important role in reinforcing the lessons learned in the D.A.R.E. program. It goes beyond don't talk to strangers. Children are no longer taught to be passive. Christine Paoli, Rebecca's mother, drilled her daughter about fighting back if ever in a dangerous situation.

The protocols at the Girls' Club changed as a result of the occurrences on January 7, 1994. As the director of the club explained, "We were funded by the United Way for part of our after-school programming and part of our childcare. The news came over the scanner that someone was in the building and the police were called. And I think that because it happened on the same day that Lewis Lent was arrested, there became a major concern over the security at childcare facilities. It was put upon us that we needed to install a security system. We worked with board members who were affiliated with City Savings Bank (now Legacy Bank). They got cameras for us. Then we worked with New England Security to install a security system that locked down all the outside doors so people could not just walk into the building. We put our security systems in place, trained our staff and parents and never looked back. We now have cameras in the parking lot and at every entrance."

A heightened awareness on the part of parents, teachers, and childcare providers has become universal protocol. Children are more closely monitored. Buildings and schools have heightened their security.

What was Next for the Major Players?

Detective Owen Boyington served with the Pittsfield Detective Bureau, earning an Honorable Service Medal for solving the murder of Earl Lewis. He took an early retirement in 2003 after twenty-six years on the force.

Amy Boyington finished her undergraduate degree from Westfield State College. She went on to pursue her true passion, becoming a beautician. She has worked as a hairdresser since 1995, for many years owning her own salon. She credits her father with being an inspiration to her, making her want to do her best.

District Attorney Gerard Downing served as Berkshire County district attorney for four terms until 2003 when he died suddenly of an apparent heart attack.

First Assistant David Capeless took over as district attorney upon the death of Gerard Downing and was then elected to the position. He remained the district attorney until his retirement in 2018.

Assistant District Attorney Anne Kendall died in 1999. The Berkshire County District Attorney's Office law library was named in her honor.

Defense Attorneys Ricard LeBlanc and Alan Rubin still serve as public defenders with the state Committee for Public Counsel.

Judge Daniel Ford served as a superior court judge until his mandatory retirement at age seventy in 2019. In his tenure as a superior court judge, he presided over cases in all the superior courts in the state of Massachusetts. In 2020, the Diocese of Springfield, MA, hired him to investigate claims of sexual abuse by the late Bishop Christopher Weldon.

Detective Thomas Bowler moved from the Pittsfield Police Department to the Berkshire County Sheriff's Department. He was elected Berkshire County sheriff in 2010 and still serves in that capacity.

Police Chief Gerald Lee retired from the Pittsfield Police Department in 1998 after twenty-nine years on the force. He was elected to the Pittsfield City Council in 2000, becoming council president in 2004. He remained a member until 2012, when he decided not to run again for office. Gerald Lee died on Christmas Day 2019.

Detective Anthony Riello became chief of the Pittsfield Police force in 1997 for eleven years, serving a total of thirty years on the force. He went on to become police chief in Falmouth, Massachusetts for five years. When he returned to Pittsfield, he was elected to the Pittsfield School Committee.

Lieutenant Robert Scott retired from the Massachusetts State Troopers in 2001, following a serious illness. Fortunately, he made a miraculous recovery. While a trooper, Scott specialized in child abuse cases, so he was a natural to work for Juvenile Court Judge Perachi as a court investigator. When Judge Perachi retired in 2009, Scott also retired from that job and to this day works part-time for a private company, doing criminal and civil records checks.

Lieutenant Jack Flaherty returned to troop headquarters as operations officer, then executive officer. From there he became commandant at the State Police

Academy. He finished his career with the State Police as commander of the troop headquarters.

Captain Frank Pace returned to Troop C. After various commands, he finished his career with the New York State Police as the task force commander for the Internet Crimes Against Children Unit, a unit within the Computer Crimes Unit, which is nationwide and funded by the Justice Department.

Paul Perachi was appointed Associate Justice of the Juvenile Court. He became First Justice of the Berkshire County Juvenile Court in 1997, serving until his retirement in 2009. Paul Perachi died in September 2021.

Phil Shallies finally, after seven months, had his truck returned to him. It took longer for law enforcement to stop poking around his house looking for clues. He still occasionally gets calls or a visit from law enforcement or a pesky author who continue to ask questions and check facts about the Lewis Lent case. He continues to work on and restore cars.

Officer Timothy Sorrell became Lanesboro, MA's chief of police in 2015. He retired in 2021 after almost thirty-three years with the department.

Captain Michael McCabe retired from the Westfield Police Department in 2021 after thirty-six years and was then elected mayor of Westfield, Massachusetts.

Sgt. Stephen Griffin retired from the Massachusetts State Police in 2013, but continued to be a resource for the ongoing Lewis Lent case.

Sgt. Michael Case retired from the Pittsfield Police Department in 2002, and was reactivated in the US Army as a master sergeant, retiring in 2009.

Captain Patricia Driscoll served with the Massachusetts State Police for thirty-one years, retiring in 2012. She moved up from the rank of sergeant in the investigation unit to captain in the uniform division as Executive Officer of Troop B in Western Massachusetts.

Rebecca Savarese just wanted her life to return to normal after this incident. She made some appearances and participated in some interviews but did not find joy in being in the spotlight. She quietly went on with her life, keeping a low profile. To this day, there is not one person involved with the Lewis Lent case who is not in awe of Rebecca. Everyone still marvels at how she had the presence of mind to outsmart a predator who remained under the police radar for years until he met his match with this amazing girl.

ACKNOWLEDGEMENTS

Owen and Amy Boyington shared with me intriguing coincidences in which both father and daughter each nabbed a criminal in Pittsfield on the same day. Years later, I decided I wanted to write a book telling their stories.

On my initial call to the Boyington house, I spoke with Owen's wife Judy, explaining what I wanted to do. Judy, knowing her husband's self-effacing nature, was skeptical about whether he would consent to being interviewed. As luck would have it, Owen agreed to talk with me. I thank Owen and Amy for their unquestioning faith in my telling a story that began with them.

It is with much gratitude that I acknowledge the wonderful people who trusted me enough to help me complete the story that began with the Boyingtons. Phillip Shallies could not have been more gracious, letting me open up a period in his and his family's life that was beyond stressful. Phil's willingness to chat with me and to share the voluminous scrapbooks of articles that his sister Sandra Prive meticulously preserved launched me into the complex world of Lewis Lent Jr. Phil's life partner Janie Ray added an extra dimension to Phil's narrative.

Many thanks to the retired Pittsfield Police officers who worked the Lent case for sharing their recollections: Thomas Bowler, Michael Case, Joseph Collias, Gerald Lee, and Anthony Riello. Pittsfield Police Lieutenant Gary Traversa served as my guide to the physical space in the police department. Thank you also to Lanesboro Police Captain Timothy Sorrell for adding to the narrative.

The Berkshire County district attorney's office provided much needed information. DA David Capeless and ADA Joseph Pieropan, who were involved in the Lent case, added firsthand accounts. Massachusetts State Trooper, then Sgt., later Captain Patricia Driscoll, added not only an important first-hand perspective, but she also steered me to the two law enforcement professionals involved in the Jamie Lusher case. These two men, Massachusetts State Police Sgt. Stephen Griffin and Westfield Police Captain Michael McCabe, also kept me up to date on Lewis Lent in the years following his initial incarceration. Ahmed Ismail was the first to provide me relevant research data that I requested. A very special shout out to Andrew McKeever, who schlepped sixteen boxes of files to the DA's office for me to peruse. He sat patiently with me for many hours, both of us masked and at extreme ends of the large conference table during the height of the COVID pandemic, while I combed through the multitude of files. Also, I want to acknowledge the assistance of the office staff in the District Clerk of Courts office.

The local history department of the Berkshire Athenaeum was a rich resource for newspaper articles. The librarians and volunteers patiently assisted me in the use of the microfilm machines. Susan Frisch Lehrer, a local historian, provided me with vivid details about the "Gilded Age" in the Berkshires.

Members of the Lewis Lent task force helped me understand the enormity of their job. New York State Police Detective Frank Pace, Massachusetts State Police Detectives Jack Flaherty, Robert Scott, and Patricia Driscoll are heroes although they would never admit it.

Judge Francis Spina and Judge Daniel Ford guided me through the legal intricacies mentioned in the book. Judge Ford generously shared his eloquent decisions, which adeptly accomplished fair, impartial, and uncontested outcomes.

Others who added to my seeing the big picture were Ben Downing, Judy Boyington, and Allison Boyington. Judy, Allison, and Ben gave me a personal glimpse into the families' perspective with a spouse and fathers in the thick of it. Judge Paul Perachi gave me a glimpse into the unassuming heroine of the story, Rebecca Savarese.

Paul Rapp, my intellectual property attorney and literary agent saw promise in a novice writer. With his acumen, and a sense of humor, advocated for me. I also thank Guyani Weerasinge and Jane Halpern for their sage advice.

Greta Valusky, owner of Berkshire Print Shop, who worked with me for years designing brochures and program books, again came to my rescue. She provided the technical know-how to guide me through my computer challenges and to prepare the photos featured in the book.

Kevin Moran, editor of the Berkshire Eagle, and Jeannie Maschino, the Eagle community news coordinator and librarian, located many of the photos which appeared years ago in the newspaper. My husband, Alan Metzger, provided additional recent photos.

The last in the series of steps in turning out my book is my publisher WildBlue Press. True professionals, the staff guided me every step of the way in the production process. They shared their professional expertise without compromising my written words. Donna Marie West provided thoughtful and constructive editing. Stephanie Johnson Lawson, production supervisor, stayed in touch and answered all my many questions, while the entire team weighed in on the book making this production a partnership.

Most of all I thank my family. From the beginning of this project my husband Alan and my daughters Shana and Mallory have been rooting for me every step of the way. My girls patiently responded to my frantic help me pleas. My husband filled in the gaps in any way that I needed him. To quote the late Queen Elizabeth, "He has been "my strength and my stay."

BIBLIOGRAPHY

Appleton, John, "18 Hudson Street." *Union News*, January 13, 1994

Appleton, John and Terault, Michael , "Serial Killer Probe Spreads Nationwide.*" Union News*, January 13, 1994

Appleton, John and Vallette, David, "North Adams Man Charged in Child Slaying, Kidnapping." *Union News*, January 11, 1994

Bahlman, D.R., "Police Cellar is Clearing House." *The Berkshire Eagle*, January 14, 1994

Bahlman, D.R., "Sara Anne Wood's Father Says DA Dragging Feet in the Lent Case." *The Berkshire Eagle*, February 8, 1994

Bahlman, D.R., "Lent Task Force Troops Soak Up Area Hospitality." *The Berkshire Eagle*, March 3, 1994

Barron, James, "A Suspect in Summer abduction of Girl." *The New York Times,* January 11, 1994

Bellow, Heather, "Shooting at Bard College at Simon' Rock/ 25 Years Later." *The Berkshire Eagle,* December 17, 2017

Bever, Frederick, "Girl Points to Lent Photo in Bennington Lineup.*" Bennington Banner*, January14, 1994

Bullard, Janice, "Kids Picked on Him Because of his Glasses." *Democrat and Chronicle* January 13, 1994

Caldwell, Jean, "Drug Abuse Resistance Education." Boston *Globe*, January 12, 1994

Caldwell, Jean, "Heroine Asked to Address Group." *Boston Globe*, January 14, 1994

Campbell, Ramsey and Lauren Ritchie, "Former Lake Man May Be Serial Killer." *Orlando Sentinel,* January 12, 1994

Carroll, Felix, "For Car Enthusiast First, Blind Guy Second, Feeling is Believing." *The Berkshire Eagle,* October 8, 2017

Connors-Wade, Joanne, *No Tomorrows.* Indiana: Author House, 2006

Cofer, Rebecca and McElligot, David, *Good Cop, Bad Cop: The True Story of Murder and Mayhem.* New Jersey: New Horizon Press, 1994

Cuyler, Lewis, "In Refreshing Adirondack Spring, Police Search for Elusive Grave." *The Berkshire Eagle,* May 4, 1994

Cuyler, Lewis, "Methodically the Search Goes On." *The Berkshire Eagle,* May5, 1994

Daley, Lynn A., "National Dare Program Hailed After Pittsfield Near Abduction." *The Berkshire Eagle,* January 16, 1994

Daley, Lynn A., "An Omission, Question of What If. " *The Berkshire Eagle,* January 17, 1994

Daley, Lynn A., "So Far No Evidence Lent's a Serial Killer." *The Berkshire Eagle*, January 19, 1994

de Bourbon, Lisi, "Lewis Lent: Man of Contradictions." *The Berkshire Eagle*, January 12, 1994 de Bourbon, Lisi, "Lent Map May Show Local Site Not NY." *The Berkshire Eagle*, September 6, 1994

Demers, Phil, "Search of Greylock Glen." *The Berkshire Eagle*, May 12, 2015

Demers, Phil, "Search Continues for Leads in Lent Killing." *The Berkshire Eagle*, May 13, 2015

Dobrowolski, Tony, "Killer Reveals 3rd Victim." *The Berkshire Eagle*, July 16, 2013

Dobrowolski, Tony, "For 'Jamie' Lusher's Family, Closure Won't Come Until Boy's Remains Are Found." *The Berkshire Eagle*, July 16, 2013

Donlan, Ann E., "Child-Slay Suspect May Have Had Multiple Personalities." *Boston Herald*, January 13, 1994

Donlan, Ann E., "Child Slay Suspect: Evil 'Stephen' Made the Kill." *Boston Herald*, January 14, 1994

Donn, Jeff, "Found Duct Tape, etc. in Lent's Van." *Union News*, October 12, 1994

Donn, Jeff, "Lent Van Held Gun." *Union News*, October 12, 1994

Donn, Jeff, "Lent Lawyers End Bid to Bar Confession." *Union News*, October 13, 1994

Donn, Jeff, *NY,* "Mass Task Force Disbanded in Lent Case." *Union News*, December 7, 1994

Douglass, John and Olshaker, Mark, *The Cases That Haunt Us*. New York: Scribner, 2000

Drohan, Glenn, "Police Quiet on Lent Case Search: Adams Search Continues in the Lent Case Probe." *The Berkshire Eagle*, July 16, 1994

Dunn, Bob, "Update Lewis Lent Case Revived with Search of Greylock Glen." *The Berkshire Eagle*, October 4, 2017

Elfinbein, Gae, "Suspect Befriended Lanesboro Family." *The Berkshire Eagle*, January 11, 1994

Elfinbein, Gae, "Car Used by Lent Impounded." *The Berkshire Eagle,* January 13, 1994

Elfinbein, Gae, "Police Check Lanesboro Cellar in Lent Probe." *The Berkshire Eagle*, February 9, 1994

Elfinbein, Gae, "Lent Trial Slated for Pittsfield." *Berkshire Eagle*, October 26, 1994

Ellement, John, "12-Year-Old Says Lent Described Murder of Boy." *Boston Globe,* January 12, 1994

Etkind, Susan, "Jurors View Simon's Rock." *Berkshire Eagle,* January 8, 1994

Etkind, Susan, "Letter from Lent: Police Don't Buy Innocence Claim." *The Berkshire Eagle,* February 11, 1994

Etkind, Susan, "Downing Defends Strategy." *Berkshire Eagle*, February 24, 1994

Etkind, Susan, "Bernardo Family Thanks Police with a Big Gesture." *The Berkshire Eagle*, February 17, 1994

Etkind, Susan, "Lewis Lent Eliminated as Suspect in 17 Cases." *The Berkshire Eagle*, April 6, 1994

Etkind, Susan, "Lewis Lent Task Force Scaling Back its Work." *The Berkshire Eagle*, April 28, 1994

Etkind, Susan, "Chief Says Imprisonment of Troopers Won't Affect Jimmy Bernardo Case, *The Berkshire Eagle*, April 30, 1994

Etkind, Susan, "Lent Took Children to Adams Site Searched by Police." *The Berkshire Eagle,* July 21, 1994

Etkind, Susan, "Lent's Kidnapping, Robbery Trial Slated for January." *The Berkshire Eagle,* October 27, 1994

Etkind, Susan, "Lent Confession Admissible." *The Berkshire Eagle*, November 2, 1994

Etkind, Susan, "Lewis Lent Takes Stand for First Time: His Lawyers Seek to Suppress Evidence." *The Berkshire Eagle*, November 3, 1994

Etkind, Susan, "Lent Was Building Boxes in Apartment, Investigator Testifies." *The Berkshire Eagle,* January 12, 1995

Etkind, Susan, "Lent is Guilty." *The Berkshire Eagle*, January 13, 1995

Etkind, Susan, "Lent Given 17-20 Years." *The Berkshire Eagle,* January 14, 1995

Etkind, Susan, "A Cowering Lent Sent to Mental Hospital," *The Berkshire Eagle*, June 21, 1995

Fisher, Ian, "In Frozen Earth, Seeking Peace: A Father's Painful Search Continues for Sara Anne Wood." *New York Times,* January 22, 1994

Foley, Rose, "Lent, in Letter, Denies Ever Kidnapping or Killing Anyone," *The Berkshire Eagle,* February 10, 1994

Gentile, Derek, "Notch Road Search Halted." *The Berkshire Eagle,* July 17, 1994

Gentile, Derek, "Lent has "Master Plan." *Berkshire Eagle*, October 8, 1994

Gramza, Janet, "Official: Lent's Letters 'A Ploy' – Lewis Lent Jr's Claims that He Never Killed Anyone Won't Stop the Search for Sara Anne Wood, Police Say." *Syracuse Post-Standard,* February 11, 1994

Gramza, Janet and Matthew Spina, "Lent Claims Didn't Kill Sara." *Syracuse Herald Journal,* February 10, 1994

Gregory, Hamilton, *McNamara's Folly: The Use of Low IQ Troops in the Vietnam War.* Pennsylvania: Infinity Publishing, 2015

Guarino, David, "FBI Behavioral Unit Does Profiles of Serial Killers." *The Transcript,* January 29, 1994

Hutchinson, Bill, Kennedy, Helen, Mallia, Joseph. *Boston Herald,* January 12, 1994

Jacobson, Murrey, "Missing teen's mom seeks TV shows' aid." *Sunday Republican,* January 3, 1993

Kates, William, "Lent's Pleas "Bittersweet' Say Officials. Lewis Lent Cops a Plea Then Changes Mind." *The Berkshire Eagle,* October 27, 1996

Kelly, Matt, "Police Eye Lent in Bennington Incident." *The Berkshire Eagle,* January 11, 1994 Kennedy, Helen, "Police Step Up Search." *Boston Herald,* January 13, 1994

King, Suzanne, "Lewis S. Lent, Jr., A Man Full of Contradictions." *Observer-Dispatch,* January 16, 1994

King, Suzanne, "Lent Spends 23 Hrs. a Day Alone in His Cell." *Observer-Dispatch,* August 15,1994

King, Suzanne with Patrick Corbett, "I Thought He Was Just Another Weirdo Walking Around Pittsfield." *Observer-Dispatch*

Lahr, Ellen G., "Ex. DA Doubts Any Lent Link to Gutkaiss." *The Berkshire Eagle,* January 9, 1994

Lahr, Ellen G., "Alert Driver is Key to Kidnap Case." *The Berkshire Eagle,* January 11, 1994

Lahr, Ellen G., "Escape May Have Saved Others." *The Berkshire Eagle*, January 11, 1994

Lahr, Ellen G., "North Adams Boy Tells Tale of Lent," *The Berkshire Eagle, January 11, 1994*

Lahr, Ellen G., "Russell Davis Change in Routine Puts Witness at Right Spot." *The Berkshire Eagle,* January 12, 1994

Lahr, Ellen G.," A Media Circus." *The Berkshire Eagle*, January 15, 1994

Lahr, Ellen G., "Unsolved Cases." *The Berkshire Eagle*, January 19, 1994

Lahr, Ellen G. "Lent's Brain is Deteriorating According to Defense Experts." *The Berkshire Eagle,* May 8, 1994

Lahr, Ellen G. *The Berkshire Eagle,* June 9, 1994.

Lahr, Ellen G., "Lent Penned Apology to Rebecca." *The Berkshire Eagle*, October 7, 1994 Lahr, Ellen G. "Jimmy Was Like a Second Son." *The Berkshire Eagle*, June 10, 1996

Lahr, Ellen G. "Lent Wins Another Round on Doctored Evidence." *The Berkshire Eagle,* April 6, 1996.

Leman, Dr. Kevin, *The Birth Order Book,* Michigan: Baker Publishing Group, 2004

Mahoney, Joe, "Lewis Lent, in Letter Denies Involvement in Wood Case." *The Berkshire Eagle*, January 6, 1995

Mahoney, Joe, "Lent's Lawyers Seek Files on Crooked Cops." *Union News*, June 26, 1994

Mahoney, Joe, "Lent says Fear Made Him Sign Murder Confession." Union News, January 25, 1995

Mattoon, Donna B., "Police Look for Links to Other Unsolved Killings." *The Berkshire Eagle,* January 11, 1994

McNamara, Sean, "Search for Sara Anne Wood Continues." *Democrat and Chronicle*, January 13, 1994

Melley, Brian, "Lent Pleads Guilty to Killing Boy." *Union News*, June 4, 1996

Moran, Kevin, "Timeline of Bernardo Murder to Lent Plea." *The Transcript*, June 4, 1996

Moran, Kevin, "D.A. Downing: Plea Came Two Years After Tumultuous Weekend in Pittsfield in 1994." *The Transcript*, June 4, 1996

Muka, Stephen Arthur, "Lent (Jr), Lewis Stephen" *New York State Police Supplemental Report,* January 9, 1994.

Murphy, Sean P., and David Armstrong, "Abuse in Lent's Family Alleged." *Boston Globe*, January 14, 1994

New York Times News Service, "Police Appeal to Tourists for Possible Lent Videos." January 27, 1994

O' Connor, Gerald B., "N.A. Man Charged with Kidnap Try." *The Berkshire Eagle*, January 8, 1994

O' Connor, Gerald B., "Said Lent Stalked Victims. " *The Berkshire Eagle*, January 13, 1994

O' Connor, Gerald B., "Lent's Tyler St. Day." *The Berkshire Eagle*, January 14, 1994

O' Connor, Gerald B., "They Traveled Hard Road Together." *The Berkshire Eagle,* January 15, 1994

O' Connor, Gerald B., "For the Bernardos and the Police a Long Road and Sad Conclusion." *The Berkshire Eagle*, January 15, 1994

O' Connor, Gerald B., "Inside the Command Center." *The Berkshire Eagle*, January 18, 1994

O' Connor, Gerald B., "Grand Jury Indicts Lent, Police Search Cinema Center." *The Berkshire Eagle,* January 22, 1994

O' Connor, Gerald B., "Lent, While at BCC, Expressed Interest in Dual Personality, His Teacher Says." *The Berkshire Eagle*, January 20, 1994

O' Connor, Gerald B., "Lent Cases Brings Separate Continuance Dates." *The Berkshire Eagle,* January 21, 1994

O' Connor, Gerald B., "Grand Jury Indicts Lent, Police Search Cinema Center." *The Berkshire Eagle*, January 22, 1994

O' Connor, Gerald B.," Police Appeal to Tourists" *The Berkshire Eagle,* January 27, 1994

O' Connor, Gerald B., "Rebecca Deals with Spotlight." *The Berkshire Eagle*, January 28, 1994

O' Connor, Gerald B., "Grand Jury Indicts Lent, Police Search Cinema Center." *The Berkshire Eagle,* January 22, 1994

O' Connor, Gerald B., "Lent Arraigned in Absentia." *The Berkshire Eagle,* January 25, 1994

O' Connor, Gerald B., "Lee Denies Allegation That Lent Was Badgered." *The Berkshire Eagle*, February 15, 1994

O' Connor, Gerald B., "Lewis Lent arraignment Came Quickly." *The Berkshire Eagle*, February 15, 1994

O' Connor, Gerald B., "Sara Anne's Body Hasn't Been Found; DA's at Odds." *The Berkshire Eagle,* February 16, 1994

O' Connor, Gerald B., "Herkimer DA Takes Steps to Bring Lent to N.Y." *The Berkshire Eagle*, February 17, 1994

O' Connor, Gerald B., "Reno to Meet with Sara Anne's Parents." *The Berkshire Eagle*, February 18, 1994

O' Connor, Gerald B., *"As Wood Continues Quest, His Friends Worry About Him."* *The Berkshire Eagle,* February 22, 1994

O' Connor, Gerald B and de Bourbon, Lisi, "Lent Gave Teens Drink Counselor Says." *The Berkshire Eagle*, January 21, 1994

O'Neill, Capt., John, *50 Murders- History of the Pittsfield Police Department 1690-2007,* Lulu Press Inc.

Powers, Ronald, "Wood Gets No Assurances from Reno." *Associated Press as it appears in the Berkshire Eagle,* February 23, 1994

Pratt, Abby, "Lent's Lawyers Seeking Dismissal of MA Murder Charges." The *Berkshire Eagle,* September 7, 1994

Pratt, Abby, "Police Testify on Statements Made by Lent." *The Berkshire Eagle*, October 6, 1994

Pratt, Abby, "Witness: Lent Said Rebecca's" *The Berkshire Eagle*, October 12, 1994

The Republican Newsroom, "Child Serial Killer Lewis Lent Confesses to murder of Jamie Lusher, Westfield teen missing for over 20 years. *The Republican (online)* Posted July, 15, 2013, updated March 24, 2019

Rowe, Claudia, *The Spider and the Fly,* New York: HarperCollins Publishers 2017

Rule, Ann, *The Stranger Beside Me,* New York, New York: Signet 1980

Scaife, Janice Beetle, "Police Theorize Teen Was Abducted." *Union-News,* January 1, 1993.

Sennott, Charles M., "Searching for Pieces in the Lent Puzzle; Task Force Seeks Links to Unsolved Killings." *Boston Globe,* January 20, 1994

Sennett, Charles M., David Armstrong, Sean Murphy, John Ellement, B.J. Roche, and Cate Chant, "Possible Serial Killings Probed." *Boston Globe,* January 12, 1994

Siemaszko, Corky, reported by Beals, Gregory, Bennington, Vt.; Sataline, Suzanne, Pittsfield, MA.; and Garcilazo, Miguel, Raquette Lake, NY, "Accused Killer Eyed in Two More Kid Cases." *Daily News,* January 14, 1994

Sliwa, Carol, "Blue or Gray Vehicle Sought in Bernardo Case." *The Berkshire Eagle,* December 13, 1990

Sliwa, Carol, "Police Unveil Evidence in Bernardo Murder." *The Berkshire Eagle,* February 20,1991

Sliwa, Carol, "Police Unveil Evidence in Bernardo Murder." *The Berkshire Eagle*, February 20, 1991

Sliwa, Carol, "Downing Makes Mass. Case for Lent Jurisdiction." *The Berkshire Eagle*, April 6, 1995

Sliwa, Carol, "50 Attend Briefing on Bernardo Case." *The Berkshire Eagle*, October 23, 1991

Sliwa, Carol, "Lo Trial Guts DA Budget." *The Berkshire Eagle*, March 4, 1994

Sliwa, Carol, "Lewis Lent Committed, Complicating Trial Prospect." *The Berkshire Eagle*, June 29, 1995

Sliwa, Carol, "SJC Rules MA Able to Try Lent." *The Berkshire Eagle*, July 18, 1995

Spina, Matthew, "Lent's Long, Winding Road." *Syracuse Herald Journal*, February 15, 1994

Stein, Theo, "Lent's Stay I Hospital Extended." *The Berkshire Eagle*, February 2, 1996

Stein, Theo, "Sanity Hearing Sought for Lent." *The Berkshire Eagle*, February 15, 1996

Stein, Theo, "Lent Faking Prosecution Witness Says." *The Berkshire Eagle*, May 10, 1996

Stein, Theo, "Lent Must Stand Trial." *The Berkshire Eagle*, May 17, 1996

Stein, Theo, "Lent's Trial Moved but Jury Won't be Sequestered in Springfield." *The Berkshire Eagle,* May 21, 1996

Stein, Theo, "Admits Killing Bernardo: To Aid search for Wood Girl.*" The Berkshire Eagle*, June 4, 1996

Stein, Theo, "Chief Lee Contends Lent Took Four Lives." *The Berkshire Eagle*. December 26, 1996

Stein, Theo, "Lee Holds Firm on Lent Allegations." *The Berkshire Eagle*, December 28, 1996

Stein, Theo, "Lent Gets Maximum." *The Berkshire Eagle,* April 12, 1997

Stein, Theo, "Instead of Closure New Questions Arise.*" The Berkshire Eagle*, April 12, 1997

Stein, Theo, "Convicted in N.Y., Lent Returned to MA." *The Berkshire Eagle*, April 18, 1997

Swan, Rhonda, "Serial Killers Don't Look Like Monsters, They Look Like Us." *Union News*, January 14, 1994

Tetrault, Michael, "Westfield Police May Aid Inquiry." *Union News*, January 2, 1993

Wentzel, Michael, "Friends of Suspect Now Feel Betrayed." *Democrat and Chronicle*, January 13, 1994

48 Hours: "Child Hunter: Lewis Lent." CBS News Archives, January 28, 1994

"Florida Woman Identifies Attacker of 15 Years Ago." *The Berkshire Eagle,* January 10, 1994

"Child Serial Killer Lewis Lent Confesses to Murder of Jamie Lusher, Westfield Teen Missing for Over 20 Years." *The Republican,* Posted July 15, 2013, updated March 24, 2019

https://en.wikipedia.org/wiki/North_Adams_Massachusetts

Court Decisions

1. Commonwealth vs. Lew Lent, Jr., MEMORANDUM OF DECISION ON DEFENDANT'S MOTION TO RECUSE, Judge Daniel A. Ford, Justice of the Superior Court, October 11, 1994, Berkshire, ss. – Superior Court No. 94-0044-0047, No. 94-0083 & 0084.

2. Commonwealth vs. Lew Lent, Jr., FINDINGS, RULINGS AND ORDER ON DEFENDANT'S MOTION TO SUPPRESS IDENTIFICATION, Judge Daniel A. Ford, Justice of the Superior Court, October 19, 1994, Berkshire, ss. – Superior Court No. 94-0044-0047.

3. Commonwealth vs. Lew Lent, Jr., MEMORANDUM OF DECISION ON DEFENDANT'S MOTION FOR TRANSFER OF TRIAL, Judge Daniel A. Ford, Justice of the Superior Court, October 19,

1994, Berkshire,ss. – Superior Court No. 94-0044-0047.

4 Commonwealth vs. Lew Lent, Jr., MEMORANDUM OF DECISION ON DEFENDANT'S MOTION FOR DISMISS INDICTMENT, Judge Daniel A. Ford, Justice of the Superior Court, October 24, 1994, Berkshire,ss. – Superior Court No.94-0045.

5 Commonwealth vs. Lew Lent, Jr., REPORT, November 1, 1994, Berkshire,ss. – Superior Court No. 94-0083.

6 Commonwealth vs. Lew Lent, Jr., MEMORANDUM OF DECISION ON DEFENDANT'S MOTION TO DISMISS FOR LACK OF JURISDICTION, Judge Daniel A. Ford, Justice of the Superior Court, November 1, 1994, Berkshire, ss. – Superior Court No. 94-0083.

7 Commonwealth vs. Lew Lent, Jr., MEMORANDUM OF DECISION ON DEFENDANT'S MOTION IN LIMINE, Judge Daniel A. Ford, Justice of the Superior Court, December 29, 1994, Berkshire, ss. – Trial Court of the Commonwealth Superior Court Department Berkshire Division, 94-0044, 0046-47, 0703.

8 Commonwealth vs. Lew Lent, Jr., 420 Mass. 764, April 5, 1995 – July 17, 1995, Berkshire County, Present: Liacos, C. J., Abrams & O' Connor, JJ.

9 Commonwealth vs. Lew Lent, Jr., MEMORANDUM OF DECISION ON DEFENSE COUNSEL'S MOTION TO WITHDRAW, Judge Daniel A. Ford, Justice of the Superior Court, April 30, 1996, Berkshire, ss. – Superior Court No. 94-0083 & 0084.

10 Commonwealth vs. Lew Lent, Jr., MEMORANDUM OF DECISION ON DEFENSE COUNSEL'S MOTION FOR TRANSFER OF TRIAL, Judge Daniel A. Ford, Justice of the Superior Court, May

29, 1996, Berkshire, ss. – Superior Court No. 94-0083 & 0084.

11 Commonwealth vs. Lew Lent, Jr., MEMORANDUM OF DECISION ON DEFENDANT'S MOTION IN LIMINE-REFERENECES TO OTHER CRIMES AND BAD ACTS, Judge Daniel A. Ford, Justice of the Superior Court, May 29, 1996, Berkshire, ss. – Superior Court No. 94-0083 & 0084.

12 Commonwealth vs. Lew Lent, Jr., TRANSCRIPT OF TAPE RECORDING OF HEARING BEFORE THE COURT ON JUNE 1, 1996, Judge Daniel A. Ford, Justice of the Superior Court, June 3, 1996, Berkshire, ss. – Superior Court No. 94-0083 & 0084.

13 Commonwealth vs. Lew Lent, Jr., MEMORANDUM OF DECISION RE: COMPETENCY, Judge Daniel A. Ford, Justice of the Superior Court, October 21, 1996, Berkshire, ss. – Superior Court No. 94-0083 & 0084.

14 Appeals Court of Massachusetts, Berkshire, Commonwealth vs. Lewis S. Lent, Jr., No. 97-P-742, Decided May 10, 1999.

Investigative Reports

1. Interview with Christopher Herbert Muka, State of New York, County of Tomkins, Town of Dryden, Investigator Ronald B. Sicina, November 21, 1990.

2. Interview with Angela Taikowski, Federal Bureau of Investigation, Special Agents Emery Joseph Adams & William J.C. Agnew, Jr., November 27, 1990

3. Interview with Mr. Andrew and Mrs. Barbara Miner, Federal Bureau of Investigation, Special Agents Charles McManagle and Brian F. McLaughlin, November 28, 1990.

4. Interview with Mr. Ronald and Mrs. Mary Bernardo, Federal Bureau of Investigation, Special Agents

Charles E. McGonagle & Brian F. McLaughlin, November 29, 1990.

5. Interview with Bernard W. Aubuchon, Federal Bureau of Investigation, Special Agent Charles E. McGonagle, December 6, 1990.

6. Pittsfield Police Statement Form, Mary Jane Ray Detective Terence Donnelly, January 7, 1994.

7. Statement by Pittsfield Police Detective Owen Boyington, January 7, 1994.

8. Statement by Pittsfield Police Detective Thomas Bowler, January 7, 1994.

9. Pittsfield Police Department Statement, Chester Forfa, Detective Joseph D. Collias, January 7, 1994.

10. Pittsfield Police Department Voluntary Statement by Lewis S. Lent, Jr., Detective Thomas Bowler, January 7, 1994.

11. Pittsfield Police Department Voluntary Statement by Lewis S. Lent, Jr., Detective Gary W. Danford, January 7, 1994.

12. Pittsfield Police Department Voluntary Statement by Lewis S. Lent, Jr., Detective Peter McGuire, January 8, 1994.

13. Pittsfield Police Department Voluntary Statement by Lewis S. Lent, Jr., Detective Gary Danford, January 8, 1994.

14. North Adams Police Department Statement by Melissa Benoit, Sargent Richard M. Smith, January 9, 1994.

15. Pittsfield Police Department Statement, Phillip Shallies, Detective Joseph D. Collias, January 8, 1994.

16. New York State Police Interview, John Wood, Investigator Frank J. Jerome, annuary 8, 1994.

17. Pittsfield Police Department Statement, John Wood, Detective Gary W. Danford, January 8, 1994.

18. Pittsfield Police Department Statement, Melissa Benoit, Officer Glen F. Decker, January 8, 1994.

19. Pittsfield Police Department Statement, Roger W. Beaudoin, Detective David R. Granger, January 8, 1994.

20. Statement by Pittsfield Police Department, Detective Gary Danford, January 8, 1994.

21. Statement by Pittsfield Police Department, Detective Peter McGuire, January 8, 1994.

22. New York State Police – Ithaca Interview with Lois S. Wood & Alfred G. Wood, Detectives Conroy and Stark, January 8, 1994.

23. Massachusetts State Police Interview with Melissa Benoit, Sargent. Richard M. Smith (Berkshire CPAC), January 9, 1994.

24. Massachusetts State Police Statement by David J. Barrett, Detectives Robert G. Scott & Richard M. Smith, January 9, 1994.

25. New York State Police Supporting Deposition by Jonathan Wood, Investigator Frank Jerome, January 9, 1994.

26. New York State Statement by Jon Wood, Trooper John Murray, January 9, 1994.

27. New York State Statement by Jon Wood, Trooper Frank Jerome, January 9, 1994.

28. North Adams Police Department Statement by Linda Domenichini, Investigator Arthur Daniels & Sargent Richard M. Smith, January 9, 1994.

29. New York State Police Interview with Stephen Domenichini, Investigator Charles Sullivan, January 9, 1994.

30. New York State Police, Supporting Deposition with Stephen Domenichini, Investigator Charles Sullivan & Detective Robert J. Canale, January 9, 1994.

31. New York State Police Voluntary Statement by Lewis S. Lent, Jr Investigators John H. Murray & James G. Ayling, January 9, 1994.

32. Voluntary Statement by Lewis S. Lent, Jr., New York State Police Investigators John H. Murray & Frank J. Lawrence, January 9, 1994.

33. New York State Police Interview with Roger W. Beaudoin, Investigator Arthur Daniels, January 9, 1994.

34. North Adams Police Department Statement by Melissa Benoit, Sargent M. Smith, January 9, 1994.

35. New York State Police Voluntary Statement by Lewis S. Lent, Investigators John F. Murray & Frank J. Lawrence.

36. Task Force Investigation Interview with Linda Domenichini, Investigators Gary Danford & John F. Murray, January 13, 1994.

37. New York State Police Support Deposition with Chester Forfa, Investigator Frank Jerome, January 13, 1994.

38. Federal Bureau of Investigation Interview with Rene Michelle Parr, Special Agent Todd Rowley, January 18, 1994.

39. Federal Bureau of Investigation Interview with Charlene Tobey, Special Agent Terry Wetmore, January 19, 1994.

40. Pittsfield Police Department Statement by Chester Forfa, Detective Owen Boyington, January 28, 1994.

41. Task Force Investigation of Lead #670 with Debra Loveless, Pittsfield Detective Joseph D. Collias, February 3, 1994.

42. Task Force Notes re: Jamie Lusher, February 21-25, 1994, March 2, 1994.

43. Westfield Police Department & Lewis S. Lent, Jr. Task Force Interview with Terrance Regan, Westfield Police Detective Joseph Maxton, Pittsfield Police

Department Officer Richard R. LeClair, March 10, 1994.

44. Lewis S. Lent, Jr. Task Force Investigative Report, New York State Police Investigator Maurice Sullivan, March 28, 1994.

45. Lewis S. Lent, Jr. Task Force Investigative Report, Massachusetts State Trooper William Murphy, Neil Dorval & Angela Govini, March 29, 1994.

46. Lewis S. Lent, Jr. Task Force Investigative Report re: Holly Piirainen, Massachusetts State Trooper William F. Murphy, March 29, 1994.

47. Lewis S. Lent, Jr. Task Force Investigation of Lead #894 rr: Richard Burnham & Debra Loveless, New York State Police Investigator James G. Ayling & Massachusetts State Trooper William F. Murphy, June 22, 1994.

48. Commonwealth of Massachusetts, Berkshire District Attorney Press Release re: Gag Order, March 1, 1996.

49. Hardy Healthcare Assoc., PC – Neurological Evaluation of Lewis Lent.

50. Public Information Office, Supreme Judicial Court, Memo to Gerard Downing, DA., Request for Direct Appellate Review.

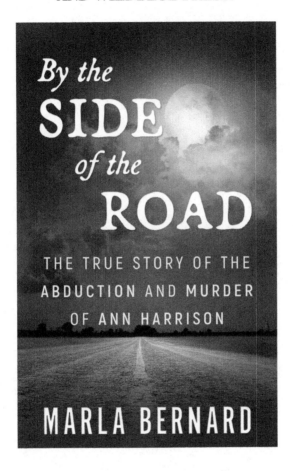

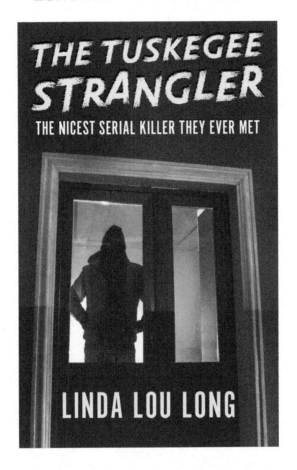

Made in the USA
Middletown, DE
04 February 2023

23936553R00166